One with the Community

One with the Community

Indicators of Engagement at Minority-Serving Institutions

Edward Zlotkowski
Rosalyn Jacobs Jones
Margarita Maria Lenk
Jennifer Meeropol
Sherril B. Gelmon
Katrina H. Norvell

Contents

iii   Acknowledgments

v   Foreword

1   Introduction

15   Contexts for Civic Engagement at HBCUs, HSIs, and TCUs

39   Engagement at Historically Black Colleges and Universities
     68   HBCU PROFILES

77   Engagement at Hispanic-Serving Institutions
     105   HSI PROFILES

113   Engagement at Tribal Colleges and Universities
     141   TCU PROFILES

149   Conclusion

155   Appendix I: Research Methodology

169   Appendix II: Campus Compact's "Indicators of Engagement" Self-Assessment Guide

197   Appendix III: Key Campus Contacts for Institutions in This Study

199   References

Acknowledgments

We would like to thank our colleagues at Campus Compact for their assistance in various aspects of this project. Elizabeth Hollander contributed to the creation of the original indicators of engagement and provided valuable guidance throughout this project. John Saltmarsh, another author of the original indicators, provided insight, direction, and feedback throughout the project. Karen Partridge served as volume editor and helped ensure the consistency and integrity of the text. Jan Torres and William Beaird guided the original proposal that funded the project.

Many directors of Campus Compact state offices identified and recommended model minority-serving institutions in their states, encouraged their members to participate in this project, made recommendations about project design and implementation, and participated in the site visits.

Dean McGovern, executive director of Montana Campus Compact; Julie Plaut, associate director of Minnesota Campus Compact; and Jean Strait, assistant professor at Hamline University in Minnesota, visited tribal colleges in their states, attended focus group meetings, reviewed chapters on Tribal colleges and universities, and drafted the profiles of Tribal institutions included in this volume.

Barbara Frankle, dean of faculty at LeMoyne-Owen College, and Stephen Rozman, co-chair of the HBCU Faculty Development Network and director of The Center for Civic Engagement and Social Responsibility at Tougaloo College, provided key input on the project and generously shared their time and expertise with us. David Ray, director of the Ford/United Negro College Fund Service-Learning Network, reviewed several sections of the monograph and provided valuable feedback. President Renee Gurneau and Academic Dean Mary Ringhand of Red Lake Nation College, and Director of Administration Deborah McArthur and grant writer Judy Fairbanks of White Earth Tribal and Community College, collaborated on the profiles of their institutions and provided valuable guidance for project staff. We are grateful for the assistance of these leaders.

Student interns Katie Donovan, Philissa Cramer, and Ji Hyun Lee assisted with project details, provided administrative support, helped to draft initial language for the monograph, assisted with fact-checking, and tracked down documentation and additional information.

We are grateful to the Carnegie Corporation of New York for their generous support of this project and to our program officer, Cynthia Gibson, for her insights and recommendations.

Finally, we wish to thank the individuals from Tribal colleges and universities, historically Black colleges and universities, and Hispanic-serving institutions who completed the survey, participated in telephone interviews, hosted the site visits, spoke with our scholars, participated in focus groups, and collected and submitted their documents for our use. Many individuals took time out of their busy lives to share their stories, successes, and challenges with us. This book would not have been possible without their generosity and commitment.

Foreword

Some time ago, a colleague remarked to me, "HBCUs [historically Black colleges and universities] have always had close ties with the community. This is nothing new. Now the majority institutions have adopted service-learning and other types of community outreach and think they've made a new discovery. Yet they get the credit because they document what they do, and we don't!"

As a matter of fact, I have heard this type of comment from more than one representative of a minority-serving institution (MSI), and it has a ring of truth to it. HBCUs and other MSIs tend to be intimately tied to their communities, but they often take this relationship for granted and do not keep a record of their history of community outreach. They have long legacies of community service—in various forms—that cry out for serious research and publication.

Campus Compact, by featuring service-learning and civic engagement at MSIs in this volume, opens the door to what will, no doubt, be follow-up studies that give further exposure to the close bonds between these institutions and their communities.

This book also casts light on the diversity of MSIs, showing both similarities and differences in the community outreach approaches of those that are predominantly African-American, Hispanic, and Native American. One similarity is that MSIs have a "less individualistic, more community-based mindset" than most mainstream institutions. Accordingly, a greater percentage of MSIs have service-learning and civic engagement programs than Campus Compact members in general, which leads Campus Compact to recommend ways of spreading the successes of engaged MSIs to other institutions.

That Campus Compact would publish a book that exalts and attempts to empower MSIs comes as no surprise. Several years ago, its executive director, Elizabeth Hollander, contacted the HBCU Faculty Development Network and registered to attend our annual HBCU Faculty Development Symposium, where we had several presentations on outstanding service-learning programs at HBCUs. The connections she established with the presenters helped pave the way for the publication of this book.

At a time when some people are either questioning the need for MSIs or are seeking to make them clones of majority institutions, Campus Compact, in this volume, makes a persuasive argument that MSIs "have much to teach the rest of higher education about how best to educate African American, Hispanic American, and Native American students for engaged citizenship."

This book has additional value in going beyond a description of MSI achievements. It also provides a guide for self-assessment designed to "gauge and further advance engagement on campus." This has been another challenge for MSIs: to assess their community outreach experiences to measure their successes and explore strategies for further enhancing their effectiveness.

The HBCU Faculty Development Network has been reaching out to other organizations engaged in faculty development to help create a network of networks. Since Campus Compact has been engaged in this same pursuit, it was probably inevitable that we would develop a collaborative relationship to promote service-learning and civic engagement. Campus Compact conducted a workshop at our recent summer institute on "Civic Engagement and Social Justice." In addition, at this writing, our two organizations are collaborating with Tougaloo College, the Gulf-South Summit on Service-Learning, and the United Negro College Fund Special Programs Corporation to co-sponsor a symposium on responding to community crisis in the aftermath of Hurricane Katrina and other recent storms.

For readers from MSIs, this publication both confirms a long track record of reaching out to the community and offers a guide for further action and documentation. For other readers, this publication will promote a greater appreciation for MSIs and the important role they play in educating minority students in a manner that enhances their existing bonds with the community and prepares them to take their place as leaders in a democratic society.

STEPHEN L. ROZMAN, PH.D.
Co-Director, HBCU Faculty Development Network
Director, Center for Civic Engagement & Social Responsibility
Tougaloo College
Tougaloo, Mississippi

Introduction

MSIs, Diversity, and Democracy

In 1903, W.E.B. Du Bois wrote that "the function of the university is not simply to teach breadwinning, or to furnish teachers for the public schools or to be a centre of polite society; it is, above all, to be the organ of that fine adjustment between real life and the growing knowledge of life, an adjustment which forms the secret of civilization."

In 21st century America, the challenge of making that fine adjustment is at the forefront of civic debate. While more individuals than ever before are attending colleges and universities, young people are increasingly removed from the real life of their democracy. And despite the slight recent bump in voting rates, the multi-decade trend toward declining civic participation has alarmed many eminent sociologists, political scientists, and government and nonprofit leaders. Their concerns were neatly summarized in the much-cited Nunn/Bennett Commission report: We have become a "nation of spectators" who have distanced ourselves from our civic responsibilities (National Commission on Civic Renewal, 1998).

Of particular concern is the lack of democratic participation among young Americans, a group especially alienated from government and deeply cynical about the political system (Sax et al., 1999; The Institute of Politics, 2000; National Association of Secretaries of State, 1999; The Mellman Group, 2000). Since it has long been a goal of American higher education to develop well-informed, critically thinking citizens, the challenge now is to harness the power of higher education to educate the next generation of active citizens.

Maintaining civil society will require an ability to work effectively across different cultures and perspectives. Minority-serving institutions of higher education (MSIs) serve as an intersection between diversity and democracy. They play a crucial role in educating minority students, and as minority populations in the United States grow, this role will continue to increase in importance. In addition, since MSIs are focused on minority populations, they have much to teach the rest of higher education about how best to educate African American, Hispanic American, and Native American students for engaged citizenship. It was for this reason that Campus Compact determined to focus a major portion of its multi-year Indicators of Engagement Project—which examines civic engagement practices at different institutional types in higher education—on MSIs.

This focus is both timely and relevant. Minority populations in the United States are increasing rapidly. In 2000, 28% of the U.S. population comprised minorities, including African Americans, Asian Americans, American Indians, and Hispanic Americans. This number is expected to grow to 36% in 2020 and 47% by 2050 (Alliance for Equity in Higher Education, www.msi-alliance.org/main.asp). As the minority population has increased, so has the number of minority students attending college. According to the American Council on Education, an increasing number of minority students are both attending and completing college. Between 1995 and 1999, minority enrollment in institutions of higher education rose by at least 3.2% each year (see Figure 1).

Figure 1: **Increase in Minority Enrollment in U.S. Colleges and Universities, 1995–1999**

YEAR	% INCREASE FROM PREVIOUS YEAR
1999	3.3
1998	3.2
1997	3.7
1996	3.2

SOURCES: Young, J.R. (2000); Young, J.R. (2002).

These statistics reflect a continuing trend of growing minority enrollment in America's colleges and universities that is expected to continue for the foreseeable future. The Educational Testing Service projects that by 2015, U.S. college and university enrollment will increase by 19% over 1995 enrollment to reach 16 million students. Minority students are expected to account for a full 80% of this increase (Carnevale, 2000).

MSIs play an important role in making higher education accessible for minority students. These institutions confer more than 20% of all college degrees and certificates that are awarded to African American, American Indian, and Hispanic students. In 2000, more than 1.8 million college students, representing more than 10% of all college students in the United States, were enrolled in MSIs (Alliance for Equity in Higher Education, www.msi-alliance.org/main.asp). According to the Hispanic Association of Colleges and Universities (HACU), although Hispanic-serving institutions (HSIs) constitute fewer than 7% of all higher education institutions, more than two-thirds of Hispanic college students attend an HSI ("HACU 101," www.hacu.net).

Clearly, minority-serving institutions play an important role in increasing the diversity of higher education, but do they also help educate students for democratic participation in our increasingly diverse democracy? Statistics show that MSIs are active in the civic engagement movement on campuses throughout the United States. According to Campus Compact's 2003 annual member survey, service-learning and civic engagement are more prevalent at MSIs by a wide margin than at other types of schools. MSIs are more likely than average to require service and service-learning for graduation; to have established service offices and staff on campus; and to form partnerships with K–12 and faith-based organizations (see Figure 2).

In 2003 the Supreme Court recognized the connections between diversity and the academic mission of higher education when it affirmed the authority of colleges and universities to consider race or ethnicity as one factor in their admissions in the landmark Gratz v. Bollinger and Grutter v. Bollinger cases. In these cases the Supreme Court concluded that higher education has a compelling interest in promoting the educational benefits of diversity.

Figure 2: Service-Learning and Civic Engagement at MSIs

	PERCENTAGE OF RESPONDING INSTITUTIONS	
	MSIs	ALL COMPACT MEMBERS
Institutions that require service for graduation	18	8
Institutions that require service-learning for graduation	17	9
Institutions with a community service or service-learning office	96	83
Institutions with a community service or service-learning director	92	80
Institutions with an existing partnership with one or more K-12 schools	100	93
Institutions with an existing partnership with one or more faith-based organizations	90	69

SOURCE: Campus Compact (2004). *2003 Service Statistics: Campus Compact's Annual Membership Survey.* Providence, RI: Campus Compact.

Higher education associations, including the Association of American Colleges and Universities (AAC&U) and the American Association for Higher Education (AAHE), have echoed the court's decision through their efforts to combine civic engagement and diversity. AAC&U has focused on diversity in higher education for more than three decades, and its work has led to the creation of an entire community of institutions that are dedicated to making diversity an integral part of both civic engagement and educational excellence. AAHE has also focused on engagement and diversity through projects like "Building Engagement and Attainment for Minority Students" (BEAMS)—a joint effort with the National Survey for Student Engagement Institute to increase campus-based student engagement—and "The Engaged Campus for a Diverse Democracy." (The

Alliance for Equity in Higher Education assumed leadership and management of the BEAMS project in May 2005 following the announcement of AAHE's decision to cease operations.)

This book focuses on the shape of civic engagement at minority-serving institutions to understand why and how MSIs engage their students. MSIs embrace diversity not only in their populations but also in the models they use. Understanding these unique institutions is an important step in helping Campus Compact and other higher education associations committed to supporting campus-based engagement broaden the civic engagement movement and connect with important new allies.

Campus Compact and the Growth of Campus Engagement

In 1985, the presidents of Brown, Georgetown, and Stanford Universities, along with the president of the Education Commission of the States, joined together to form Campus Compact, a coalition of college and university presidents committed to fulfilling the civic purposes of higher education. Member presidents believe that by creating a supportive campus environment for engagement in community service, colleges and universities can best prepare their students to be active, committed, and informed citizens and community leaders.

Campus Compact's growth in membership is one strong indicator of higher education's renewed commitment to its civic mission. Membership has grown by more than 40% in the past five years to more than 950 member institutions. Furthermore, the rich diversity of Campus Compact's membership reflects the civic commitment of institutions across the spectrum of higher education: 52% of member campuses are public and 48% are private, encompassing women's, faith-based, historically Black, Hispanic-serving, and Tribal institutions.

As campus-based civic engagement has grown, finding ways to measure, assess, expand, and improve engagement efforts has become an increasingly important priority. To meet this need, Campus Compact developed the Pyramid of Service-Learning and Civic Engagement, a schematic representation of the developmental levels of service-learning and civic engagement on campuses (see Figure 3).

The pyramid has three levels: Introductory, Intermediate, and Advanced. Each level has a set of characteristics appropriate for the constituency involved (see Figure 4). Thus, the full picture of each level is quite complex, defined as it is by the roles and needs of multiple constituencies that act both as stakeholders and as agents of institutional change: presidents, chief academic officers, faculty, community service and service-learning coordinators and directors, community partners, and students.

The advanced level represents the fully "engaged campus"—an institution whose mission, purpose, and support structures are aligned with the needs of the local community. The engaged campus has been described as having "an integrated approach to fostering students' citizenship skills through both educational and co-curricular programs and activities, and conscious modeling of good institutional citizenship through external partnerships and activities" (Thomas, 2000, p. 66). This level also reflects full acceptance of that larger sense of institutional alignment Ernest Boyer identified as "the scholarship of engagement"; namely, scholarship that "connect[s] the rich resources of the university to our most pressing social, civic, and ethical problems" (Boyer, 1996).

The three levels of the pyramid reflect the journey of an institution in achieving a richer and deeper commitment to service-learning, civic engagement, and the scholarship of engagement. A number of key indicators serve to mark the institution's progress.

The Indicators of Engagement

The indicators of engagement were developed by Campus Compact executive director Elizabeth Hollander, project director John Saltmarsh, and senior faculty fellow Edward Zlotkowski (Hollander & Saltmarsh, 2000; Hollander, Saltmarsh, &

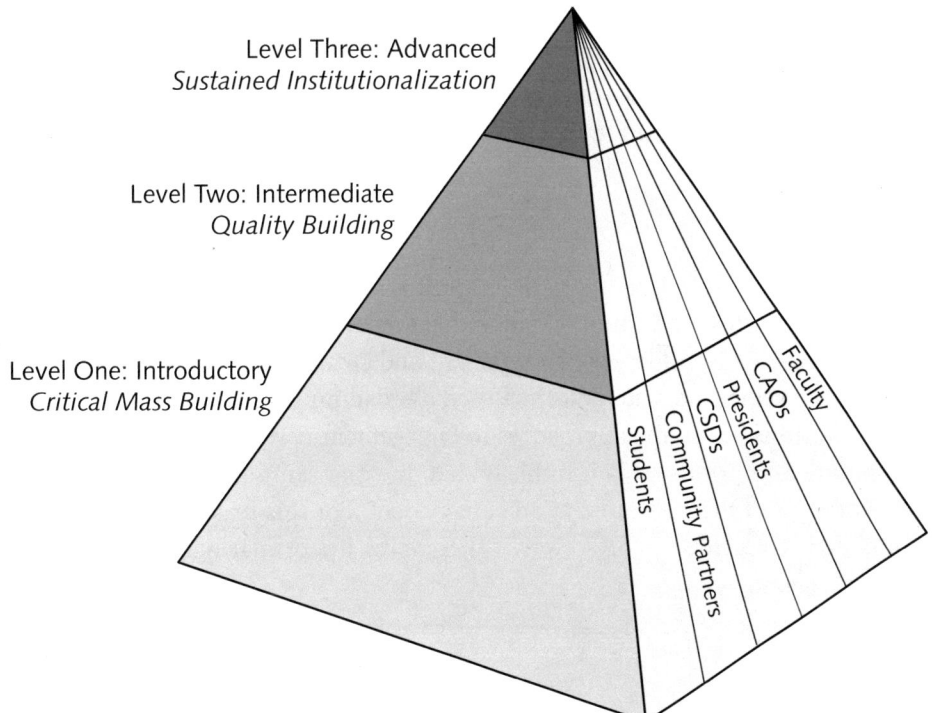

Figure 3: **Campus Compact Civic Engagement/Service-Learning Pyramid**

Level Three: Advanced
Sustained Institutionalization

Level Two: Intermediate
Quality Building

Level One: Introductory
Critical Mass Building

Faculty, CAOs, Presidents, CSDs, Community Partners, Students

> **Figure 4: Campus Characteristics at Each Level of Engagement**
>
> **INSTITUTIONAL CHARACTERISTICS OF LEVEL ONE: INTRODUCTORY PRACTICE**
> Level One is the *Critical Mass Building* stage (Furco, 2001). At this stage campuses are beginning to recognize service-learning and civic engagement and are building a campus-wide constituency for the effort.
>
> Campuses at the introductory stage are building awareness among faculty, students, and community partners; debating, discussing, and clarifying the meaning of service-learning and civic engagement in the context of institutional mission; and considering the need for institutional support.
>
> **INSTITUTIONAL CHARACTERISTICS OF LEVEL TWO: INTERMEDIATE PRACTICE**
> Level Two is the *Quality Building* stage. At this stage campuses focus on ensuring the development of "quality" engagement activities; the quality of activities begins to supercede their quantity.
>
> Intermediate campuses have a critical mass of faculty involvement and support, multiple student opportunities for service and civic engagement, sound community partnerships, and a funded infrastructure on campus.
>
> **INSTITUTIONAL CHARACTERISTICS OF LEVEL THREE: ADVANCED PRACTICE**
> Level Three is the *Sustained Institutionalization* stage. It is at this stage that a campus has fully integrated service-learning and civic engagement into the fabric of the institution, creating an "engaged campus" characterized by recognizable institutional activities, policies, and structures.
>
> Institutionalization is evident in the alignment of civic engagement with institutional mission. Faculty have incentives and rewards for implementing an engaged pedagogy. Students exercise high levels of leadership and are also rewarded for engagement. The community is a partner in the educational process, and the institution regularly assesses and plans its ongoing engagement efforts.

Zlotkowski, 2001) to capture the various approaches to engagement they observed at institutions across the country. The indicators are designed to help campuses both assess their current level of engagement and create strategies to deepen their work. The developers of the indicators used a broad range of criteria, recognizing that institutions utilize the approaches to engagement best suited to their particular culture and priorities. It is unlikely that any one campus, however engaged, will exhibit all of the indicators to an equal extent. For this reason, the indicators should not be regarded as prescriptive; their value lies primarily in the possibilities they suggest.

The 13 indicators of engagement are defined as follows:

1) **Mission and purpose** explicitly articulate a commitment to the public purposes of higher education.

2) **Administrative and academic leadership** (president, trustees, provost) is in the forefront of institutional transformation that supports civic engagement.

3) **Departments, disciplines, and interdisciplinary work** have incorporated community-based education, allowing it to penetrate across disciplines and reach the institution's academic core.

4) **Teaching and learning** incorporate a community-based, public problem-solving approach.

5) **Faculty development** opportunities are available for faculty to retool their teaching and redesign their curricula to incorporate community-based activities and reflection on those activities within the context of the course.

6) **Faculty roles and rewards,** including promotion and tenure guidelines and review, reflect a reconsideration of scholarship that embraces a scholarship of engagement.

7) **Support structures and resources** are present in the form of visible and easily accessible structures (e.g., centers, offices) on campus to assist faculty with community-based teaching and to broker community partnerships.

8) **Internal budget and resource allocation** is adequate for establishing, enhancing, and deepening community-based work on campus—for faculty, students, and programs that involve community partners.

9) **Community voice** deepens the role of community partners in contributing to community-based education and shaping outcomes that benefit the community.

10) **External resource allocations** are made available for community partners to create richer learning environments for students and for community-building efforts in local neighborhoods.

11) **Coordination of community-based activities** is a priority, with structures to weave together student service, service-learning, and other community engagement activities on campus.

12) **Forums for fostering public dialogue** are created that include multiple stakeholders in public problem-solving.

13) **Student voice** is cultivated in a way that recognizes students as key partners in their own education and civic development and supports their efforts to act on issues important to them and their peers.

Campus Compact's Indicators of Engagement Project

Higher education institutions are eager for reliable information about how to become an engaged campus. This is evident from Campus Compact's annual member survey; in 2003, respondents identified Campus Compact's most valuable services as providing resource materials (97%) and identifying model programs (93%). National leaders have also called upon Campus Compact to provide more information on campus engagement practices, seeing such information as an essential tool in advancing national policy. However, several barriers exist to gathering such information. One is the need for a conceptual framework that respects the tremendous diversity of American colleges and universities. Another is the difficulty of capturing all of the relevant practices on a campus and determining whether, in fact, they represent "models" of engagement. Finally, there is the challenge of documenting practice with enough specificity to be truly useful.

Campus Compact has experimented with a number of ways to develop model program information, including self-reports of best practice, small grants to campuses to document their practice, and self-evaluation grants made available by state Campus Compact offices. Each strategy has produced some useful information, but none has been organized in a way that can powerfully effect change.

In May 2002 Campus Compact received a three-year grant from the Carnegie Corporation of New York to combine documentation and dissemination of best practices of civic engagement with an organizing effort to help campuses achieve broader institutionalization of that engagement. In structuring the resulting Indicators of Engagement Project (IOEP), Campus Compact realized that higher education's segmentation based on institutional type, region, and peer group—as well as the significance of an institution's place, history, and local identity—limits the usefulness of any single "engaged campus" model across higher education. Instead, campuses need a *variety* of exemplary practices that they can use to create civic engagement strategies appropriate to their particular type of institution and their specific community assets and needs.

Hence, the IOEP seeks to identify, document, and disseminate best practices of civic engagement at different types of institutions. Each year of the grant focuses on a different institutional type: community colleges in year one, minority-serving institutions in year two, and comprehensive institutions in year three. In all cases, the project seeks to capture the diversity within each institutional type by including broad representation based on geography, setting (e.g., urban, rural, suburban), size, and other characteristics. The 13 indicators of engagement are the organizing framework for this documentation effort.

Minority-Serving Institutions and the IOEP

As discussed earlier, Campus Compact's most recent member survey has found a significant culture of community engagement at minority-serving institutions. Yet despite this culture of engagement, MSIs do not have a great deal of visibility in the world of campus-based service-learning and civic engagement. Major service-learning conferences certainly do not showcase the work of MSIs to the extent that practice on these campuses merits. This monograph, and other work springing from the IOEP, serves to help fill this gap. In detailing best practices of engagement from a range of institutions, we hope to provide models not only for MSIs but for all of higher education.

Project Methodology

The relevance of civic engagement to minority-serving institutions is clearly illustrated in the exemplary work of the historically Black colleges and universities (HBCUs), Hispanic-serving institutions (HSIs), and Tribal colleges and universities (TCUs) highlighted in this monograph. Project staff used a variety of research tools to identify these schools. First, all MSIs were invited to participate in the project by completing a web-based survey to identify promising practices. Project staff then conducted follow-up telephone interviews to identify exemplary approaches. Finally, project staff conducted site visits at selected institutions to document exemplary practices in depth (see Figure 5). Site visitors and interviewers used protocols developed for assessment across multiple sites and researchers, including standardized interview protocols for each indicator of engagement and each stakeholder group. (Additional information about the research methodology, including how and why project staff chose to utilize a different approach to document indicators of engagement at Tribal institutions, appears in Appendix I.) Examples and quotations included in this monograph were collected during these interviews and site visits.

This project encompasses most, but not all, institutions that fall within the broad category of MSIs. In addition to HBCUs, HSIs, and TCUs, minority-serving institutions exist that serve native Alaskan and native Hawaiian populations, among others. Project staff narrowed the scope of their research to three types of institutions to ensure adequate breadth of coverage within each type without glossing over individual schools' unique qualities. They chose to follow the example of other recent MSI initiatives, including the well-known Kellogg Alliance, in focusing on HBCUs, HSIs, and TCUs to remain in line with the focus of recent scholarship in this field.

Another factor affecting the comprehensiveness of this analysis is the characteristics of Hispanic-serving institutions. Unlike HBCUs and TCUs, which have many historical similarities, there is significant diversity within HSIs. They serve multi-

Figure 5: Minority-Serving Institutions Visited for This Project

HISTORICALLY BLACK COLLEGES AND UNIVERSITIES
Benedict College, SC
Johnson C. Smith University, NC
LeMoyne-Owen College, TN
North Carolina Central University, NC
Xavier University of Louisiana, LA

HISPANIC-SERVING INSTITUTIONS
California State University, Stanislaus, CA
Heritage University, WA
Our Lady of the Lake University, TX
St. Edward's University, TX
West Hills Community College District, CA

TRIBAL COLLEGES AND UNIVERSITIES
Red Lake Nation College, MN
Salish Kootenai College, MT
White Earth Tribal and Community College, MN

In addition, the following Tribal institutions sent representatives to focus group discussions conducted as part of the IOEP:

Bemidji State University, MN*
Diné College, AZ
Leech Lake Tribal College, MN
Red Lake Nation College, MN
Southwestern Indian Polytechnic Institute, NM
University of New Mexico, NM*
White Earth Tribal and Community College, MN

*Although not Tribal colleges, these institutions educate a significant number of Native American students and are committed to serving Native populations.

ple populations, including students whose families come from Puerto Rico, Mexico, Cuba, and Central and South America. For the purposes of this project, staff planned to work with schools that served all of these populations; however, the institutions that completed the survey of exemplary approaches all served primarily Mexican-American students. The reasons for this degree of self-selection are unclear, although staff expected a preponderance of these institutions, given that Mexican Americans make up by far the largest proportion of Hispanic Americans (see the chapter titled "Contexts for Civic Engagement at Minority-Serving Institutions" for more detail). Project staff would expect to have found some differences in approach among schools serving other populations, but the findings here are necessarily limited to the institutions that chose to participate.

Another consideration is that HSIs do not necessarily serve their student populations and communities the same way that TCUs or HBCUs do. Whereas the latter institutions have historical mandates to serve Native American and African American students and communities respectively, "Hispanic-serving institution" is a government designation (conferred on institutions meeting certain demographic criteria) that may or may not play out in the mission and purpose of the institution. For the purposes of this project, staff members decided to focus on institutions whose institutional missions and cultures reflect a commitment to serving Hispanic students and communities, since these schools embody the spirit of traditional MSIs.

About This Volume

The present volume seeks to address a variety of constituencies: faculty, students, administrators, and others in the higher education community interested in civic engagement, as well as community leaders seeking to partner with minority-serving institutions. Campus Compact hopes the volume's documentation will be sufficiently persuasive to make a strong case for continued and even increased support for local, state, and national policies and programs that support civic engagement at MSIs. In addition, it is our hope that other higher education institutions will learn from the successes of MSIs in engaging their students and adapt some of the best practices here for use in their institutions.

In the course of this research, the authors found that while MSIs share some important similarities, they also have substantial differences in the ways they approach civic and community engagement. Therefore, the project findings are separated into three sections, one for each institutional type. This organization recognizes that programs and approaches that are successful at one type of school may not be the most effective ways of engaging students at other types, and allows each chapter to focus on the specifics of engagement at HBCUs, HSIs, and TCUs.

In addition to organizing the findings by institutional type, they have also been grouped into five thematic clusters rather than deal with each indicator separately (see Figure 6). This approach, which reflects work with community colleges in the first year of the project, minimizes repetition while allowing the creation of larger units of coherence with which to explore the engaged campus. In addition, organizing each of these three main findings chapters around the same five thematic groupings of the indicators allows comparisons and contrasts to be drawn among these three institutional types.

The text of this volume is divided into five chapters. The first chapter, **Contexts for Civic Engagement at HBCUs, HSIs, and TCUs,** provides context for the project findings. This framing chapter explores the history of MSIs in the United States and locates the current project within the context of earlier initiatives to encourage engagement at these schools.

The three findings chapters highlight the work of MSIs that excel in certain aspects of engagement. **Engagement at Historically Black Colleges and Universities** explores best practices among HBCUs and examines how the history, culture, and missions of these schools affect their engagement efforts. Profiles of five HBCUs detail a range of institutional approaches to engagement. **Engagement**

Figure 6: Five Thematic Groupings of the Indicators of Engagement

1. **Institutional Culture** acknowledges that a wide spectrum of possibilities exists for understanding and acting on a college or university's connection to its community. These sections examine indicators that help establish a broad culture of engagement—a culture that demonstrably affects the ways in which faculty, students, and community partners experience the goals and priorities of the institution. These indicators include *mission and purpose* and *administrative and academic leadership*.

2. **Curriculum and Pedagogy** focuses on one of the most important lessons of the last decade: civic engagement must be rooted in the core work of the college or university if it is to be effectively spread throughout the institution. Since the core work of the institution is teaching and learning, civic engagement must be linked directly to the curriculum. This section looks at those indicators—*disciplines, departments, and interdisciplinary work* and *teaching and learning*—that measure the degree to which community-related work has become part of the institution's teaching and learning activities.

3. **Faculty Culture** examines issues of faculty identity. If faculty feel neither prepared nor rewarded for their engaged work, the curricular connection cannot long survive. Therefore, this section examines faculty culture and the two indicators, *faculty development* and *faculty roles and rewards*, that suggest faculty are getting the support they need to undertake the task of linking the curriculum to the community.

4. **Mechanisms and Resources** recognizes that successful engagement depends not only on institutional culture and faculty self-understanding; it also depends directly on the concrete and specific resources the college is willing to commit to support civic engagement. Such a commitment must be deep enough to survive the pressures of competing priorities and difficult economic times. This section looks at indicators that determine whether community concerns can hold their own in the face of decisions regarding the bottom line. It also explores the ways in which students themselves are empowered to support the engagement process. The indicators included here are *internal budget and resource allocation, support structures and resources, coordination of community-based activities,* and *student voice*.

5. **Community-Campus Exchange** turns to the off-campus community itself. Civic engagement means more than successful "outreach" in the traditional sense. It also presupposes an important shift in the way in which the higher education institution regards the surrounding community. No longer does the college act on its own, however benign its intentions. Instead, it recognizes the community as an equal partner, fully entitled to participate in all matters affecting the two. This section explores indicators that measure the community role in the engagement process: *external resource allocations, community voice,* and *forums for fostering public dialogue*.

at **Hispanic-Serving Institutions** explores how HSIs incorporate their commitment to educating the whole student, often from a cultural perspective that values family and community-strengthening activities, into their civic engagement efforts. It concludes with profiles of HSIs visited for the IOEP that discuss their institution-wide approach to engagement. The last findings chapter, **Engagement** at Tribal Colleges and Universities, explores approaches to engagement at Tribal institutions and examines how well the indicators capture activity at these institutions. This chapter also includes profiles of several TCUs with exemplary approaches to engagement.

The **Conclusion** focuses on the implications of the project's findings. Reviewing those findings in the context of the civic engagement movement as a whole, this chapter discusses the importance of recognizing—and supporting—the role of MSIs in creating the next generation of active citizens and recommends ways of spreading the successes of engaged MSIs to other institutions.

Finally, the appendices include a discussion of **project methodology**, which addresses the research approach utilized here and evaluates key decisions, outcomes, and project findings; **a self-assessment guide** for using the indicators to gauge and further advance engagement on campus; and a list of **key contacts** at the colleges studied for this project.

* * * *

Biographical Notes on Volume Authors

Edward Zlotkowski is the senior scholar for Campus Compact's three-year Indicators of Engagement Project. Dr. Zlotkowski is a professor of English at Bentley College in Waltham, MA, where he founded the Bentley College Service-Learning Center in 1990. As the Senior Faculty Fellow at Campus Compact, he directs the organization's initiative on service-learning in the disciplines. He is the editor of *Successful Service-Learning Programs (Anker Publishing, 1998) and Service-Learning and the First-Year Experience* (Resource Center for the First-Year Experience and Students in Transition, University of South Carolina, 2002). He also served as series editor of the American Association for Higher Education (AAHE)/Campus Compact 20-volume series on service-learning in the disciplines. Dr. Zlotkowski drafted the findings chapters and the conclusion and served as the volume editor.

Rosalyn Jacobs Jones is a Campus Compact engaged scholar for the second year of the Indicators of Engagement Project and dean at Johnson C. Smith University in Charlotte, NC (one of the schools included in this project). She is also an associate professor in English and a member of the Honors College Core Faculty. Dr. Jones has been instrumental in incorporating service-learning in the liberal studies core curriculum and major-level courses and has spent many years working on institutionalizing service-learning at Johnson C. Smith University. Dr. Jones conducted the initial review of all the documentation provided by the HBCUs, which established a foundation for the third chapter of this book. In addition, Dr. Jones wrote the profiles of the HBCUs included in Chapter 3 and drafted the section on the history of HBCUs in Chapter 1.

Margarita Maria Lenk, also an engaged scholar for the second year of the IOEP, is an associate professor in the Departments of Computer Information Systems and Accounting in the College of Business at Colorado State University, where she is also a service-learning fellow. Dr. Lenk was the first chair of the Active Learning Committee within the American Accounting Association, and is a member of the Minority Initiatives Committee of the American Institute of Certified Public Accountants. Her work has had a common theme of creating long-term partnerships among industry, professionals, nonprofits, and the university—work that led to her being named Colorado's Outstanding Accounting Professor in 1996. Dr. Lenk conducted the initial review of the documentation provided by HSIs, which established a foundation for the fourth chapter of this book. In addition, she wrote the profiles of the HSIs included in Chapter 4 and drafted the section on the history of HSIs in Chapter 1.

Jennifer Meeropol is the project associate for Campus Compact's Integrating Service with Academic Study Department. Ms. Meeropol has worked in higher education administration at Harvard Medical School and at Brown University. She has also served as Campus Compact's resource coordinator and project coordinator for the IOEP. Ms. Meeropol oversees the daily management of all project activities and coordinates the efforts of internal and external project staff. Ms. Meeropol wrote the Introduction to the monograph, edited the context chapter, drafted the sidebars in the three findings chapters, and managed the process of writing the monograph.

Sherril B. Gelmon, professor of public health at Portland State University and Campus Compact engaged scholar on assessment, is the evaluation director for the IOEP. Dr. Gelmon has extensive experience in designing and evaluating multi-institutional and interdisciplinary projects related to civic engagement and service-learning. She is lead author of the seminal assessment guide *Assessing Service-Learning and Civic Engagement: Principles and Techniques* (Campus Compact, 2001) and a co-author of *The Engaged Department Toolkit* (Campus Compact, 2003). As the engaged scholar on assessment, she has provided evaluative consultation to Campus Compact's work on civic engagement in the disciplines over the past three years. Dr. Gelmon was the primary author of the appendix on project methodology.

Katrina H. Norvell is a doctoral student in the public administration and policy program at Portland State University. She assists in program evaluation of projects on community-based nursing education and nonprofit leadership development in minority communities. Ms. Norvell assisted Dr. Gelmon in evaluating the project and writing the methodology appendix.

Contexts for Civic Engagement at HBCUs, HSIs, and TCUs

In recent years, changes in student demographics have combined with interest in connecting the burgeoning civic engagement and diversity movements on campus to focus attention on the education of minority students, including the role of minority-serving institutions. Higher education associations, government agencies, and private foundations are investing significant resources in documenting the achievements and challenges of minority students and assisting higher education institutions in meeting the needs of these students.

Although educating these students is not—and should not be—solely the concern of minority-serving institutions, the reality is that a disproportional percentage of minority students attend MSIs, and these schools have been more successful than majority-white institutions in retaining and graduating these students (Merisotis & O'Brien, 1998). Historically Black colleges and universities (HBCUs) account for just 4% of all the four-year colleges and universities in the United States, but they enroll 26% of all African American students and award 28% of the bachelor's degrees earned by African Americans. Hispanic-serving institutions (HSIs) account for 52% of total Latino postsecondary student enrollment (including enrollment in two-year institutions) and 41% of the baccalaureate recipients (Swail, Redd, & Perna, 2003). The situation is similar for Native American students; according to the Alliance for Equity in Higher Education (www.msi-alliance.org), Tribal colleges and universities (TCUs), most of which are two-year institutions, award 19% of all associate's degrees received by American Indians. Clearly, those interested in increasing the educational attainment and civic engagement of minority students have much to learn from these institutions.

Although MSIs have much in common, they also have many important differences. These differences include their institutional characteristics (two-year or four-year, public or private, faith-based or secular), the resources they can draw upon (ranging from institutions with very limited means to private universities with substantial endowments), and the demographics of their student populations (including institutions with a majority of Caucasian students and those composed almost entirely of minority students). These institutions also have different approaches to civic and community engagement; thus, a program that is successful at a number of TCUs may not be successful at an HSI or HBCU, and vice versa.

Some of these differences can be explained by the diverse historical and social contexts that surrounded the formation and growth of these different types of institutions. HBCUs were established to educate a population explicitly excluded from traditional institutions of higher education (namely, freed slaves). In contrast, TCUs were established to offer alternatives for Native American students who had suffered through forced attendance at schools established by the majority society to ensure their assimilation into that society. HSIs differ from both in that they were not necessarily formed to be Hispanic institutions. "Hispanic-serving institution" is a government designation for an institution whose enrollment of Hispanic students reaches or exceeds 25% of full-time equivalent undergraduate enrollment. This designation can be applied years after an institution is founded; it is based on demographic composition, not on institutional mission or purpose. Although in some cases the institutional mission is in line with the demographic reality—as in the HSIs discussed in this book—this is not always the case.

Given the many differences among minority-serving institutions, to understand fully their current efforts to educate and engage their students it is necessary to explore the discrete histories of the HBCU, HSI, and TCU movements and the different ways these schools have explored and expressed their civic and community engagement. Therefore, this chapter focuses on these movements and the establishment and growth of the institutions that grew out of them. It also examines the organizations that have supported the growth of these institutions, key legislation that has guided their development, and the challenges they have faced.

HBCUs and the Tradition of Engagement

> "These institutions [HBCUs] represent, in many ways, one of the most remarkable stories of education-against-the-odds of any set of schools in America."
>
> HENRY N. DREWRY AND HUMPRHEY DOERMANN (2001)

The Origins of Black Colleges

The history of HBCUs is linked inextricably to the history of the struggle on the part of African Americans for all the rights and privileges of citizenship in the United States. The Civil War left 4 million newly emancipated slaves in need of transition services such as the provision of food, clothing, housing, medical care, and, of course, education, to which they had been denied access. In 1865 Congress created the Freedmen's Bureau to assist in this effort and, most notably, to foster education. As the South began to struggle through Reconstruction, religious missionaries had started to set up schools in church basements and former army campsites. The Freedmen's Bureau provided oversight and funding, helping to build and staff some 1,000 schools.

Many HBCUs were founded during this period, including Clark Atlanta, Fisk, Hampton, Howard, Lincoln, Morehouse, and Spelman. Dedicated to the "uplift" of the race, these institutions, which were supported primarily by black churches and community groups, educated more than 70% of the nation's early African American teachers. The impact of this work was huge. In 1870, 80% of all African American adults were illiterate; just 30 years later more than half could read or write (Franklin, 2000, p. 48).

The research of John Hope Franklin, noted scholar and author of the seminal book *From Slavery to Freedom: A History of African-Americans* (originally published in 1947), reveals a race spiritually bound to social activism. In the latter part of the 19th century, much of this activism—spearheaded in large measure by religious leaders—focused on education. In 1865 a group of 500 illiterate slaves joined together to explore ways to provide an education for their children; two years later, Episcopal clergy members helped them set up Talladega College for the education of freed slaves. In 1866, the American Missionary Association established Fisk (now Fisk University) in a wooden shack on confiscated confederate land. The Missionary Association also founded Tougaloo College when it purchased a 500-acre plantation for that purpose in 1869. (Interestingly, the school's purpose was to train young people "irrespective of religious tenets, and conducted on the most liberal principles for the benefit of our citizens in general.") Spelman College began in the damp, dirt-floor basement of Friendship Church in Atlanta. Shaw University was founded as a Bible instruction school to train newly freed slaves to start churches and church organizations.

A landmark in African-American education was the founding of Tuskegee Institute in 1881 under the leadership of Booker T. Washington. Washington, who had attended Hampton Institute—a Black college that emphasized manual training—started with a strong vision that included creating new educators, teaching occupational skills, and building moral character.

Before Washington could take charge of the school, he had to build it. Teachers and students made the bricks that were used to erect their labs, dormitories, and library. They stuffed the mattresses they slept on and raised the food they ate. These activities fit well with Washington's philosophy. He firmly believed that the best interests of black people would be realized through industrial education, intelligent farm management and land ownership, the cultivation of such worthy habits as patience and thrift, and the application of good manners and high morals. He believed that such skill and character would win a place of security and benevolence for his people within Southern society and ensure a sound base from which to advance (Washington, 1901).

Other leaders of the time followed Washington's model of occupational training and outreach. Tuskegee graduates went on to found numerous other schools—dubbed "little Tuskegees"—based on Tuskegee's principles. George Washington Carver, who worked at Tuskegee, taught agricultural practices to black farmers (and won international fame for his research on the uses of peanuts). In 1904, Mary McLeod Bethune, the 17th child of former slaves, founded the Daytona Educational and Industrial Training School for Negro Girls, which later became Bethune-Cookman College.

In addition to advancement through practical education and community skills training, early HBCUs strived to serve the larger African American community through a combination of intellectual development and direct service. W.E.B. Du Bois, in *The Souls of Black Folk* (1903), formulated the idea that an educated black elite should lead African Americans to liberation. North Carolina Central University was founded under this premise in 1910 in order to "seek the regeneration of the Negro," as Du Bois outlined it. The college's history notes that "from the beginning, North Carolina Central University has declared its purpose to be the development in young men and women of the character and sound academic training requisite for real service to the nation" (www.nccu.edu/about/history.shtml).

Into the 20th Century

As Black colleges proliferated, they preserved their emphasis on service. The number of Black colleges increased from just 1 in 1854 to more than 100 by the middle of the next century. These colleges were diverse in many ways, representing a mixture of church-related, privately endowed, and public institutions—but most noted as part of their mission the education of citizens who would provide service to the nation.

According to scholar Beverly W. Jones (1998), service and cooperative work are natural extensions of the African heritage of African Americans. She believes that this ethic is rooted in an African tradition of connectedness and intergenerational obligation, which emphasized "three basic aspects of humanity":

> The first is the idea that individuals and communities have the capacity to celebrate life, even in despairing situations. The second idea is that individuals and communities are visionaries who have the creative power to manifest their

visions. The third idea is that individual identity is communal. The individual operates in a network that provides economic, religious, and political functions (p. 110).

Jones believes that this "communal nature" became a part of the fabric of slave communities, helping slaves survive the harsh conditions under which they lived. Slaves formed several voluntary, benevolent organizations within their communities to provide support where it was most needed. "Family" was often viewed as a combination of extended family and friends in the community. The young were nurtured and taught by elders, and in turn they respected and took care of the elders.

This tradition of helping each other when no help was available from other sources became part of the fabric of HBCUs. For example, African American sororities and fraternities were created in response to discriminating practices that kept students from joining white organizations. These organizations are dedicated not only to promoting academic excellence but also to improving community life through an array of programs and volunteer services.

HBCUs also played a role in fostering the Civil Rights movement, dating back to well before the highly publicized events of the 1960s. In *Civilities and Civil Rights* (1981), William Chafe describes Bennett College, a private, all-female college in Greensboro, North Carolina, as a "model of racial strength" where leaders maintained a standard of independence that suffused the campus. Chafe relates that David Jones, president of the college from 1926 to 1956, instructed his students not to spend money where they were mistreated and always to devote part of their week to helping the community (p. 26). In the 1930s Bennett students helped to lead a boycott of downtown movie theaters in protest against Hollywood's restriction of black actors to stereotyped roles. In 1951, Bennett College and the Greensboro Citizen's Association mobilized the largest and most effective voter registration campaign ever held in Greensboro.

Students at HBCUs were a vital part of the change, growth, and development of the Civil Rights movement during the early 1960s. In some instances, administrators at HBCUs were reluctant to issue public edicts regarding the movement, but they generally recognized its importance and did what they could to support students. The first sit-in, which occurred in February 1960, was initiated by four students at North Carolina A&T University. Their actions sparked the student phase of the Civil Rights revolution, providing an important model for other students. Sit-ins spread rapidly throughout the South, eventually involving more than 70,000 participants.

An essential element of their success was the founding of the Student Nonviolent Coordinating Committee (SNCC) at Shaw University. Started just two months after the first sit-in, SNCC coordinated and publicized protest activity. The organization transformed and solidified student involvement in the movement and placed students in leadership roles. It became a sustained force that would challenge racism throughout America. As the protest movement grew, HBCU students began to recognize that they had the power to effect change in the system. Within a year, more than 100 cities had engaged in at least some desegregation of public facilities in response to student-led demonstrations (Chafe, 1981).

Involvement in the Civil Rights movement became a catalyst for a wave of protest activity among HBCU students in the late 1960s and early 1970s. This was the era of the Vietnam War, which students (and others) saw as a war in which blacks fought for the freedom and rights of others when they were not entitled to those same rights at home. Even more, a disproportionate number of soldiers in Vietnam were black. They fought, died, or returned home altered psychologically, spiritually, and physically. Unrest among HBCU students, many of whom knew these soldiers personally, was widespread. Black students protested not just against the war but also for full enfranchisement and for a voice in their education.

Ironically, the very desegregation the Civil Rights movement helped bring about may also have served to deflect, at least temporarily, some HBCUs from their historic commitment to engagement. As Jones (1998, p. 112) notes in an essay entitled "Rediscovering Our Heritage: Community Service and the Historically Black University":

> Not surprisingly, African-American universities were originally commissioned to serve local community needs and to solve community problems. However, in the wake of desegregation, many of these universities neglected their service focus in order to emulate and compete with white institutions. Thus, over time, instead of working to improve the nation's poor urban communities, HBCUs…abandoned them altogether, opting instead for purely academic/theoretical goals.

This retreat from community engagement has been short-lived, however. Jones notes that "a number of HBCUs have begun to reassert themselves as community partners by tapping the rich source of helping hands and positive role models in their student bodies and faculties." Our research bears out this reassertion; in the course of our site visits, many community partners noted increased community engagement on the part of their local HBCU beginning 10–15 years ago.

The Current State of Engagement

HBCUs have been hugely successful in contributing to society through their education mission. President Ronald Reagan proclaimed September 26, 1983, National Historically Black Colleges Day "because the 103 HBCUs in the United States have contributed substantially to the growth and enrichment of the nation." The proclamation goes to say, "they have awarded degrees to 85% of the country's black lawyers and doctors and 50% of its black business executives. Throughout the years, these institutions have helped many underprivileged students to attain their full potential through higher education" (Presidential Proclamation 5099, 1983).

HBCUs have also maintained their tradition of strong ties to their communities. For many, this is a matter not only of principle but also of self-preservation. HBCUs are often located in deteriorating urban communities; as Beverly W. Jones (1998) notes, they cannot be oblivious to community issues because their future is tied to the fate of their communities. For this reason and many others, community involvement remains at the heart of engagement at HBCUs.

One recent milestone in the history of engagement at HBCUs is the Ford Foundation/United Negro College Fund (UNCF) Community Service Partnership Project, which focused on service-learning. Initiated in 1993, the project provided $2.7 million in grant money to link direct service and learning on 10 UNCF campuses. The project both drew from and enhanced the strong tradition of service and local community outreach at HBCUs by promoting partnerships between HBCUs and their surrounding communities.

In the program's first three years, 3,600 students at the 10 schools participated in service-learning projects, and more than 60 faculty members across disciplines incorporated service-learning into their course curricula. In some cases, service-learning became a graduation requirement. Most impressive is the number of community partnerships established; participating colleges and universities worked with more than 200 nonprofit organizations to improve local communities. Building on the success of this project, the same groups more recently launched the Ford/UNCF Service Learning Network (SLN), whose goal is to expand and enhance service-learning at HBCUs through comprehensive instructional services.

Whether through service-learning or other types of activity, civic engagement at HBCUs rests on the foundation of concern, conviction, and commitment to the community—a foundation that is also at the core of the HBCU mission. Activism and community service are considered part of the education of students at these institutions. Many within the HBCU community believe that the partnership between communities and HBCUs is essential for community empowerment and positive change. They make sure students are introduced early to the heritage of their institution and encouraged to see service not only as a moral responsibility but also as a reciprocal activity with manifold advantages for all concerned.

Resources for and about HBCUs

BILL AND MELINDA GATES FOUNDATION
www.gmsp.org
This website provides information about the Gates Millennium Scholars program for African American, American Indian, and Hispanic students.

BLACK EXCEL
www.blackexcel.org
With a focus on helping minority students navigate the college admission process, this site lists scholarships, fellowships, financial aid information, and more.

DIVERSE: ISSUES IN HIGHER EDUCATION (FORMERLY BLACK ISSUES IN HIGHER EDUCATION)
www.diverseeducation.com
This site provides news and commentary on recent issues affecting minority participation in higher education.

HBCU FACULTY DEVELOPMENT NETWORK
www.hbcufdn.org
This site discusses programs and strategies that enhance the teaching and learning process at HBCUs and provides leadership and coordination for collaborative efforts at HBCUs.

NATIONAL URBAN LEAGUE
www.nul.org
This site includes information about issues relating to economic empowerment, civic engagement, leadership, civil rights, health, quality of life, and racial justice.

SALLIE MAE FUND
www.thesalliemaefund.org
The fund's site includes information about scholarships, support programs, and initiatives that increase access to higher education and encourage volunteerism and community service.

THURGOOD MARSHALL SCHOLARSHIP FUND
www.thurgoodmarshallfund.org
In addition to discussing the contributions of HBCUs, this site offerse information on programs, legislative agendas, scholarships, jobs, and training events for minority students.

UNITED NEGRO COLLEGE FUND (UNCF)
www.uncf.org
This site offers information about scholarships and internships for students as well as faculty and administrative training. Information about the Ford/UNCF Service-Learning Network is at www.uncf.org/Ford; UNCF special projects, including the Health and Community Development Division, is at www.uncfsp.org.

El Compromiso a la Corresponsabilidad Social: HSIs and the Commitment to Community Stewardship

"Tell me what you pay attention to and I will tell you who you are."

JOSÉ ORTEGA Y GASSET

Attention and action-oriented commitment to the welfare of the families and organizations in their communities is a shared trait of Hispanic-serving institutions of higher education. This "we" rather than "me" frame of reference guides the policies, strategies, and partnerships of HSIs; it is evidenced by their willingness to share significant resources to improve factors such as health care, education, economic opportunity, and social justice within their communities. Often the boundaries between these institutions and their communities are difficult to articulate, as many funds and programs are co-owned.

While one may argue that this philosophical description is not unique to Hispanic American cultures or institutions, several factors may explain the differentiated journey of civic engagement at HSIs. First, as noted earlier, HSIs did not originate from a specific federal program or uniform plan. Rather, HSIs evolved primarily because of the growth of Hispanic ethnic and cultural concentrations and/or isolation that occurred in certain communities (Holmes, 2000). The HSI faculty, staff, students, and partners do not just do their civic engagement work in the community, they are that community—and they are living and working together to improve their own future. This spontaneous inception of HSIs increases the philosophical similarities between these schools and community colleges, as both of their missions are closely tied to responding to the specific needs of their communities (Zlotkowski et al., 2004).

Second, consistent with why most Hispanic American families originally moved to the United States, there is a strong focus within HSIs on helping their communities collectively achieve the "American dream" by making sustainable economic or quality of life improvements in the community. The HSI civic engagement projects observed in research for the Indicators of Engagement Project reflect this framework. Because HSI students usually already have a well-developed understanding of the social conditions in their community, engagement activities on these campuses are less focused on awareness-building than at many other institutions and more focused on developing long-term relationships and networks, leadership skills, resource capacity, and advocacy efforts addressing local family, economic, and social issues.

Finally, Catholic traditions have historically influenced much of the Hispanic American value system. While these traditions have more recently expanded to include other religious traditions, the common underlying value system prioritizes service for the betterment of families, the poor, the sick, the hungry, the uneducated, and the otherwise downtrodden in their communities. This tradition of co-ownership and stewardship of community welfare may make civic engagement initiatives an easier "sell" at HSIs than at many other types of institutions. It may also help to reduce the turf battles that commonly slow joint progress toward community goals.

The Development of HSIs and Civic Engagement

Just as the Civil Rights movement is associated with the 1950s and 1960s, and work for Tribal and women's rights with the 1970s, the 1980s and 1990s may very well be remembered as the era of the "Hispanic American civil rights in education" movement. The first formal advocacy group for Hispanic American higher

ONE WITH THE COMMUNITY

The Linguistics of Engagement at HSIs

The literal translation of "civic engagement" in Spanish is a contract, agreement, or obligation with the local government. The terms commonly utilized in Latin America and Spain for this concept are *compromiso, corresponsabilidad,* and *participacion cuidadana*. In this context, *compromiso* is used to mean a personal or collective internal commitment or closely held value. *Corresponsabilidad* denotes a joint or mutual external social responsibility most closely resembling the English concept of "shared stewardship." *Participacion cuidadana* means citizen participation. In contrast to the way "civic engagement" is used in the United States, these terms are typically utilized to discuss one target social condition (poverty, public health, literacy, justice, etc.). Adding social, as in *corresponsabilidad social,* provides the amplitude of meaning to imply stewardship across all social issues and conditions.

Interestingly, many different Spanish-speaking countries use the same words to mean civic responsibility and engagement. This is notable because these countries commonly utilize different words for the same idea, and the same words often have different meanings in different countries. Moreover, the context in which these words are used often influences their meanings. These customary cultural or linguistic differences seem to have been set aside for the discussion of civic engagement—a phenomenon that may result in important synergies in international policy, practice, and research.

---

education began in 1986, when 18 colleges and universities came together to create the Hispanic Association of Colleges and Universities (HACU). HACU's philosophy is that the future economic and social success of the United States will be in part determined by the education, skills, and knowledge of the growing Hispanic American population, and that higher education institutions that serve Hispanic Americans and their communities therefore need to be promoted and developed.

By 1992, just six years after its formation, HACU leadership and members had persuaded the U.S. Congress to amend the Higher Education Act (Title III, sections 316 and 360) to create a separate federal designation for colleges and universities whose student body comprised at least 25% Hispanic Americans. In 1994, with Executive Order 12900, President Clinton formed the first President's Advisory Commission on Educational Excellence for Hispanic Americans to provide advice and input regarding federal education initiatives to improve the education of Hispanic American students.

By 1995, approximately $12 million in federal grants had been awarded to HACU member institutions. Simultaneously, momentum for this movement gained a boost from educators who published influential articles on multiculturalism.

Padilla and Chavez (1995) wrote that the practice of democracy is a daily act based on personal agency and a conviction for action, dialogue, and interaction with those who differ from us. Aguirre (1996) argued that the responsibility of modern higher education is not to reflect the look of diverse cultures but rather to incorporate the multicultural character of the United States.

Despite these advances, in 1997 a report from the U.S. Department of Education revealed that expenditures at HSIs were well below average among all of higher education. Compared with other postsecondary institutions, HSIs were spending just 73 cents to the dollar for student services, 49 cents for academic support services, and 57 cents for instruction. The differences in these expenditures were a direct result of the fact that HSIs were receiving 42% less revenue per FTE and 91% less in endowment revenues overall than other postsecondary institutions (Merisotis & O'Brien, 1998). This data helped to fuel further support for HSIs.

In 1998, the U.S. Congress responded by voting to expand educational opportunities for institutions that serve large numbers of Hispanic Americans by amending Title V of the 1965 Higher Education Act. In order to qualify for Title V funding, HSIs need to have at least 25% Hispanic American enrollment, and at least 50% of all students must qualify as low-income individuals. This amendment opened the door for many more federal grants to support long-term capacity-building investments at HSIs, such as building construction, program and course expansion, teacher education programs, technology resources, faculty and curriculum development programs, joint-use facilities, tutoring and other academic success programs, and community outreach programs.

During this same time period, William Bowen and Derek Bok, the former presidents of Princeton and Harvard Universities, published *The Shape of the River: Long-Term Consequences of Considering Race in College and University Admissions* (1998). The data presented in this book provided strong empirical evidence that minority students were more likely to become leaders in their communities than were their non-minority peers. The conclusion was that universities have a responsibility to create and nurture new opportunities to support the educational needs of these future leaders (Keohane, 1999).

The HSIs that participated in this research clearly demonstrated an awareness and commitment to their responsibility to nurture, train, and develop future leaders for their respective communities. Since most of the HSIs in this study are located in smaller towns or cities that have suffered significant "brain drain" (where graduates leave the area after their education) in the past, their civic engagement programs have been especially effective in developing committed local leaders for the future.

Advances in the New Century

In 2001, Chapter VI of Title 34, part 606, in the Code of Federal Regulations was amended to include language supporting the development of HSIs. The same year, President George W. Bush formally recognized the educational achievement gap of Hispanic American children by signing Executive Order 13230. This order charged a new Presidential Advisory Commission on Educational Excellence for Hispanic Americans to develop an action plan to close this gap. In 2002, Representative Howard P. MeKeon (R-CA) successfully put forward a resolution in the U.S. House of Representatives that honored the important contributions and vital role played by HSIs in the United States.

In 2003, the Presidential Commission submitted its final report, *From Risk to Opportunity: Fulfilling the Educational Needs of Hispanic Americans in the 21st Century*. This report documented severe deficiencies in the education of Hispanic American children at all levels (K-16). In terms of the higher education findings, the report demonstrated a deep cultural expectations gap and a lack of federal support, both of which are most strongly evidenced by a startling statistic from the U.S. Census Bureau (2003): no more than 10% of Hispanic Americans attending four-year institutions were graduating, with fewer than 100,000 Hispanic Americans graduating from college each year in the entire United States. The report's recommendations include the development of better programs for managing expectations, No Child Left Behind Act provisions, teacher education programs focusing on the instruction of diverse students, federal research into Hispanic American education, the development of pathways to college graduation for Hispanic Americans, and improved federal accountability and coordination of related federal funds.

This report coincided with the release of the 2003 Census Bureau finding that Hispanic Americans were now the largest minority group in the United States, totaling more than 37 million people, or 12.5% of the population. Figure 1 depicts the 2002 U.S. Census Report data on Hispanic Americans by origin, illustrating a wide diversity of cultures from Europe, South America, the Caribbean, and Central America. These cultural differences are important to consider for civic engagement work, as Hispanic Americans are often incorrectly characterized as a homogeneous group. Oftentimes, with the exception of the Spanish language and a commitment to families and communities, there may be little overlap between cultures.

In 2003, Partners in Hispanic Education (PHE) was formed. The PHE is the first national-level coalition of federal agencies, Hispanic organizations, private organizations, and corporations focused on the importance of leveraging and empowering the Hispanic American community in efforts to improve Hispanic American education. This program embodies a democratic process consistent with the philosophies of civic engagement and community-based research, and has been a recent springboard for many civic engagement programs.

The first action steps of the PHE have been to develop and provide multi-dimensional educational programs in seven pilot cities around the United States. The PHE local members work together with local families, schools, organizations, and businesses to increase the quality of education and the number of Hispanic Americans prepared for, admitted to, and graduating from college. The pilot cities are San Diego, Miami, New York (specifically, the Bronx), Tucson, Albuquerque, El Paso, and Las Cruces. Each city will develop steering committees and programs that include town hall planning meetings and conference sessions to share information, help families have realistic expectations and increase participation, provide students and their families with tools needed for successful education, and create mentoring, tutoring, and scholarship programs.

Figure 1: **Description of Hispanic Americans by Type**

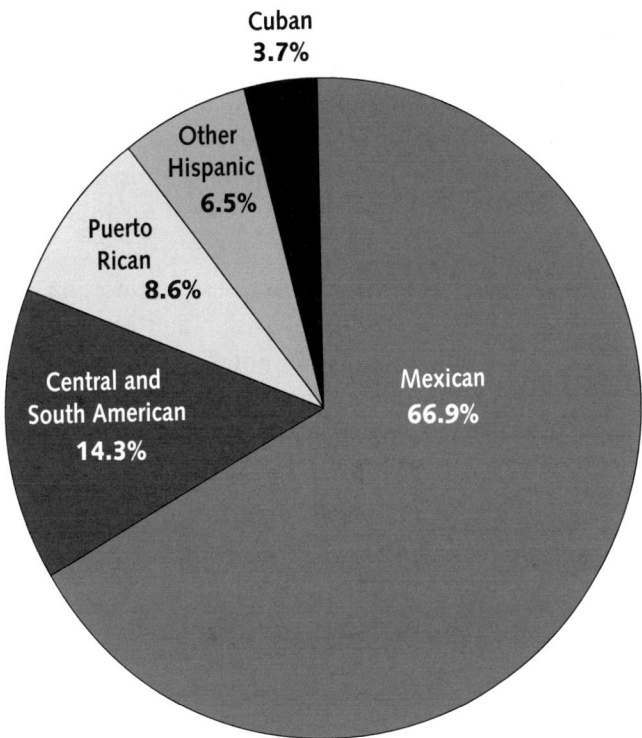

SOURCE: U.S. Census Bureau (2002).

Several other sources of federal funding also support HSIs. These sources include the Strengthening Institutions Program, the International Education and Graduate Programs, TRIO Programs, the Fund for the Improvement of Postsecondary Education, the GEAR UP Program, and specifically earmarked grants from the U.S. Department of Defense, the Department of Housing and Urban Develop-ment HSI Program, and the Department of Transporta-tion.

In 2004, two developments provided further incentives to increase both the amount and the sophistication of civic engagement and community-based research at HSIs. First, a new federal grant program, Hispanic-Serving Institutions Assisting Communities (HSIAC), was initiated to help HSIs lead their communities in sharing ownership and responsibility for work to address community development needs. Administered through the Office of University Partnerships at the U.S. Department of Housing and Urban Development (HUD), the HSIAC program is designed to support initiatives such as neighborhood revitalization, housing and facilities improvements, and economic development, similar to the Community Develop-ment Block Grant program.

Second, U.S. Secretary of Education Rodney Paige and HACU President and CEO Antonio R. Flores signed a memorandum of understanding for a new Joint Leadership Group to oversee the growing number of federal resources flowing into HSIs and their surrounding communities. The purpose of the Joint Leadership Group is to help increase the leadership for, capacities of, and opportunities for successful education and research at HSIs as well as internship and employment in the communities. As Flores noted, "With Hispanics already making up one of every three new workers joining the U.S. labor force today, we all have a stake in the work of the Leadership Group to equip our Hispanic students with access to the advanced knowledge and skills they must have to excel for their communities and for the future of our country."

This mounting support has resulted in steady increases in federal funding for HSIs. By mid-2004, less than ten years after the first federal grants, HSIs had received federal grant money totaling approximately $94 million. President Bush's 2005 budget, which passed in March

---

Partners in Hispanic Education

The Partners in Hispanic Education include leaders from the White house Initiative on Educational Excellence for Hispanic Americans, the United States Department of Education, the United States Hispanic Chamber of Commerce Foundation (USHCCF), MANA (a national Latina organization), Girl Scouts of the USA, the Hispanic Association of Colleges and Universities (HACU), the National Council for Community and Education Partnerships (NCCEP), State Farm Insurance Companies, the League of United Latin American Citizens (LULAC), the National Association of Hispanic Publications (NAHP), the United States Army, the Hispanic College Fund (HCF), the Hispanic Council for Reform and Educational Options (CREO), the National Society of Hispanic MBAs (NSHMBA), the Association for the Advancement of Mexican Americans (AAMA), the Cuban American National Council (CNC), El Valor, and the College for Texans Campaign, Texas Higher Education Coordinating Board.

2004, included $95.9 million for the Title V program, representing a 3.5% increase over the previous year, and a 783% increase over the total for Title V in the 1995 budget. The playing field is still not level; even with these increases, HSIs received less than half of the total amount of 2004 federal funding per student that non-HSI institutions received. Yet even with these significant differences in funding per student, HSIs have been able to organize and mobilize their internal resources to sustain exemplary civic engagement and community development programs that involve significant amounts of externally shared resources.

HSI organizational growth has kept pace with financial gains. HACU has grown to become an international association with approximately 350 U.S. colleges and universities as members. The organization now also numbers many government, nonprofit, and business organizations as partners. These broad-based partnerships are helping to develop programs targeting college preparation, financial aid awareness, scholarships, internships, college retention and advancement, workforce development, technology use, technical training, and faculty development.

Resources for and about HSIs

COLLEGIATE LEADERSHIP NETWORK (CLN)
www.xnetworks.com/nhinet/cln
A program of the National Hispanic Institute.
PO Box 220, Maxwell, TX 78656; 512/357-6137

CONGRESSIONAL HISPANIC CAUCUS INSTITUTE (CHCI)
www.chci.org
911 2nd Street NE; Washington, DC 20002;
202/543-1771 or 800-EXCEL-DC

HISPANIC ASSOCIATION OF COLLEGES AND UNIVERSITIES (HACU)
www.hacu.net
4204 Gardendale Street, Suite 216, San Antonio, TX 78229; 210/692-3805; email: hacu@hacu.net

INTER-UNIVERSITY PROGRAM FOR LATINO RESEARCH
www.nd.edu/~iuplr
PO Box 8180, Austin, TX 78705

NATIONAL HISPANIC INSTITUTE (NHI)
www.nhi-net.org
PO Box 220, Maxwell, TX 78656-0220; 512/357-6137; email: info@nhimail.com

U.S. OFFICE OF UNIVERSITY PARTNERSHIPS, HISPANIC-SERVING INSTITUTIONS ASSISTING COMMUNITIES (HSIAC) PROGRAM
www.oup.org/about/abouthsiac.html

WHITE HOUSE INITIATIVE ON EDUCATIONAL EXCELLENCE FOR HISPANIC AMERICANS
www.yic.gov
400 Maryland Ave., SW, Room 5E110, Washington, DC 20202-3601; 202/401-1411; email: white_house_init_hispanic_ed@ed.gov

While HACU member colleges and universities account for only 7% of all U.S. institutions of higher education, more than 65% of all Hispanic American postsecondary students in the United States attend HACU member institutions (see www.hacu.net).

Cultural Traditions and Community at TCUs

> "Without question, the most significant development in American Indian communities since World War II was the creation of tribally controlled colleges."
>
> PAUL BOYER

Historically, the Native American population has not been well served by the mainstream higher education system. The American Indian Higher Education Consortium (AIHEC) puts it this way: "The history of American Indian higher education over the last several hundred years is one of compulsory Western methods of learning, recurring attempts to eradicate tribal culture, and high dropout rates by American Indian students" (1999, p. A2). The colleges of the 1800s served only a tiny fraction of Native students, and well into the 20th century mainstream colleges had a 90% attrition rate for Native students (Reyhner & Eder, 2004).

During the 1940s and 1950s, many tribal leaders became increasingly dissatisfied with the practice among many majority institutions of pushing Native Americans to embrace Western teaching and culture and neglect their Indian heritage. They also began to see the links between low education achievement and high rates of poverty on the reservations. Two U.S. government policies contributed to a change in the approach of tribal leaders to higher education: the "termination" policies of the 1950s, which proposed to eliminate reservations and tribal affiliations and shifted administration of American Indian programs to the states; and the opposing "self-determination" policies, which began in the 1960s and encouraged maximum choice for American Indians (Cunningham & Parker, 1998). The former policy revealed to tribal leaders their vulnerability to shifts in government policy; the latter led many tribes to create their own institutions and define their own policies.

The opportunities opened up by self-determination eventually led to the creation in 1968 of the first U.S. Tribal college, Navajo Community College (now Diné College). The Navajo Community College Act of 1971 supported this move by providing federal funds "to assist the Navajo Tribe of Indians in providing education to the members of the tribe and other qualified applicants through a community college." Other colleges followed in short order. In 1978, Congress passed the Tribally Controlled Community College Act, which provided funding for

Tribal institutions and opened the door for further growth. The United States now has 34 TCUs that serve some 30,000 students representing more than 250 tribes.

TCU Structure and Purpose

From their inception, TCUs have used the community college as a model for scope and purpose. Each Tribal college began as a two-year institution, although some now offer four-year degrees. True to community college form, vocational education and job training are central to the TCU curriculum, as are disciplinary courses that can be transferred to four-year institutions.

Part of what makes TCUs unique is that cultural studies are a core component of the curriculum. General education requirements typically include courses in Native American culture, and traditional native languages are taught and often used on campuses. In addition, many TCUs are home to annual powwows that celebrate traditional dance, drumming, and other Indian arts.

TCUs expand both the reach and the benefits of higher education. They often serve students in remote areas who would not otherwise have a chance to attend college. They also have a high percentage of "non-traditional" students; according to the American Indian College Fund (AICF), "the average tribal college student is female, age 30, a single mother responsible for two dependent family members, and is often the first in her family to attend college" (AICF fact sheet, www.collegefund.org). Many operate on economically depressed reservations, where job preparation is a particular boon. Studies have found that TCU graduates have substantially higher employment rates than those found on the reservation as a whole (Boyer, 1997).

For TCUs, serving the community is as important as serving students.

The Beginning of the Tribal College Movement

"U.S. Rep. Wayne Aspinall (D-CO) was one of the most powerful men in Congress as chairman of the House Interior Committee in the 1960s and 1970s. Never considered a friend to American Indian causes, Aspinall was cajoled by Ruth Roessel (Navajo) to attend the groundbreaking ceremony for Navajo Community College in Tsaile, AZ, the nation's first tribal college and thus the first to seek federal funding.

At the groundbreaking, Aspinall and several others held onto the *gish*, the traditional digging stick. During the lengthy ceremony, Bob Roessel [one of the college founders] grew increasingly alarmed. The day was hot; the Congressman was elderly; and Aspinall was stooped over, his hands below the others on the *gish*. At the end, he released the stick and slowly stood up, calling Bob Roessel to his side. 'I have been to mosques; I have been to synagogues; I've been to churches all over the world. But I felt God when I felt that stick. You will get your college,' he said. True to his word, Aspinall shouted down congressional and Bureau of Indian Affairs (BIA) opponents, and the Navajo Community College Act of 1971 became law."

Ambler, M. (2002, Winter). Thirty years strong. *Tribal College Journal of American Indian Higher Education, 14 (2),* 6–10. Reprinted with permission from *Tribal College Journal of American Indian Higher Education,* a quarterly magazine published at P.O. Box 720, Mancos, CO 81328. For information call (888) 899-6693, e-mail info@tribalcollegejournal.org, or see the website at www.tribalcollegejournal.org.

Active engagement in community life has always come naturally to these colleges because of their origins. Tribal colleges were created by leaders frustrated with the economic, social, and political realities of life on the reservation. The mission statements of most TCUs are explicitly linked to meeting community needs, and the engagement work found on these campuses is designed to provide direct benefit to the community.

In many areas, community constituents depend heavily on college-sponsored education and other programs. Among other strategies, TCUs utilize grants provided by the U.S. Department of Housing to promote community development; resulting programs focus on employment, crime prevention, child care, health care, drug abuse prevention and treatment, education, fair housing, counseling, energy conservation, and recreational needs (Office of University Partnerships, 2003). With education a priority, many TCUs either work with area K-12 schools or offer their own programs in adult basic education, remedial tutoring, and high school equivalency preparation. Local economic development is also a major focus. TCUs offer courses, technical assistance, and advice; some also sponsor small business centers or provide training in and access to technology. Information about and access to health screening, disease prevention, and health care services are additional key areas of outreach for TCUs.

Recent Legislative Action

The success of TCUs stems in part from government and organizational support. Although gaining government support has been a long and difficult struggle, recent trends highlight efforts by the federal government to aid TCUs. Most recent legislation has focused on acknowledging the special place of TCUs in the United States and the importance of preserving tribal culture through these institutions.

One key piece of legislation is the Native American Languages Act of 1990, which recognizes the unique status of the cultures and languages of Native Americans and notes that the government has a responsibility to act together with Native Americans to ensure the survival of these unique cultures and languages. The act also states that "there is convincing evidence that student achievement and performance, community and school pride, and educational opportunity is clearly and directly tied to respect for, and support of, the first language of the child or student." This act, designed to counter historical attempts to suppress Native languages, supports bilingual education and Native language revitalization.

In 1991, the U.S. Department of Education issued a report titled *Indian Nations at Risk: An Educational Strategy for Action*, which provided support for the Native American Languages Act and the idea of TCUs in general. The report, which presented findings of the Indian Nations at Risk Task Force, argued that well-educated American Indian and Alaskan Native populations, together with a renewal of the language and culture base of the American Native community, would strengthen self-determination and economic well-being among native peoples. A key finding was that "schools that respect and support a student's language and culture are significantly more successful in educating those students" (Indian Nations at Risk Task Force, 1991).

Another key move came in 1994, when Congress awarded TCUs land-grant status, giving them access to a range of federal assistance programs. This designation was a direct outgrowth of the work of TCUs in their communities; according to AIHEC (1999), land-grant status was conferred "in recognition of the essential ties between the colleges, tribal lands, and local economic development" (p. A45).

A land-grant college or university is entitled to receive benefits under the Morrill Acts of 1862 and 1890, which established lands and financial support for higher education institutions to give members of the working class both a practical (mainly agricultural and technical) and an academic education. The conference of land-grant status on TCUs authorized the creation of a $23 million endowment over five years, with interest payments going to the colleges. The legislation also authorized a $1.7 million challenge grant initiative and other funds for higher education programs in agriculture and natural resources. In addition, the act provided funds for the Cooperative Extension Service, through which other land-grand institutions cooperate with TCUs in their state to set up joint agricultural extension programs to meet specific needs identified by the TCUs.

A key challenge for TCUs has been to gain the full benefit of the authorized appropriations under the act. AIHEC notes that funding for schools under Title I of the act has never matched authorized levels; actual funding per student in 1999 was less than half of the authorized amount of $6,000. In addition, growth in the number of schools covered and in overall enrollment in Tribal colleges have kept per-student appropriations stagnant.

In 2002, President George W. Bush issued an executive order establishing a Board of Advisors on Tribal Colleges and Universities to ensure that these institutions have full access to federal and private programs and funds that benefit other higher education institutions. The board is also charged with making recommendations to the President and the Secretary of Education on ways the federal government and the private sector can help Tribal colleges strengthen and expand their resources, programs, facilities, and use of technologies. Actions and initiatives the board considers include long-term development strategies such as creating endowments; other financial security measures, including obtaining private-sector funding and expanding federal education initiatives; using new technology to develop institutional capacity; and implementing the No Child Left Behind Act of 2001 in conjunction with TCUs and their communities.

Organizational Support

Numerous organizations provide financial and other assistance to TCUs and their students. Many were formed and are sustained by education and other leaders within the Native American population. The American Indian Higher Education Consortium, founded in 1972 by the presidents of the first six Tribal colleges, is a key organization. Its mission is "to nurture, advocate, and protect American Indian history, culture, art and language, and the legal and human rights of American Indian people to their own sense of identity and heritage" (www.aihec.org/mission.htm). To accomplish this mission, AIHEC promotes and encourages the development of new TCUs and assists existing Tribal institutions in maintaining high educational standards, developing an accrediting body, and reaching out to other national education organizations. AIHEC also promotes national policy and legislation that strengthen American Indian higher education and provides technical assistance to member institutions. AIHEC's membership includes all 34 U.S. TCUs, across 12 states (as well as one college in Canada).

AIHEC's influence has been far-reaching. In 1978, the organization persuaded Congress to pass the Tribally Controlled Community College Act to provide federal support for Tribal colleges. In the early 1990s AIHEC launched a two-year campaign that was instrumental in persuading Congress to confer land-grant status on the Tribal colleges. In November 1994, the board of the National Association of State Universities and Land-Grant Colleges (NASULGC), which had strongly endorsed the campaign, voted to admit AIHEC as a system member of the association.

Another influential organization is the American Indian College Fund (AICF), a nonprofit association founded by the Tribal colleges in 1989. The AICF provides scholarships for American Indian college students and supports TCUs through endowments, operating monies, and programs in teacher training, facilities construction, and cultural preservation. The AICF is the nation's largest provider of privately funded scholarships for American Indian students.

Also important to the TCU movement is the Native American Higher Education Initiative (NAHEI), a five-year, $22.2 million project funded by the W.K. Kellogg Foundation and involving the AIHEC, the AICF, the National Institute for Native Leadership in Higher Education, and AIHEC's Student Congress, as well as more than 75 mainstream higher education institutions and community organizations. Among other goals, this initiative worked to strengthen TCUs in order to improve educational opportunities for Native Americans, boost the success rates of Indian students at mainstream institutions, and increase the ability of existing organizations to provide financial support and advocacy. Another key goal was to help TCUs use their new land-grant status to improve the quality of the education they provide and to offer more outreach programs to communities. (A project profile is available at www.wkkf.org/Programming/Overview.aspx?CID=165.)

Evolving Roles

The influx of legislative and organizational support since the 1990s, as well as increasing interest and enrollment in Tribal colleges, has allowed these institutions to expand both their scope and their stature. Many of these colleges have sought to become four-year independent institutions. AIHEC has lobbied for accreditation of TCUs and of Native American studies programs, increasing their "legitimacy" among the mainstream academy. In addition, the past five years have seen increased interest in master's programs, teacher education programs, and language certificates for Native students.

Alongside this support has been controversy within the tribal community over funding for TCUs and over the role these institutions play on reservations and in Native communities. Part of this controversy is based on diverging visions for tribal education, with more traditional leaders advocating for a strong focus on preserving tribal culture and others arguing for a greater emphasis on preparing students to enter the workforce or transfer to four-year colleges off of the reservation. One resident of the Rosebud Sioux reservation sums up the former point of view this way: "separate but equal is just fine with us" (Boyer, 1989, p. 2).

After centuries of fighting to preserve their language, culture, and identity, many educators at TCUs are understandably divided over the relative value of integration into mainstream institutions and separation from them. Adherents to both points of view, however, are committed to improving not just the lives of students but also the health of their communities.

Minority-Serving Institutions and Social Advancement

Despite the numerous historical and cultural differences among and between HBCUs, HSIs, and TCUs—and the communities they serve—they are united by several deeply held beliefs and commitments. First, and perhaps most fundamental, is the value they place on family and community. All of these institutions are committed to creating long-term partnerships that share resources to improve both the economy and the quality of life in their surrounding communities. The mainstream emphasis on the individual as the measure of thinking and planning gives way here to an appreciation of the community/family/ethnic group as the ultimate touchstone of the value of any individual effort.

This less individualistic, more community-based mindset has important implications for engagement at minority-serving institutions. One is that MSIs regard their impact on the lives of the families and organizations in their community as

Resources for and about TCUs

AMERICAN INDIAN COLLEGE FUND (AICF)
www.collegefund.org
This website provides information about scholarships and fellowships as well as about Tribal colleges.

AMERICAN INDIAN GRADUATE CENTER (AIGC)
www.aigc.com
This site provides information on fellowships, scholarships, and job opportunities, as well as a community bulletin board, publications, event listings, and a student directory.

AMERICAN INDIAN HIGHER EDUCATION CONSORTIUM (AIHEC)
www.aihec.org
The AIHEC site provides profiles of TCUs, information on student populations and legislative priorities, and links to relevant websites, resources, and publications.

AMERICAN INDIAN SCIENCE AND ENGINEERING SOCIETY (AISES)
www.aises.org
AISES provides education opportunities to bridge Native American traditions with recent technology. The site provides information on events, scholarships, resources, and career services for students.

THE INSTITUTE FOR HIGHER EDUCATION POLICY (IHEP)
www.ihep.com
This site provides information and links on education policy, as well as information about ongoing projects such as the Alliance for Equity in Higher Education.

NATIONAL CONGRESS OF AMERICAN INDIANS (NCAI)
www.ncai.org
This site provides information on issues important to American Indians, from legislation to current events, as well as legislative links, a tribal directory, and internship opportunities.

NATIONAL INDIAN EDUCATION ASSOCIATION (NIEA)
www.niea.org
This site offerse a newsletter, information on upcoming events and speakers, and links relevant to Native American education.

TRIBAL COLLEGE JOURNAL OF AMERICAN INDIAN HIGHER EDUCATION
www.tribalcollegejournal.org
This culture-based publication addresses subjects of importance to the American Indian and Alaska Native communities. It features both journalistic and scholarly articles, as well as information on careers, internships, and scholarships.

WHITE HOUSE INITIATIVE ON TRIBAL COLLEGES AND UNIVERSITIES (WHITCU)
www.ed.gov/about/inits/list/whtc/edlite-index.html
This government site has information for TCU students, parents, teachers, and administrators, including information on scholarships and financial aid, recent legislation, and research and statistics.

an important measure of their success. Another is that MSIs do not view their students as customers to be served, but rather as owners of their communities and as part of a larger social advancement system that is owned by all participating parties, not just the campus administration or faculty. This is evidenced by the many cultural traditions at MSIs that celebrate partnerships and community achievements. These traditions can be informal—such as cultural festivals—or official ceremonies and events that include influential community members.

The future holds much promise for civic engagement at MSIs. This promise stems perhaps most from the community partnerships and cultural infrastructures they already have in place, and from their commitment to achieving the American dream. It is our hope that this book will help share the innovative and transforming programs and approaches of these institutions with the rest of higher education, both to increase support for these programs and to encourage majority-serving institutions to follow their lead.

Engagement at Historically Black Colleges and Universities

The Service Mandate of HBCUs

Among minority-serving institutions, those with the longest service tradition are historically Black colleges and universities (HBCUs). It is important to appreciate the degree to which interest in campus-based community engagement, a recent phenomenon for many institutions, has always been part of the core mission of HBCUs. Whether one looks at one of the original HBCUs like Johnson C. Smith University (JCSU), founded under the auspices of the Freedman's Bureau in the years immediately following the Civil War, or one of the "younger" public HBCUs like North Carolina Central University (NCCU), founded early in the 20th century at the height of Jim Crow repression, one is immediately struck by the direct connection between these schools and education for the public good.

As is also true with regard to other kinds of MSIs, it is not easy to capture the distinctive quality of engagement at HBCUs—especially in and through a set of specific policies and practices. Although no objective measurement criteria can fully capture either the historical urgency of these campuses' commitment to engagement or the broad integrity that informs their work, Campus Compact's indicators of engagement help document a remarkable set of commitments, initiatives, and programs.

Institutional Culture

Best Practices

- Include specific and concrete expressions of commitment to civic and community engagement in the college's mission statement.

- Expose new students to the college's service tradition early and often in their academic careers.

- Lead by example; make sure college administrators and faculty are involved in the community.

ONE WITH THE COMMUNITY

- Encourage the Board of Trustees to institutionalize support for service and engagement.

Mission and Purpose

A key way to create a culture of engagement is to include explicit language in the institution's mission statement—hence the inclusion of "Mission and Purpose" as the first indicator of engagement. Jones (1998) notes that NCCU began seriously reconnecting with its historic commitment to civic and community engagement in 1993, when, as part of a "dramatic repositioning" (p. 112), the institution's mission statement was rewritten to stress its new vision. Not only would NCCU seek to "prepare students academically and professionally," it would also seek to "promote consciousness of social responsibility and dedication to the advancement of the general welfare of the people of North Carolina, the United States, and the world" (see www.nccu.edu/about/mission).

With this explicit commitment both to promote social responsibility and to advance the public's general welfare, the university positioned itself to make the kinds of strategic investments that would allow it to turn rhetoric into reality. For example, in 1995, NCCU became one of the first HBCUs to join Campus Compact and to align itself with the national movement to prepare students for active citizenship. This move indicated a willingness to allocate scarce resources to achieving this goal.

Other HBCUs have made comparable commitments in and through their mission and purpose. For the 100 years of its existence, Bethune-Cookman College's motto has always been "Enter to Learn. Depart to Serve." Understandably, community

---

**Examples from the Field:
Mission Statements with Civic Emphasis**

FROM JOHNSON C. SMITH UNIVERSITY:

[Johnson C. Smith University] provides an environment in which students can fulfill their physical, social, cultural, spiritual and other personal needs and in which they can develop a compelling sense of social and civic responsibility for leadership and service in a dynamic, multicultural society. Likewise, the university embraces its responsibility to provide leadership and lifelong learning to the larger community.

SOURCE: Johnson C. Smith University, www.jcsu.edu/friends/about.htm.

FROM LEMOYNE-OWEN COLLEGE:

LeMoyne-Owen College is a private, historically black liberal arts institution, distinguished by diverse faculty, rigorous academic programs, and success in preparing students for professional careers, leadership, and service in the local and global community.

SOURCE: LeMoyne-Owen College, www.loc.edu/welcome/mission.htm.

FROM XAVIER UNIVERSITY OF LOUISIANA:

Xavier University of Louisiana is Catholic and historically Black. The ultimate purpose of the University is the promotion of a more just and humane society. To this end, Xavier prepares its students to assume roles of leadership and service in society. This preparation takes place in a pluralistic teaching and learning environment that incorporates all relevant educational means, including research and community service.

SOURCE: Xavier University, www.xula.edu/mission.html.

engagement, outreach, volunteerism, and service are core components of the college's mission, and service-learning has been institutionalized—embedded across the college's practice—for more than a decade.

Another example, Benedict College, in Columbia, South Carolina, identifies as one of its primary teaching goals instilling in students "a desire for public service," with graduates "committed to making the world a better place" (www.benedict.edu/divisions/inseff/research/bc_research_college_mission.html). It is not just through teaching that Benedict explicitly commits itself to the public good. Its mission statement goes on to endorse "research [that] will contribute to discovery and implementation of better policies and programs in the public and private sectors to advance all Americans to full and complete equality."

Given Benedict's status as an HBCU, its emphasis on equality is not especially noteworthy. What is noteworthy is the college's understanding of research as leading not just to the discovery of better policies and programs but also to their implementation. This view mirrors the spirit of Ernest Boyer's "scholarship of engagement" (1996); for Boyer, such scholarship leads students and faculty to view campuses "not as isolated islands but as staging grounds for action" (p. 119). This also seems to be Benedict's goal.

In its understanding of service, the third of the academy's traditional concerns (after teaching and research), Benedict does not shy away from a concrete understanding of the college as a staging ground for action, pledging "to provide direct service in the local community and throughout South Carolina." This commitment to service that includes direct assistance, combined with teaching that highlights public service and research that contributes to the creation of better public policies, sets the Benedict mission statement apart from the more typical generic expressions of public purpose.

Other schools, such as Morehouse College and Talladega College, focus on service leadership. Morehouse's strategic plan focuses in part on developing students "intellectually and ethically for service to local, national, and international communities." In addition, "Morehouse works to produce students who have the knowledge, values, and practical skills necessary to become civic leaders in every corner of our world" (www.morehouse.edu/aboutmc/strategicplan/index.php). The mission statement of Talladega College is similarly concerned with leadership through service: "Talladega College is dedicated to producing humane, well-rounded leaders who think independently, are secure in their sense of themselves, are open to intellectual growth, and prompted to serve their community."

This commitment to practices and policies that make a *demonstrable* difference in the lives of non-academics is a distinctive feature of the way in which many

HBCUs understand their mission. At LeMoyne-Owen College in Memphis, a recent strategic planning document called "The Renaissance Begins" (2003) is referring not just to a campus undertaking; seeing the future of the college as fundamentally tied to the future of the surrounding community, the plan identifies "community revitalization" as its very first expected outcome. The document goes on to embrace the community as a "hands-on laboratory where students and faculty… engage directly in projects with their neighbors, developing their expertise in community development, team collaboration, and civic engagement." This view echoes the powerful connection between academic work and community problem-solving that characterized the birth of American universities in the late 19th century (Harkavy, 2000).

Such a resemblance has more than curiosity value. In an essay titled "Institutional Identity and Social Responsibility in Higher Education," William Sullivan (2000) writes that "Despite its great size and prestige, much of American higher education today suffers from a sense of demoralization and decline" (p. 21). According to Sullivan, one important source of this malaise has to do directly with the indicator we've titled "Mission and Purpose":

> In the absence of an updated version of its founding conception of itself as a participant in the life of civil society, as a citizen of American democracy, much of higher education has come to operate on a sort of default program of instrumental individualism. This is the familiar notion that the academy exists to research and disseminate knowledge and skills as tools for [private sector] economic development and the upward mobility of individuals. This "default program" of instrumental individualism leaves the larger questions of social, political, and moral purpose out of explicit consideration (p. 21).

Whatever else one might say about the guiding documents of engaged HBCUs, one can hardly accuse them of failing to consider explicitly these larger questions of purpose. In an age when market considerations saturate almost all public discourse, many HBCUs continue to speak the language of community obligation and democratic promise.

It is, moreover, a language the colleges' students quickly appropriate. It is no coincidence that schools like NCCU, Benedict, and LeMoyne-Owen are among the relatively few higher education institutions in the country that require either community service or service-learning for students to graduate. However, even more important than this requirement itself is the student attitude toward it. At Johnson C. Smith University (JCSU) in Charlotte, NC—another HBCU with a service graduation requirement—a senior remarked that doing community service is "just like walking and putting on your shoes." Since his arrival at the university, he had logged approximately 20 hours per month of community work and had become one of the school's Student Ambassadors, responsible for supervising other students at community sites. One faculty member noted that the verse from the Gospel of St. Matthew to the effect that "from those to whom much has been given, much is expected" almost functioned as a JCSU mantra. Another faculty member suggested that since she first arrived at the college more than 25 years ago, she had "never heard a student object" to its service graduation requirement.

Many factors help account for such widespread student acceptance of service as an essential part of their education, but one of the more important institutional factors is the willingness of engaged HBCUs to help new students adopt their college's service tradition. At Xavier University of Louisiana's orientation, students not only learn about the history of the institution, with its roots in the service commitment of St. Catherine of Drexel, they also learn why "giving back to the community" should be one of their own personal priorities. At NCCU, all students are required to take a course called Dimensions of Learning. Among the topics covered is the history and mission of the institution. Early on, they learn why the school's motto is "Truth and Service."

Administrative and Academic Leadership

A campus culture in which service and civic engagement are accepted as a natural part of what one does clearly requires more than a powerful mission statement. A second, complementary indicator, "Administrative and Academic Leadership," helps make what is on paper more than a paper commitment. This, of course, requires commitment from the top. When NCCU began its "dramatic repositioning," it did so as a "top-down strategy" initiated by then-Chancellor Julius Chambers (Jones, 1998, p.112). Similarly, LeMoyne-Owen's strategic plan notes that

> Upon arriving in September 2002, President James Wingate set priorities... [that] have included reconnecting with the college's various constituencies [and] strengthening LeMoyne-Owen's role as...a partner to schools, communities, agencies, and other greater Memphis institutions.

According to some of the college's community partners, it was the president's willingness to speak personally to the importance of community engagement that led every department in the college to embrace such work.

At Xavier University of New Orleans, President Norman Francis has noted that when the university's stated purpose of promoting "a just and humane society" is applied to the communities that surround the campus, questions of justice and humanity almost "jump out at you." Under President Francis's leadership, Xavier has actively embraced its responsibility to act, in his words, "as a catalytic agent" "to invest resources, particularly human resources, and use moral authority to get city agencies to do more." The president's commitment and example have led faculty, staff, and students to become actively involved in programs that help Xavier fulfill the community responsibilities inherent in both its "Black and Catholic heritages" (see www.xula.edu/planning/documents/2003-XULA-goals.pdf). This commitment extends to offering staff release time to work in the local community.

President David Swinton of Benedict College also sees his students and faculty as "community resources." When he first arrived at Benedict 10 years ago, he found the community surrounding the college so troubled it was dangerous to walk down some streets. Immediately he began partnering with community organizations not just to clean up but to transform the neighborhood. Local crack houses were shut down; underage drinking was curbed; and housing was rehabilitated. Given this agenda, it is not surprising that in 1998 President Swinton became the first African-American chair of the Greater Columbia Chamber of Commerce and in 1999 "helped organize a group of 50 investors … to preserve the only minority bank in South Carolina" (see www.benedict.edu/exec_admin/presid/bc-president-bio.html).

Although it would be hard to underestimate the importance of presidential leadership, it is, of course, not only the president or chancellor who helps make an engaged mission statement real. At Benedict College, the president has strongly encouraged all faculty and administrators to become actively engaged in the community, as well as to promote service among those they supervise. Especially impressive has been the commitment of David Whaley, vice president for Student Affairs, whose efforts have earned him a place on the Columbia Housing Authority's community "Wall of Fame." The wall pays tribute to individuals who grew up in the area and have made significant contributions to the community. The college has invited those featured on the wall to campus to present their stories to help students gain an understanding of how community leaders can make a difference.

Many HBCUs can boast strong community commitment from all tiers of academic and administrative leaders. For example, LeMoyne-Owen College's chief academic officer (CAO), Barbara Frankle, sees her main job as "bringing full academic support to the college's engagement agenda." At JCSU, both the provost, Marilyn Sutton-Haywood, and the dean of Arts and Sciences, Rosalyn Jones, have emerged as significant spokespersons for the legitimacy of academically based service.

Finally, it is important to note that at these schools the board of trustees has more often than not played a critical role in facilitating institutional support for service and engagement. For example, the board played a very supportive role in establishing JCSU's Service-Learning Center at a time when such centers were still relatively rare. Similarly, the board at LeMoyne-Owen has been strongly behind that institution's community-based learning initiatives and has backed President Wingate's plans to strengthen the college's partnership with South Memphis.

Such widespread institutional leadership, coupled with unambiguous mission statements and planning documents, helps create a climate that fosters civic and community engagement among faculty, staff, and students. That said, it takes much more than a supportive culture to make academy-community partnerships both successful and significant. The next pair of indicators helps identify specific ways in which engagement is facilitated in and through academic programs and practice.

Curriculum and Pedagogy

Best Practices
- Incorporate service-learning into courses across the curriculum.
- Encourage students to participate in service-learning courses from the beginning of their academic careers.
- Require service-learning for graduation.
- Develop curricular mechanisms that allow students to link service activities to traditional courses.

As noted elsewhere, at most American colleges and universities an enormous gap exists between civic/community engagement as a component of the mission statement and engagement as a core part of the institution's curriculum. To some degree, this gap also exists at HBCUs insofar as their exceptionally engaged mission statements do not always translate into a correspondingly full spectrum of community-based courses. However, strategic use of service-learning, in conjunction with other mechanisms to promote student and faculty community involvement, does result in a set of practices and programs that do justice to stated institutional priorities.

Departments, Disciplines, and Interdisciplinary Work

"Departments, Disciplines, and Interdisciplinary Work," the first of two indicators of engagement in the Curriculum and Pedagogy category, refers to the ways in which an institution makes civic and community engagement a part of its core teaching agenda. At schools like NCCU—one of the first HBCUs to realize the potential of course-based service—service-learning has, for some time, found broad representation across the entire academic spectrum. For example, the university's Faculty Fellows—"persons who have shown exemplary work in service-learning in their classes or have supported service-learning" (www.nccu.edu/commserv/facultyfellows.htm)—include faculty from 13 academic areas, including art, music, theater, English, biology, geography, political science, and several health-related disciplines. A list of courses for which the service-learning office plans to post syllabi spans not only those disciplines but also sociology, criminal justice, and education. Clearly, NCCU is well on its way to achieving what Assistant Provost and Associate Vice Chancellor Franklin Carver calls the goal of incorporating service-learning into "every area of the university."

Other HBCUs have also been successful in integrating service-learning into courses across the curriculum. However, such broad curricular representation is not the only strategy used to make community-based course work part of a school's engagement strategy. LeMoyne-Owen set up a faculty committee to explore ways in which each of the college's five divisions could infuse service into its curriculum. In the end, each division was tasked with developing a core competency related to "service to humanity," together with vehicles through which that competency can be demonstrated. In addition, to ensure that its students participate in community-based work in and through the curriculum, LeMoyne-Owen also

---

Example from the Field: A Service-Learning Plan

Agency: Agricultural Extension Service, Desert Rock, CA

Assignment: To form a youth club in a barrio neighborhood for urban teenagers who do not respond to the regular 4-H program; to introduce nutrition information for club members.

Time Commitment: Ten hours per week for one semester.

Agency Supervisor: Ernie Powers, Youth Liaison Officer

Faculty Advisor: Alicia Gibson, Professor of Psychology

SERVICE OBJECTIVES

- To form a club of young people under 15 years of age from the Northside neighborhood by March 1.

- To plan and implement a nutrition education program for the club by May 31.

SERVICE ACTIVITIES

1. To become familiar with the Agricultural Extension Service, especially its youth outreach program.

2. To become acquainted with the Desert Rock community, especially young people, their parents, and teachers at the Casa Loma School.

3. To help draw up club by-laws, elect officers, and establish a committee system.

4. To introduce club members to recreational activities and audiovisual materials giving nutrition information.

EVALUATION OF SERVICE

I will meet with the Ernie Powers [the agency supervisor] once a week to:

- Discuss problems and ask questions related to my assignment.

- Receive verbal feedback from him about my progress.

Upon completion of my assignment, I will have an exit interview with Ernie Powers. There will be no written evaluation from the host agency.

CONTINUED NEXT PAGE, BOTTOM

requires students to complete a first-year service-learning experience as well as two elective upper-level service-learning courses. As the college's CAO and one of her faculty colleagues have explained:

> Service-learning was deemed so important to personal and academic growth that the faculty decided students should encounter it at the very beginning of their college careers. Faculty also believed this experience would be so rewarding it would encourage service in subsequent years. Consequently, service-learning was integrated into the freshman-level social science class Power and Society (Frankle & Ajanaku, 2002, p.109).

Benedict College has employed a similar strategy. Benedict students are required to enroll in both Freshman Seminar I and II, and Sophomore Seminar I and II, all of which include a service-learning component. As President Swinton notes, Benedict does not want to graduate students who look at the community and simply see that something is wrong but rather students who, when they see a problem, immediately begin figuring out how to take corrective action.

Example from the Field: A Service-Learning Plan *(continued from previous page)*

LEARNING OBJECTIVES

- To understand the impact of barrio environment on teenage development.
- To test a variety of organizing techniques that I studied last year in a Social Psychology course.

AVAILABLE RESOURCES

1. Ernie Powers will give me four hours of on-site orientation.
2. I will have access to the reference library of the Extension Service.
3. I will attend Extension Service staff meetings once a month.

LEARNING ACTIVITIES

1. To keep a journal about my expectations and observations of the teenagers; their responses to different organizational techniques; how they change and how I change during the course of the semester.
2. To read ten selected books on adolescent development.
3. To compile an annotated bibliography of my reading list.

EVALUATION OF LEARNING

1. Professor Gibson will meet with me once every two weeks to discuss the assigned readings.
2. Professor Gibson will also visit with Ernie Powers and me at the site to discuss the project.
3. I will submit my journal to her once a month and upon completion of my project.
4. I will write a short self-evaluation for Professor Gibson, consisting of excerpts from my journal, from my readings, and from the feedback that I receive from Ernie Powers during the semester. Professor Gibson will evaluate me on the extent to which my self-evaluation reveals understanding of factors influencing teenage development in the barrio.

SOURCE: Johnson C. Smith University Service-Learning Center/Student Union Student Information Guide, Angela Jeter, Service-Learning Coordinator. Used by permission.

Service-learning as a graduation requirement, or as a required component of a required course, is still relatively rare in American higher education. Also rare is a substantive community service requirement (as opposed to the widespread practice of including a one-time service event in a first-year seminar). It is therefore notable that of the five HBCUs visited for the Indicators of Engagement Project, four have such a substantive community service graduation requirement. (The fifth requires service activities of every student organization every semester as a condition of institutional support.)

These requirements are manifestations of the major role service plays in the educational philosophy of HBCUs. For engaged HBCUs, social responsibility is as fundamental to their understanding of what it means to be an educated person as are critical thinking and communication skills. As one Benedict College administrator explains: "Community service is seen as the essence of going to college."

This linking of service and education has powerful antecedents. In an article entitled "Unrecognized Roots of Service-Learning in African American Social Thought and Action, 1890-1930" (2003), Charles Stevens argues that much of what we today identify as exemplary service-learning practice was clearly if not formally anticipated in the work of black educators and activists more than 100 years ago.

> In the black American experience, there is a long-standing interest in the community service ideal. This perspective in the context of African American social thought is manifested as a racial legacy dedicated to strengthening community to deal with internal problems and promote broader social change. Responding to the urgency in African American social thought, the community service perspective is conceived as a social obligation and organizing principle for blacks actively committed to the social advancement of American black communities (pp. 25–26).

From this perspective, it is easy to understand the logic of seeing community service as the "essence of going to college" and hence of requiring service as a significant part of the college experience. When HBCUs require that all first-year students understand the history of their institution, and when they make service a required part of the first-year experience as well as a requirement for graduation, they are themselves responding to that same "urgency" in African American social thought that Stevens discusses. Even where community engagement is not specified as a curricular requirement, it is more than a casual undertaking meant to fill extracurricular time.

Given this essential link between the idea of education and that of engagement, individual strategies for introducing service as part of the student experience are far less important than is a general, ongoing commitment to making community work as unexceptional—and as essential—as "walking and putting on your shoes."

To help students find natural venues for their service interests and make progress toward their service graduation requirement, NCCU, JCSU, and Lemoyne-Owen have all developed a curricular mechanism that allows students to link service activities to a wide range of traditional courses. Hence, in addition to those courses where community-based work has been designed as a formal course component, students are encouraged to look for additional opportunities where they can take the initiative to make a curriculum-community connection (with their instructor's consent). At Johnson C. Smith, students' service interests also find expression in many of the required senior papers as well as in research projects identified by the faculty's multidisciplinary Urban Research Group.

HBCUs also have a variety of specific academic programs where engagement is especially prominent. At NCCU, the political science department is looking for funding to extend the activities of the Institute of Civic Engagement it pioneered several years ago. No student can get a degree in political science without doing engaged work. The university's criminal justice department has also developed an exemplary set of community-based initiatives. At JCSU, the teacher education program has so comprehensively embraced service-learning that it has become an "engaged department"—what Campus Compact identifies as a department in which engagement is part of the collective culture and is infused throughout the curriculum. From sophomore through senior year, education majors must take a sequence of courses (developmental psychology, educational methods, children's literature) that contain a service-learning component. The program also features several elective courses that include service-learning. A similar situation exists at Benedict, where service to the community drives the entire teacher education program.

Teaching and Learning

Institutions that make available so many opportunities to link the curriculum and community service are clearly not locked into a narrow understanding of what counts as legitimate academic work. This flexibility is evident in "Teaching and Learning," the second of the two indicators that constitute the Curriculum and Pedagogy unit. Unlike institutions where the operating assumption seems to be that developing the "life of the mind" requires separation from life as it is actually lived, engaged HBCUs not only sanction experiential education but celebrate it.

One especially striking example can be found in LeMoyne-Owen's 2003 strategic planning document, "The Renaissance Begins." The first of the document's five goals calls for the institution to "develop and enhance the life and leadership skills of students through a culturally and academically challenging experience grounded in the unique history and heritage of the region." The second, related, goal speaks of providing "world-class quality programs and services using community resources," while the third goal envisions the creation of Centers of Excellence: "communities of learners using multiple perspectives to develop breadth and depth of knowledge about the disciplines and practitioners in the fields." Such centers will allow students to "gain valuable experience through internships, community projects, performances and presentation."

This overt embracing of the value of community-based experience as a core educational strategy helps account for several distinctive features of the way in which the schools we looked at approach engagement. For example, if experience is seen as central rather than as marginal to the education process, early preparation of students for off-campus work becomes almost a necessity. At JCSU, a special preparation unit taught by the service-learning coordinator has been incorporated into the first-year seminar all students must take. Nearly a third of those students are also enrolled in a learning community that focuses on issues of African American identity. All of the sections in this course require service-learning.

As noted earlier, students at Benedict are required to take a four-seminar sequence in their first and second years, each unit of which requires service-learning. Such a program gives faculty and administrators a solid foundation on which to build throughout students' college experience. In discussing the school's new strategic plan, administrators noted:

> One of its main goals is to get the students off the campus into the community into various work environments, especially in the upper level courses. The question is continually asked, "Do we have the experiences in those courses that require students to move into the community?"

This goal relates directly to a second feature of engagement at the schools we visited: a focus on career development, specifically in public service. If experience is expected and practitioners are seen as valued educational allies, it is only natural that civic engagement and career exploration begin to overlap.

Especially important in this regard are the American Humanics programs hosted by several HBCUs, including Xavier and LeMoyne-Owen. Working with a range of community-based organizations, both programs not only give students an opportunity to "give back"; they also give them an opportunity to prepare for a career in the nonprofit sector. The success of these initiatives is evident in one particularly impressive finding: at virtually all the schools visited, whether or not they have an American Humanics program, many of the institutions' key community partners are their own former students. "Leadership and service" is an almost constant HBCU coupling, and leadership often takes the concrete form of harnessing one's college education to the work of a service-based organization.

This link between service and career opportunities points to another way HBCUs create context for—and see the results of—their focus on the student service experience. If a school like Xavier sees serving as "a catalytic agent" to improve the local community as one of its key responsibilities, it should hardly be surprising that New Orleans' first black mayor, Ernest Morial, was a Xavier graduate. And while some schools are concerned that service could lead to political action, Xavier's President Francis laments that service has not led to *enough* political action. For him, and for other leaders of engaged HBCUs, politics must be part of the engagement experience.

This is because engagement is not intended as window dressing for an otherwise "unthreatening" education; it is meant to produce community change agents. Like other HBCU leaders, Bessie Gage, chair of JCSU's education department, notes that students need to understand the philosophy behind engagement so they will develop into citizens who can provide solutions to problems. She doesn't want her students simply to learn to work with homeless children: they must also learn to become those children's "advocates."

> **American Humanics**
>
> Founded in 1948, American Humanics (AH) is a national alliance of colleges, universities, and nonprofit organizations devoted to preparing college students for careers in nonprofit youth and human service organizations. The program incorporates service-learning classes into the curriculum in order to qualify students for professional employment opportunities in these agencies.
>
> The AH program is in place at more than 70 colleges and universities nationwide. Partners include the American Red Cross, Big Brothers Big Sisters of America, and the United Way.
>
> The AH program is a supplement rather than a separate degree. In addition to the requirements for their major, students must compete two AH core courses as well as five AH-related courses, with requirements varying from major to major. Students must also fulfill a 300-hour internship/practicum at an approved site. In addition, students are required to participate in co-curricular activities coordinated by the American Humanics Student Association and to attend at least one session of the AH Management Institute, held at various locations across the United States.
>
> Students are evaluated using 14 core skill and knowledge competencies in nonprofit youth and human service management, including communication skills, historical and philosophical foundations, fundraising principles and practices, and nonprofit marketing.

Thus, the importance of "Teaching and Learning" as an indicator of engagement at HBCUs far transcends the idea that experiential learning has real academic value. For these schools, it points not just to a way of knowing but to a way of living; not just to legitimate knowledge but to embodied knowledge. Community-based teaching and learning does not embellish the academic resume. It informs that resume and transforms it into a tool of social justice. The next pair of indicators begins the process of documenting support for those who guide the development of this tool.

Faculty Culture

Best Practices

- Offer in-house service-learning trainings.
- Provide written materials to help faculty understand and implement service-learning projects.
- Obtain outside support, through grants and independent organizations, to create and sustain faculty development opportunities.
- Include service and engagement in faculty evaluation documents.
- Welcome new approaches to teaching and learning.
- Informally recognize faculty service and engagement.

Although institutional culture and faculty culture are in many ways related, they are by no means identical. While it is hard to imagine strong faculty support for engaged work at a school where both key documents and key administrators seem to point in another direction, it is easy to find examples of institutions where a strong mission and top-down leadership have not resulted in faculty engagement. For the latter to occur, faculty need to feel both competent in and recognized for their dealings with the community.

Faculty Development

The "Faculty Development" indicator addresses the need of faculty members to feel competent. By and large, HBCU strategies in this area do not differ significantly from those at other kinds of engaged institutions. At several of the schools we visited, in-house service-learning trainings are offered on a regular or frequent basis, and all of the schools provide written material to help faculty understand and implement quality service-learning projects. In addition, NCCU has developed an extensive website hosted by the Academic Community Service Learning Center. The site offers information, forms, and other resources useful to faculty, students, and staff (www.nccu.edu/commserv).

Approaches to faculty development vary, but hands-on training is a common element. Faculty development for service-learning at the University of the Virgin Islands occurs primarily in a pilot project developed with grant funding. The program educates faculty about service-learning principles and practices, supports faculty participation in regional conferences, and provides stipends to support work on revising syllabi to incorporate service-learning.

At JCSU, faculty development is not only available; it is required. Before a faculty member can offer a service-learning course, she or he must take a service-learning workshop and have the course design approved by both the service-learning coordinator and the dean of arts and sciences. JCSU also requires faculty to fill out a post-course assessment sheet. Xavier, which more recently began developing its service-learning program, similarly requires faculty developing a new service-learning course to attend a service-learning institute. This work is supported by a grant from the Corporation for National and Community Service (CNCS). The same grant has allowed Xavier to strengthen the skills of experienced service-learning faculty and to set up a peer mentoring system.

Xavier's CNCS grant, which it shares with two other HBCUs, points to the special role outside resources play in creating and sustaining faculty development opportunities at HBCUs. What CNCS provides for Xavier, North Carolina Campus Compact provides for NCCU. As noted earlier, NCCU was one of the first HBCUs to join Campus Compact. When an affiliated state office in North Carolina was founded in 2002, NCCU (together with JCSU) was one of its founding members. As North Carolina Campus Compact has successfully sought funding for a statewide faculty development effort, NCCU has been able to see a tangible return on its long-term investment in Campus Compact membership.

Given the more or less chronically tight fiscal situation at many HBCUs, such outside support is often essential. Although release time for community-based projects is rare, and most engaged HBCUs try to find sufficient internal funding to support at least some faculty travel, payment for such items as travel by institutional teams, faculty mini-grants, and external trainers/speakers would not possible at many schools without the support of outside organizations.

Of these supporting organizations, none has been more important than the United Negro College Fund (UNCF). Founded in 1944, the UNCF has long supported both the academic pursuits and the community initiatives of HBCUs. As one of the leading supporters of minority students—second only to the federal government—the UNCF has distributed millions of dollars to individual students and to institutions and programs designed to improve the black student college experience. One of the organization's most productive ventures has been its decade-long partnership with the Ford Foundation to fund the UNCF/Ford Community Service Partnership Project. This project aims to strengthen service-learning efforts at member campuses. The first set of grant recipients, named in 1993, included Benedict College, JCSU, and LeMoyne-Owen; hence, it is not surprising that these institutions have been pioneers in developing formal service-learning programs.

The partnership's components offer a variety of support mechanisms for HBCUs that are developing such programs. The Ford/UNCF Clearinghouse for Service Learning is an information-gathering resource that makes member HBCUs aware of model programs and best practices. The partnership also produces a regular newsletter describing the accomplishments and goals of service-learning at HBCUs, and provides assistance in navigating the logistical challenges of implementing new and dynamic programming. Finally, a faculty development institute trains faculty members from a diverse set of academic fields to incorporate service-learning into their classes. By encouraging HBCUs to formalize service-learning, the UNCF helps them become eligible for other service-learning funding while bringing the schools closer to their communities, thus allowing them to reclaim their historic legacy of engagement.

Faculty Roles and Rewards

"Faculty Roles and Rewards" complements "Faculty Development" in creating a culture favorable to community-based academic work. Across higher education, the lack of faculty rewards is often the single greatest obstacle to sustained faculty engagement. To some extent, the powerful ratification of campus-community partnerships by top administrators, together with their willingness to utilize pro-service mission statements as a kind of touchstone for new initiatives and strategic priorities, ensures that faculty at the schools we looked at can expect to be recognized rather than punished for their community-based interests. However, equally important is the determination of schools like Benedict, LeMoyne-Owen, and NCCU to see that engagement is accepted and appropriated by academic divisions and departments across the institution. At many schools—both minority-serving and others—a considerable gulf exists between the genuine but generic support of the central administration and the agenda of individual academic units.

Most striking about the HBCU approach to "Faculty Roles and Rewards" is the way in which service is positioned in faculty evaluation documents. We have already noted that for many HBCUs, an engaged mission statement serves as a touchstone for actual policies and practices; this extends to faculty evaluation procedures. Both established programs like that at LeMoyne-Owen and newer programs like that at Xavier testify to this point. LeMoyne-Owen's faculty evaluation criteria include a reminder that "service to the community reflects the institutional commitment to outreach." Xavier's faculty handbook (www.xula.edu/academic-affairs/handbook/handbook.htm) makes a similar point:

> When faculty serve outside the University in their academic roles, that activity...furthers Xavier's mission. For using one's disciplinary expertise to benefit the greater community brings the University into the community, bridging the gap between academic theory and the world outside the academy. In addition, the University highly values faculty service in a just cause.

Invoking the school's engaged mission in the context of faculty evaluation is a natural way to build engagement into faculty rewards. Some schools use the same practice in considering faculty appointments in the first place. Xavier faculty noted that the social justice component of the university's mission, as well as service-learning as a mechanism for manifesting that component, is built into the faculty selection process. "You come to Xavier to serve the mission. If you don't support the mission, you don't get hired," one faculty member explained. "Candidates are asked about how their teaching, research, and administrative work will fulfill the mission." At LeMoyne-Owen, community members are included on some faculty hiring committees, depending on the discipline or division involved.

Complementing this up-front emphasis on service and engagement is the way in which HBCU promotion and tenure documents frame the three traditional areas of faculty responsibility: teaching, scholarship, and service. Excellence in teaching, HBCUs emphasize, can be demonstrated in part through the introduction of new pedagogies. Effective innovation is to be encouraged—and rewarded. As a faculty member at Johnson C. Smith noted, "JCSU has long been an innovative, risk-taking campus." In such an environment, new approaches to teaching and learning, including experimentation in and through community work, are welcome.

This type of innovation is valued not only as an indication of excellence in teaching but also as a way of approaching research, including pedagogical research. As the LeMoyne-Owen faculty handbook notes,

> Professional growth...may include learning new instructional strategies and techniques, honing scholarship and research skills, increasing knowledge about the discipline and/or educational trends, or the development of grant proposals.

Research can be directed toward creating a new course or substantially revising an established course. Professional meetings related to pedagogy are as welcome as meetings related to one's academic discipline. Xavier's faculty handbook states that scholarship can take many forms, including the scholarship of teaching:

Example from the Field: Community Engagement as Part of Faculty Evaluation

SERVICE TO THE COLLEGE AND COMMUNITY (10% MINIMUM)

The faculty is responsible for the development, maintenance, and evaluation of a sound academic program. Service to the College constitutes the contributions in this role, reflecting active College and divisional participation in governance and committee work. Service to the community reflects the institutional commitment to outreach, and may include providing expertise, service on boards, or volunteer efforts.

3.01　Develop new programs for the campus

3.02　Develop new programs for the community

3.03　Service on civic boards or committees (national, state, or local)

3.04　Volunteer service on campus (tutoring, etc.)

3.05　Assume a fair share in divisional tasks

3.06　Assume a fair share in area tasks

3.07　Provide leadership in campus activities

3.08　Participate in College recruitment activities

SOURCE: LeMoyne-Owen College Faculty Evaluation Criteria and Forms, p. 6. Used by permission.

[Here] defined as making public, in a conference presentation or pedagogical journal, for example, the results from studying a problem about an issue of teaching or learning through methods consistent with disciplinary epistemologies, with the end of enhancing student learning.

In defining is faculty service, HBCU documents emphasize that service to the community is valued no less than service to the institution, a department, or a discipline. In evaluating faculty, LeMoyne-Owen accepts "providing expertise," "service on boards," and even "volunteer efforts" as demonstrations of service. Xavier's categories are comparable: consulting within an area of expertise, serving on boards, and "performing regularly any volunteer activity undertaken to enhance the well-being of the community." Thus, service includes not only work in the community but even work in the community that does not necessarily draw on academic expertise, as long as it enhances the community's "well-being."

Such a broad approach to defining faculty service is perfectly consonant with the HBCU emphasis on meaningful engagement and social responsibility as the driving forces behind student service. This broader mandate finds expression in, for example, the expectation at NCCU that serious community work will be a part of every faculty portfolio; and, in fact, the faculty senate recently formalized the evaluation process for the service component of faculty evaluation. Similarly, faculty at Benedict note that their annual evaluation specifically asks what they have done beyond the scope of their academic area. Some schools attach a specific value to engaged work. At Benedict, for example, community service counts for approximately 10% of a faculty member's evaluation.

Other aspects of the engaged HBCU approach to "Faculty Roles and Rewards" are important but less distinctive. NCCU's Faculty Fellows program is an honorific as well as a practical resource. Certificates, luncheons, and recognition in print are common at most schools. In contrast to the situation at many other kinds of institutions, at engaged HBCUs the faculty reward system does not appear to impede engaged work in any way. Any impediments are more likely to lie elsewhere.

Mechanisms and Resources

Best Practices

- Staff an office to facilitate student service.
- Publish and disseminate guidebooks to keep constituencies informed of functions, opportunities, and resources related to service and engagement.
- Create a service-learning website with basic information, evaluation and feedback forms, statistical analyses, and databases of community placements and projects.

- Establish programs to recruit and train students to lead and facilitate community-related work.
- Encourage students to serve on institutional committees.

The indicators included in this unit—"Internal Budget and Resource Allocation," "Support Structures and Resources," "Coordination of Community-Based Activities," and "Student Voice"—collectively point to the infrastructure that makes it possible for an institution to fulfill its engaged mission without demanding superhuman effort on the part of any one stakeholder group. It seeks to identify ways in which faculty receive both professional and logistical support, staff gain the resources they need to do their work, community members are easily able to navigate institutional programs and players, and students are tapped to play structural and leadership roles. Since the work of engaged institutions is ultimately of a piece, a number of the issues referred to in this unit have already surfaced elsewhere. Indeed, the practices covered by the first three of this unit's four indicators are sufficiently interrelated to justify discussing them as a group.

Internal Budget and Resource Allocation, Support Structures and Resources, and Coordination of Community-Based Activities

Like almost all engaged institutions, engaged HBCUs invariably staff a special office to facilitate student-related service. Such offices vary in size from a single key individual (e.g., JCSU) to a number of complementary positions (e.g., Benedict, with five staff positions). When NCCU first established its program in 1995, it created a staff of five: a director, an assistant director, a service-learning coordinator, a student placement coordinator, and an administrative assistant. Since then, NCCU has gone on to develop several supplementary operations. For example, once a semester it hosts a "service-learning circle" that brings together representatives of all major stakeholder groups to share information, work on grants, and complete program work.

At Howard University, the Center for the Advancement of Service Learning (CASL) coordinates service opportunities. In conjunction with other parts of the university and its community partners, CASL plans and coordinates both one-time, campus-wide service events and service-learning courses. The office makes extensive outreach efforts to inform community and service organizations about the service-learning program and encourages these organizations to partner with the university in order to recruit volunteers and access other university resources of interest.

One of the primary responsibilities of any service-learning office is keeping its many constituencies informed of functions, opportunities, and resources. To accomplish this task, HBCU programs, like programs at other kinds of schools,

> **Example from the Field:**
> **Staff and Functions of a Service-Learning Office**
>
> North Carolina Central University's service-learning office has five staff positions, structured as follows:
>
> | POSITION | FUNCTION |
> |---|---|
> | Director | Develops policy and funding |
> | Assistant Director | Coordinates departmental functions and maintains daily operations |
> | Service-Learning Coordinator | Designs and implements specific service-learning projects |
> | Student Placement Coordinator | Oversees the service graduation requirement |
> | Administrative Assistant | Runs office operations |

publish and disseminate guidebooks. For the most part, these guidebooks do not differ significantly from their counterparts elsewhere. They explain both service-learning in general and a school's particular program model, identify principles of good practice, and provide sample forms. Benedict College's Community Partners Guide has an especially useful section in which it uses a question-and-answer format to discuss 23 frequently recurring topics. LeMoyne-Owen's Service-Learning Manual includes a set of reflection questions that capture, among other topics, the importance of the civic dimension in community-based work. Drawing upon the work of Barber and Battistoni (1993), one question asks students to consider what it means to be a citizen of Memphis as well as the United States, and what responsibilities such citizenship implies.

Recently, NCCU has also developed an important virtual infrastructure. This has allowed its Academic Community Service Learning Program (ACSLP) to put basic information, evaluation and feedback forms, and statistical analyses online. Users can access three different databases to facilitate community placements and projects—one that lists agencies looking for volunteers, one that lists one-time events in the area, and one that identifies ACSLP programs. So far the new resource has been a resounding success. According to the ACSLP, figures from the 2003-2004 academic year (through mid-March) suggest that the new databases and website have "dramatically increased both the number of students participating in service and the number of hours completed." The program attributes this increase to the ease with which students can now find suitable service opportunities.

An earlier section of this chapter discussed some of the ways in which engaged HBCUs seek to introduce service-learning and prepare students for community-based work at the very start of their academic careers. At JCSU, this task falls to Angela Jeter, service-learning coordinator, who not only teaches a service-learning module in all first-year seminars but also designed and maintains the protocols that track the student service graduation requirement. Jeter's office, originally established in 1994 with grant funding from UNCF/Ford, has remained a high enough institutional priority that it has survived intact many years of difficult fiscal decisions. Through a steady stream of grants, Jeter has even been able to support such things as faculty travel when departmental funding has not been available. Building effective bonds with new students and new faculty (through a new faculty orientation program), Jeter sees herself as perhaps the "most loved person on campus."

Nearly all of the HBCU campuses that took part in the Indicators project had similar stories about how the service-learning office has come to be seen as a psychological center of the campus. At Benedict, the office is lodged in what students fondly refer to as "The White House," a building in the middle of the campus. At NCCU, student evaluations regularly give the ACSLP some of the highest marks of any office on campus. At LeMoyne-Owen, the administration thought the service-learning program central enough to the college's identity to link it formally to the Center for African and African American Studies. At Xavier, the service-learning office is part of the Center for Student Leadership and Service.

Although two of these programs (Benedict and Xavier) are structurally located in Student Affairs and three (JCSU, NCCU, and LeMoyne-Owen) in Academic Affairs, this distinction seems to be far less significant in an HBCU context than it is in some other higher education sectors. Faculty often see service-learning efforts that are linked with Student Affairs as having less than full academic legitimacy, but among HBCUs, there was no evidence to suggest this was the case. In addition, the fact that many of these programs handle both community service as a graduation requirement and strictly academic service-learning suggests that the service-learning/community service distinction is less philosophically important among these institutions than it is among some of their peers.

This is not to say that HBCUs do not make a distinction between community service and service-learning. All constituencies on these campuses—faculty, students, staff, and community partners—could clearly distinguish between the two. Many of the programs publish guidebooks that begin by making this very distinction. The ease with which community service and service-learning sit side by side without in any way compromising the academic legitimacy of the latter seems instead to be a reflection of institutional culture. At engaged HBCUs, the responsibility of the institution to serve the community in whatever way it can, together with the African American tradition of linking education and social activism, results in such a fundamental linking of "truth and service" (the NCCU school motto) that pursuit of the former simply does not need to be protected from the demands of the latter.

One important ancillary benefit of this flow between academic and co-curricular service is that many HBCUs are able to achieve a marked degree of coherence and coordination in their service programming. Some of this coherence flows simply from the fact that many HBCUs are relatively small institutions, but at least a portion of their success in this area can be attributed to design considerations. According to Angela Jeter, when JCSU first established its service-learning center, it did so deliberately "to overcome the fragmentation of the university's service efforts." By locating in one office support for service-learning courses, tracking of student service hours required for graduation, and coordination of the various service requests the university receives, JCSU is not only able to provide "one-stop shopping" for its various constituencies; it is also able to help focus university resources for maximum community effectiveness. At JCSU and the other engaged HBCUs, community partners frequently referred to situations where the service-learning office was able to "guarantee" sufficient support to achieve some goal.

Another important coordinating unit on many campuses is the president's or provost's office. As noted earlier, HBCUs do not shy away from providing direct services in addition to the resources that result from engaged teaching, learning, and scholarship. In the case of JCSU, Benedict, LeMoyne-Owen, and Xavier, a college/university-affiliated community development corporation (CDC) facilitates some of that direct service. (An additional school, NCCU, is affiliated with Durham's Eagle Village Community Development Corporation.) Since the work of these CDCs, as independently chartered organizations, is too broad to be accommodated to the resources of a school's service-learning office, top administrators are needed to play an appropriate bridging role. At LeMoyne-Owen, the CAO, who is responsible for academic planning (including community-based academic work) is also the person who works with the CDC director on grants that affect the greater Memphis community. At Benedict, the president has personally committed his office to community transformation. It is therefore only natural that that office should also play an important role in coordinating initiatives across the college's divisions.

Student Voice

One other form of coordination leads directly into this unit's fourth indicator, "Student Voice." A number of HBCUs, including Benedict, JCSU, and NCCU, have a student coordinator or "ambassador" program that recruits and trains undergraduates to lead and facilitate community-related work. The students are chosen on the basis of faculty recommendations, interviews, and a demonstrated commitment to service. Benedict calls its program PLUS (Preparation for Leadership and Unity through Service) and describes it as having been established to build "advocacy and administrative leadership among students." Participants are trained to coordinate outreach, service, and leadership projects, including developing and implementing activities and recruiting student teams. Other student coordinators are trained to assist faculty with service-learning courses and community partners with site supervision.

What is especially notable about such programs is the way in which they embody one of the most distinctive features of civic and community engagement as it is understood and practiced at HBCUs: an explicit linking of service with leadership and character development. Hence, the Benedict service-learning office works closely with the college's Student Leadership Development Program. At Xavier, the service-learning office works under the auspices of the Office for Student Leadership and Service. At LeMoyne-Owen, it is allied with the Student Community Leadership Initiative. In one sense, this link is not surprising, or even unusual. At most colleges and universities, service is seen as an important way to develop leadership skills. But the mix as it exists at engaged HBCUs goes much deeper than at many other institutions. The service-leadership connection is not casual or merely functional. To be a leader means to provide service. At Benedict, the School of Honors has actually taken as its motto "I serve."

Of course, service and leadership do not coexist at all times, but it is not an exaggeration to say that this nexus is an overt institutional goal. To a degree unusual elsewhere, engaged HBCUs seek to bring together emphases that often are pursued more or less separately: namely, civic engagement and character education, with the former emphasizing the importance of addressing *public* issues and problems, and the latter, the development of a *personal* code of values and behavior.

These two emphases, sometimes seen as being at odds, are, in this model, two aspects of the same goal. As the title and subtitle of a recent book by Anne Colby and colleagues (2003) suggest, *Educating Citizens* involves *Preparing America's Undergraduates for Lives of Moral and Civic Responsibility*. As the authors explain:

> …the moral and the civic are inseparable. Because we understand the term *morality* to describe prescriptive judgments about how one ought to act in relation to other people, it follows that many core democratic principles…are grounded in moral principles…. A person can become civically and politically active without good judgment and a strong moral compass, but it is hardly wise to promote that kind of involvement (pp. 15–16).

Of course, it is possible to develop "good judgment and a strong moral compass" and never see the necessity of bringing these strengths into the domain of public problem solving. This is emphatically not the vision of those who lead engaged HBCUs, however. Benedict's President Swinton believes that students should "develop into citizens who can provide solutions to problems and help resolve them." At Xavier, President Francis noted that his students are "volunteering and doing community service," but that he wants them to become more "engaged in the political process." Again and again, at all the schools included in this chapter, leaders used the term "change agents" to describe their vision for their students.

Perhaps this is also why so many of these schools actually want their students to serve on institutional committees. Xavier has two student seats on every committee except for Promotion and Tenure. At NCCU, almost every committee has a student representative, and the current administration has made room for students on the Curriculum Committee so they have more of an influence over service-learning policy.

Community-Campus Exchange

Best Practices

- Invite community representatives to interview potential new hires, speak at departmental events, and serve on public panels.
- Involve community representatives in the college's service-learning program by encouraging them to help shape courses.
- Host town meetings and forums for public dialogue on issues of interest to the community.
- Explore ways to share funds (college or grant) to benefit the community.

Nothing is more characteristic of engagement at HBCUs than the emphasis they place on community progress. Within this category, the Indicators of Engagement Project includes three indicators: "Community Voice," "Forums for Fostering Public Dialogue," and "External Resource Allocations." Taken together, these indicators begin to illustrate just how responsible effective engaged HBCUs have been in tending to the community side of the campus-community exchange.

Community Voice

"Community Voice" makes itself heard in many ways. At LeMoyne-Owen, community representatives are invited to interview potential new hires in some departments. When President Wingate took office, he commissioned a "Strategic Environmental Scan" to determine how engaged the campus was. Not only did the school use the results of the scan to shape the goals and objectives of a new strategic plan, it asked community representatives to comment on the plan and suggest ways to improve it. President Wingate continues to meets twice yearly with a community group called Friends of LOC (LeMoyne-Owen College) to exchange information and coordinate activities. At NCCU, the service-learning circles mentioned earlier play a similar role. Furthermore, to help new faculty better understand where their students come from, NCCU's chancellor, James Ammons, recently took those faculty on a state-wide bus tour of some of the students' home communities.

Another important dimension of Community Voice is the community's impact on the teaching-learning process. Here the degree of engagement is rare even among schools with well-developed service-learning programs. At Benedict, part of the students' four-semester seminar sequence includes assembly programs that feature local and regional speakers who address topical community concerns. In this way community voice is integrated into the very core of the college's general education program. Community representatives are also invited to speak at departmental events and to serve on public panels.

At LeMoyne-Owen, the community has even played a role in shaping certain courses. Central to Lemoyne-Owen's general education strategy is a required "Power and Society" course that, among other things, introduces students to service-learning. According to CAO Barbara Frankle, community representatives had a strong impact on the development of this course, especially its service-learning component. Faculty note that the community has had a shaping influence on other service-related courses as well.

A natural question is why engaged HBCUs are willing to give the community access to the curriculum development process when such access is so rare elsewhere. The answer seems to be that engaged HBCUs are unusually committed to erasing the boundary between the campus and the community. Leaders at these institutions are as committed both to making the community feel at home on campus and to making staff, faculty, and students see themselves as members of the larger community. They appear to be succeeding in this endeavor. One of Johnson C. Smith's community partners noted that JCSU students respond to the children in her program much better than do many students from other higher education institutions because "they tend to see the local kids as 'their' kids."

Forums for Fostering Public Dialogue

"Forums for Fostering Public Dialogue" is closely related to "Community Voice" but with the emphasis less on community input than on shared, open deliberation. Occasions on which an institution calls upon the community to discuss matters of common concern could probably be placed under either indicator. Thus, for example, when President Swinton of Benedict College schedules public hearings to discuss some new college initiative, such hearings can be seen as fostering public dialogue as well as providing an opportunity to listen to the community's voice. However, in its role as institutional citizen, Benedict also hosts many town meetings where the agenda is not necessarily college plans. Recently the college hosted a "civic engagement roundtable" that included students, faculty, neighborhood representatives, community activists, and local entrepreneurs.

Public dialogues are common among engaged HBCUs. South Carolina State University has held public dialogues on a range of topics, including HIV/AIDS and bioterrorism. Both Benedict and Xavier have hosted forums that make use of technology to reach a larger community population. Xavier produces a weekly public affairs program aired on public television, while Benedict hosts an annual teleconference that reaches out to high schools as well as other colleges.

Xavier is so committed to open dialogue that it has created a center dedicated to that effort. The Brueggeman Center's goal is "to serve as an incubator for programs emerging out of dialogue with partners and potential partners" (www.xu.edu/dialogue/programs_activities.cfm). The center's programs are free and open to the public. Community members are invited not only to participate in programming but also to suggest program ideas.

External Resource Allocations

The final indicator, "External Resource Allocations," captures the kinds of commitments a school is willing to make to help create concrete community assets. Here again, engaged HBCUs set a very high standard. Although the internal resources of these schools are often scarce, their willingness to share is equaled by very few institutions.

Take, for example, Xavier's commitment to the "Xavier Triangle" and to the adjacent Gert Town community in particular. The Audubon Arts Center, located in Gert Town, provides life skills enhancement and cultural enrichment opportunities for community residents. The university pays half the salary of a Family Resource Center Director and subsidizes the Bolden Childcare Center. The university's College of Pharmacy services the Community Health Center. Vans and no-cost space on campus are made available to community organizations. The library is open to community members, as are professional development opportunities such as grant-writing seminars. The university has donated computers to local organizations and even picks up overhead costs for many of them. The university also leases land to community organizations or one dollar a year. And yet, despite all these initiatives, President Francis has recently created a position to help him review the overall partnering picture with an eye toward improving town-gown relations.

The story at other engaged HBCUs is similar. As was mentioned earlier, Benedict College has been a leader in enhancing the quality of life in Columbia's Waverly Community, especially with regard to housing and safety. In 1999 the college created the Division of Community Development (DCD) to examine issues, as the division newsletter puts it, that affect "children and families, business and economic development, democracy and government, and educational excellence through research, public service, and teaching." The DCD oversees the Benedict-

Allen Community Development Corporation as well as the Business Development Center, The Center for Excellence for the Education and Equity of African American Students, and the Child Development Center. The DCD is also responsible for traditional programs like Upward Bound and a new 21st Century Community Learning Center.

Like Benedict, Fayetteville State University is deeply engaged in the revitalization of its community—the downtown area of Fayetteville, North Carolina—through its involvement in the Murchison Road/College Heights Master Plan. Funding for this project comes from local and federal government agencies as well as local businesses. Grants from the city and the U.S. Department of Housing and Urban Development have allowed the university to fund housing units and a small-business incubator.

Other engaged HBCUs have similar campus-community commitments: LeMoyne-Owen and South Memphis; NCCU and the Eagle Village neighborhood in Durham; JCSU and Charlotte's Northwest Corridor communities. However, as important as these broad institutional relationships are, and as critical as is the work of HBCU-affiliated community development organizations, community partners came back to one point again and again: nothing can replace the active engagement of the students themselves. As one of NCCU's community partners remarked, his organization "could not function without the students."

Unlike much of the cost sharing and material asset creation identified above, students as a community resource can be found at many kinds of institutions. They are, in fact, the major "investment" most engaged institutions make in their local communities. Still, it is unusual to find students making the kind of commitment that translates not just into habits of civic engagement but also into measurable community change.

One outstanding example of such change can be found in the work of the Saturday Academy created by JCSU. The Saturday Academy program began in 1999 with grant money from North Carolina's Historically Minority College and University Consortium, which aimed to improve minority student achievement and strengthen ties between elementary schools and colleges. Targeting fourth- and fifth-grade students at the Thomasboro Elementary School who tested below grade level, JCSU introduced a tutoring program to improve test scores, provide cultural enrichment activities, and increase parental involvement in their children's education. The program was designed to allow JCSU students to fill all support roles and also serve as role models for the younger students.

The latter responded well to the enrichment classes, and partially as a result, their scores went up so far that the school moved from being the lowest-performing in

Example from the Field: Allocating Resources to Revitalize Communities
From Fayetteville State University

MURCHISON ROAD IS NEWEST ADDITION TO DOWNTOWN PLANNING

Among the many exciting developments that have occurred in the past year that signal great things for Fayetteville's downtown revitalization efforts has been the unveiling of a Murchison Road/College Heights Master Plan. Aimed at outlining the abundant business investment opportunities along this long-neglected gateway to the city, the Master Plan identifies 14 potential business and housing sites and suggests possible projects for each. A recently awarded U.S. Department of Housing and Urban Development (HUD) grant of $365,897 will be leveraged with private investments to begin construction soon on one of the projects, a retail and restaurant plaza near the FSU campus called 'Bronco Square.'

The lynchpin of the Murchison Road/College Heights Plan is a new Business Incubator that will nurture small start-up ventures to success with office or manufacturing space and consulting support from students and faculty of FSU's School of Business and Economics. Initial funding of $790,000 for construction and operations of the incubator has been obtained in HUD and Community Block Development grants.

MASTER PLAN OUTLINES POTENTIAL FOR MURCHISON ROAD/COLLEGE HEIGHTS

Developed by the FSU School of Business and Economics with the assistance of a $50,000 grant from the City of Fayetteville, the Murchison Road/College Heights Master Plan was completed in 1998. The purpose of the plan is to present to private and public investors alike the potential for creating several new business and housing opportunities in the six-square-mile area surrounding Murchison Road from Rowan Street to McLamb Street. With this kind of investment in our community will come the jobs, wealth creation, and beautification that contribute to desired outcomes like reducing crime and attracting more business to the area.

FSU's Master Plan suggests two commercial projects along Murchison Road that will generate 55,300 square feet of retail space, create new businesses with new permanent jobs, and capture an additional $7,000,000 for the local market. A $365,897 HUD grant awarded in September 1998 ensures that one of these will be under way by next year. The proposed housing projects in the plan will generate 150 units of new homes priced between $59,500 and $74,950 and affordable for families with incomes as low as $12,500. An additional 254 units of much-needed rental housing are suggested to accommodate the elderly, families, and university students.

EXCITING FUTURE AHEAD FOR MURCHISON ROAD/COLLEGE HEIGHTS

As soon as this fall, we will begin to see a difference in the Murchison Road/College Heights area as the City of Fayetteville undertakes a beautification program along lower Murchison Road. With the current strengths of the area, plans moving along for the opening of a new Business Incubator, and a Master Plan in place that will help attract additional private and public investment, the Murchison Road/College Heights corridor has a bright and exciting future ahead of it. In presenting this plan, Fayetteville State University is pleased to be a partner with our community and to play a role in creating a better environment and new opportunities for our students, faculty, and staff; for the residents of Murchison Road/College Heights; and for the citizens of our city and county.

SOURCE: Excerpted from a statement by Fayetteville State University Chancellor Willis McLeod, November 2000 (http://community.uncfsu.edu/MurchDev/chancellor.htm).

the district to the second-highest. Currently, 75% of the school's students test at or above their grade level, compared with 39% before the partnership began. This success has resulted in the program's being expanded to include a second elementary school, and an even larger number of JCSU students has become involved, often spending far more time than needed to satisfy the university's service requirement.

Youth outreach—tutoring, mentoring, outings, and activities—is by far the largest area of HBCU student service and the area the students themselves, like their peers elsewhere, seem to prefer. But the effectiveness of their efforts testifies less to personal preference than to personal responsibility. Administrators and faculty at both Benedict and JCSU spoke of students who would go to their service sites "day in and day out," so that eventually the children came to look on them "as part of their family." At NCCU, students develop relationships not only with younger students but also with those students' parents. Almost all the schools discussed in this chapter have developed special initiatives to include parents in the activities the colleges' students help facilitate. At engaged HBCUs, it would seem, the idea of "family" is literally inclusive.

HBCU Profiles

Benedict College

Benedict College was founded in 1870 in Columbia, South Carolina, under the auspices of the American Baptist Home Mission Society. Maintaining a liberal arts tradition, Benedict offers a bachelor degree program in 29 areas of study. It has an enrollment of 3,000 students.

Benedict's motto, "Learning to Be the Best: A Power for Good in the Twenty-first Century," characterizes the college's commitment to continuous improvement in the community. President David Swinton listed service-learning as one of his primary initiatives when he began his presidency at the institution 10 years ago. He believes that service-learning provides Benedict students with an opportunity to put what they are learning into practice. Furthermore, he thinks that it helps them sharpen their leadership skills and to develop confidence in their ability to provide work of value to society.

Developing Student Leaders

Benedict students are introduced to service-learning and the community early in their college career. All freshmen are required to attend a "Service-Learning Freshman Experience" featuring a panel of community and civic leaders who engage the students in interactive dialogue concentrating on public issues and community history. Since service-learning is linked with student leadership development, designated Service-Learning Student Coordinators play a key role in designing and implementing service initiatives. These student leaders help serve in the capacity as extended staff and advisory team members. They develop, coordinate, and supervise outreach service initiatives. In addition, they serve as advocates for the program and recruit other students.

Benedict has a 120-credit service-learning requirement for graduation. Students fulfill this requirement through participation in Leadership Development Seminars and designated departmental courses. The freshman, sophomore, and junior Leadership Development Seminars are departmental courses that utilize service-learning to enhance students' development. All departments have developed at least one upper-level service-learning course. In the School of Honors, four courses are designated as both honors and service-learning courses. Honors Scholars engage in three service-learning activities each semester. Each department has also identified a faculty member to serve on the Service-Learning Advisory Team; this person is responsible for mentoring other faculty members in their department. All service activities are documented and included in faculty performance portfolios as a part of promotion and tenure decisions.

Benedict's service-learning program has received national recognition for its commitment to student learning through community engagement. A Ford/UNCF grant originally funded the service-learning office in 1995. Today the office has sustained funding from the college and a five-member staff dedicated to implementing the service-learning program and allocating resources. The service-learning office is located within Student Affairs and works closely with the Student Leadership Program to coordinate activities.

Community Redevelopment

Each year the college sponsors the Service-Learning Expo for community partners to receive an orientation. The college plans time for partners to become familiar with the school's *Service Learning Handbook,* talk about best practices, and meet students and staff. Part of the event is dedicated to naming a "Partner of the Year." Another annual event is a college-wide day of service, in which administrators, faculty, students, staff, and community residents participate. Projects focus on community health care and other issues; students also participate in intergenerational projects and community recreation events.

Benedict is credited with making a huge difference in the community. The college's Division of Community Development has been in the forefront in redeveloping the surrounding community. This redevelopment program serves as a model for other projects throughout the nation.

Johnson C. Smith University

Founded in 1867, Johnson C. Smith University, located in Charlotte, North Carolina, is one of the oldest HBCUs in the country. JCSU is a private liberal arts institution that offers 32 fields of study and bachelor's degrees in the arts, sciences, and social work to its 1,500 students.

The university sees itself as a leader in community-based work. Its history of civic engagement is reflected in the active role of its students during the Civil Rights movement. Its ongoing commitment to the community is evident in its 40-hour community service graduation requirement and its service-learning courses. Students learn that being an educated person means being connected to one's community.

Service figures in the lives of the students from their freshman year, when they are required to take a one-credit "orientation" course that includes the service tradition embedded in the university. This focus carries on through their senior year, when many students reflect on their community experiences for their mandatory senior paper. In this and other ways, community-based academic work is seen as extending the university's core vision and mission.

Faculty Involvement

Faculty as well as students are intimately involved with the community. Low-key but firm support from the top administration encourages both student service-learning experiences and faculty community-based research. Since the mid-1990s, faculty development efforts have consistently included a community-based teaching and learning component. Faculty workshops are offered at the beginning and end of every academic year, and a special orientation on community-based work is available for new faculty. According to Vice President for Academic Affairs Marilyn Sutton-Haywood and Executive Vice President Nathaniel Pollard, the service-learning program has a "legitimizing" effect—that is, it makes service seem worthwhile—because it links service with academic study.

An essential source of support for the campus's efforts is the Service Learning Center, established in 1994. The office is completely sustainable and receives considerable grant funding, in addition to support from alumni and institutional advancement efforts. It acts as the campus clearinghouse for all community service and service-learning activities by training faculty who want to offer service-learning courses, matching students with appropriate service activities, tracking service hours required for graduation, and even providing free bus passes for student community work. The center's director, Angela Jeter, is known as a strong and much-loved leader. She stretches limited resources for maximum impact and is known for willingly sharing those resources with others.

Embracing Service

Perhaps what is most notable about JCSU's engagement work is the students' attitude toward the service requirement. There is an ethos that one will give back to the community, an assumption that one will help. Aware of the school's service tradition, students do not complain about the 40-hour community service graduation requirement. Instead, they embrace community service and personalize it. For example, much of the community-based work and many of the service-learning courses focus on working with children, and JCSU students tend to see local children as their own. As one student stresses, "Mentoring young people is especially important." One such initiative is JCSU's Saturday Academy, which has been successful in dramatically improving grade school students' performance on statewide standardized tests.

LeMoyne-Owen College

LeMoyne-Owen College is a private HBCU located in Memphis, Tennessee. The college offers the bachelor's degrees in arts and sciences and administration degrees to its approximately 800 enrolled students.

Service is explicit in the mission of the college: "LeMoyne-Owen College prepares students in a nurturing and student centered community for lives of success and service." Furthermore, the college "strives to become a resource to address social and economic issues of the community." The mission statement is clear and firm in its commitment both to developing the service role of students and to sustaining an institutional presence in the community. A recent framework for long-range strategic planning reconfirmed the college's commitment to the community.

Neighborhood Renaissance

LeMoyne-Owen is actively engaged with its neighbors in the renaissance of the South Memphis community. In its work, the college has established itself as a model for campus-community partnerships and student involvement in community-based learning. It has received national as well as local recognition for its community development efforts and its service-learning program.

The college has formed numerous partnerships with social service and other agencies to help the community advance. This focus on neighborhood development provides a wide range of learning opportunities for students, the development of sustained relationships with community stakeholders, and the possibility for real transformation. Success in instilling an ethic of service in its students has helped the college continue to build strong relationships with community organizations: an impressive number of alumni work in nonprofit community agencies and return to campus to recruit and train undergraduate students.

One of many partnerships is with the Soulsville, Inc., redevelopment effort, which works with a museum and a music academy for minority youth. Another example is a shared facility, opened in the fall of 2004, which houses the college's Division of Business and Entrepreneurship, the neighborhood association for public housing development, the Boys & Girls Clubs, and a police precinct. In addition, the college's technology laboratory is used evenings and weekends to provide community training, and a faculty member is available to provide business development and accounting assistance to minority-owned businesses.

Valuing Service and Service-Learning

All students at LeMoyne-Owen are introduced to the value of service early on in a required social science course. This and other service-learning activities are coordinated by the college's service-learning center. The center's director and coordinator are both faculty members, and a steering committee comprises faculty representatives from all of the academic divisions.

In addition to traditional service-learning courses, the college offers a multidisciplinary service-learning course. In addition, students can add a "one plus" option to a course in any discipline, which means they can undertake a project related to their coursework and get an additional credit hour. The one plus option offers opportunities for students to relate service to any discipline.

The college acknowledges service both formally and informally. Credit for service is explicitly included in the promotion and tenure evaluation for faculty. Each year, the college holds an awards banquet to recognize outstanding service. In addition to internal recognition, LeMoyne-Owen receives recognition from the community as a "college that cares."

North Carolina Central University

Founded in 1910, North Carolina Central University was the nation's first state-supported liberal arts college for African American students. Located in Durham, NCCU has an enrollment of 8,000 students and offers both undergraduate and graduate programs in liberal arts and professional studies. The university has a 120-hour community service requirement for graduation.

Consciousness of Social Responsibility

The mission of the university is to prepare students academically and professionally and to promote consciousness of social responsibility and dedication to the advancement of the general welfare of the people of North Carolina, the United States, and the world.

In support of the university's guiding principle, the Academic Community Service Learning Program (ACSLP) was established with a mission to serve the local and global community through teaching, research, and service.

ACSLP directors are some of the institution's biggest assets. They offer individualized faculty training, workshops, community partner matching, and a host of other services to strengthen service-learning and civic engagement on campus. A 15-member Community Service Advisory Committee, comprising faculty members, students, and community representatives, developed the ACSLP's mission, goals, and program activities. To ensure an ongoing commitment, the Council of Deans has developed an administrative framework for continuously engaging in outreach activities. Eventually, every area will be involved in outreach activities.

An interesting facet of NCCU's work is the use of technology to support service-learning. The ACSLP has its own website with information for students, faculty, staff, and community agencies, including open positions, procedures, registration and other forms, and a host of other information (see http://ariel.acc.nccu.edu/commserv/acslp.html). NCCU is a prime example of how a large public institution can effectively manage a community service requirement through a comprehensive web-based program that is easy to use and has multiple capabilities.

Student and Faculty Work

At NCCU, faculty who are experienced in incorporating community service modules into academic courses are called Faculty Service-Learning Fellows. This experience allows the Faculty Service-Learning Fellows to supervise students who are involved in community service projects. These faculty members are also available as mentors who share their experiences with other faculty, administrators, and staff interested in academic community service-learning.

NCCU is a member of North Carolina Campus Compact, a statewide consortium through which campus members sponsor and attend faculty development workshops and participate in videoconferences and other activities. Among other programs, North Carolina Campus Compact has provided funds for faculty to redesign courses to include service-learning. NCCU gives annual awards to faculty who do exceptional work in the community, and civic engagement is critical to tenure and promotion decisions.

One of NCCU's successful endeavors is the Service-Learning Ambassadors program. Service-Learning Ambassadors are experienced students charged with recruiting, monitoring, and promoting the mission of the ACSLP. Ambassadors serve as coaches for student groups in organizing and conducting group sessions, meeting, surveys and other skills needed in community work.

Neighborhood Adoption

NCCU has adopted the surrounding neighborhood known as Eagle Village. The university's Community Economic Development Initiative focuses on revitalizing the neighborhood's commercial district and enhancing job and business opportunities for low-income residents. The initiative operates in collaboration with the School of Business, Academic Service-Learning, and the Eagle Village Community Development Corporation. Through this initiative, community residents receive computer training, tutoring, and mentoring in a Saturday Academy. In addition, houses are being revitalized and a shopping center is under construction.

Xavier University of Louisiana

Xavier University of Louisiana in New Orleans is a private Catholic institution with an enrollment of nearly 4,000 students. The university's social justice mission is perpetuated by numerous civic engagement projects. President Norman Francis, who has served in that role for the past 30 years, is deeply committed to making the university a mechanism for social change by educating students for community responsibility. The ultimate purpose of the university is the promotion of a more just and humane society. To accomplish this task, students at Xavier are academically prepared to be resources to the community. This preparation takes place in a teaching and learning environment that incorporates research and community service.

Students, Service, and Service-Learning

The importance of service-learning and community service is cultivated in students beginning in their freshman year during New Student Orientation Week and throughout the year. Xavier faculty and students participate in service activities throughout the city.

In addition, a the university's Emerging Leaders program requires participants to complete at least 20 hours of community service, and all registered organizations and clubs are required to complete at least three community service activities each semester.

Over the past four years Xavier has involved more than 1,200 students in service-learning. Last year more than 20% of its undergraduate students participated in ongoing (at least 3 hours per week) service activities. Another 10% participated in one-time community service activities.

Internal and External Support

Faculty and students receive help from a service-learning coordinator who is located within Student Affairs. In addition, students and community agencies receive guidance and support from the Center for Student Leadership and Service and its six-member staff. Financial support comes in part from Learn and Serve America, from which Xavier has received grants both as an individual institution and as part of a consortium.

In addition, faculty members have received faculty development grants to assist them in developing courses integrating model service-learning practices and ensuring meaningful experiences for both students and the community. Community service continues to be a tenure requirement for faculty.

A Vital Community Role

Xavier University's administration, faculty, staff, and students play a vital role in the development of surrounding neighborhoods. The university has donated land for a community swimming pool, funds and operates a childcare center, and was instrumental in establishing a health clinic and lobbying for a bus route serving the neighborhoods. In addition, the Xavier Triangle community development corporation helps neighboring communities develop and rehabilitate houses.

Xavier is also an active voting member of the Gert Town Revitalization Initiative, a project launched to reinvigorate the struggling Gert Town neighborhood of New Orleans. Members of the initiative meet with Xavier's president several times a year to discuss accomplishments, as well as concerns and challenges. The university provides release time for the assistant dean of students to participate. Other campus members are also actively involved. For example, toxicology professor Marcus Iszard recently conducted a study that found high levels of soil and water contamination near a defunct chemical plant. His findings have led to a call for the city and national governments to speed removal of the contaminants.

Community partnerships are strengthened through a community partnership luncheon at the beginning of each year. Community agencies are encouraged to recruit Xavier students through the annual Volunteer Fair, and the university offers space to participating agencies to facilitate their training.

Engagement at Hispanic-Serving Institutions

Unlike the other kinds of colleges and universities discussed in this book, Hispanic-serving institutions (HSIs) do not represent a distinct institutional type. While HBCUs were founded to serve primarily the African-American community and TCUs clearly focus on the needs of Native Americans, most HSIs do not even have a majority Hispanic student body. Instead, "Hispanic-serving" is a the government's way of identifying colleges and universities that have an undergraduate enrollment comprises at least 25% Hispanic students, of whom no fewer than 50% are low-income individuals (U.S. Department of Education). Furthermore, HSIs do not conform to a particular institutional type. Unlike HBCUs, which are four-year institutions and tend to be near cities—even if small cities—and TCUs, which are predominantly two-year schools located in rural areas, HSIs can be two-year or four-year, and are as likely to be located in cities as in rural areas.

For all these reasons, it is difficult to describe a set of exemplary practices related to civic and community engagement at HSIs as a group. Whether a particular school focuses its engagement efforts more on teaching and learning strategies or on community economic development, on making it possible for its students to find adequate daycare or on validating their cultural identity, depends directly on the particular needs, circumstances, and traditions that define that institution. This is also to some extent true of individual HBCUs and TCUs, but in their case it is also much easier to identify cross-institutional strategies and considerations. Hence, one can with greater confidence predict that a promising practice found at one school will likely be of interest and use to others.

Fortunately, it is precisely such heterogeneity that Campus Compact's Indicators of Engagement Project was designed to accommodate. Knowing that no single model of the "engaged campus" exists, staff defined the 13 indicators to make it easier for institutions to identify their strengths and weaknesses, as well as specific practices for bolstering the former and addressing the latter.

What complicates this strategy in the case of HSIs is that the absence of a generic type multiplies the need for models exponentially: an effective mission statement for one kind of HSI may be inappropriate for another; an enabling mechanism used successfully at school A may not be feasible at school B, for reasons that have nothing to do with available resources or institutional commitment. Ideally, we would have looked at dozens of schools to begin to do justice to the complexity of the HSI institutional range. In the aggregate of the examples here, however, we offer a wealth of information to enrich the thinking of those concerned with the education of Hispanic students and the well-being of Hispanic communities.

One additional consideration deserves mention. Because HSIs are not necessarily culturally Hispanic, it is often not possible to identify specific practices as culturally distinctive. Functional effectiveness and cultural identity are not necessarily congruent categories. Thus, much of what we found to be exemplary—while strengthening the institution's commitment to policies and programs that benefit Hispanic students and Hispanic communities—is not necessarily tied to Hispanic culture. Where such policies and practices do suggest a distinctive cultural dimension, we have called attention to that fact.

Institutional Culture

Best Practices

- Include a commitment to serving populations underrepresented in higher education in the college's mission statement.
- Include specific community goals in the college's mission statement.
- Develop concrete action plans to implement civic engagement goals.
- Make community service a top priority for administrators and faculty.

Mission and Purpose

Because of the institutional differences among HSIs, the ways that the first indicator in this area, "Mission and Purpose," plays out on campus are highly variable. At Our Lady of the Lake University (OLLU) in San Antonio, the mission statement identifies three specific goals to which the school is committed. Of these, the third is explicitly related to engagement: "To graduate individuals who are competent and committed to service" (www.ollusa.edu/_welcome_center/olluinfo/unmission.html). However, it is the accompanying "Statement of Values and Beliefs" that captures most powerfully the university's understanding of engagement. The statement identifies as a special area of concern "persons whose access [to higher education] has been limited, especially women and minorities." Further, the university's emphasis on a "values-based" education is linked not only with Catholic tradition but also with the "Hispanic heritage of the region." The university's vision statement bears out this emphasis: "Our Lady of the Lake University will be a leading comprehensive university known for its Catholic values, its preparation of emerging leaders in the Southwest, and its expertise in Hispanic cultures."

Such an explicit commitment to a population whose access to higher education has often been limited also appears in the key documents of several other schools we visited. At Heritage University on the Yakama Indian Reservation in Toppenish, Washington, Hispanic and Native American students constitute almost 70% of the student body (54% and 14% respectively), and this is clearly by design. Founded in 1981 to serve the people of the Yakama Valley, the college has grown from 85 to more than 1,200 students by remaining faithful to its mission of "providing a quality, accessible higher education to multicultural students who have been educationally isolated" (www.heritage.edu/about/topabout.htm).

Without the active collaboration of the local community, Heritage would never have been founded—a fact clearly reflected in the university's 2003 strategic planning document, "Blueprint for the Future." Not only is one of the college's eight operating principles "grass-roots community involvement"; its very first strategic goal is to "provide high-quality educational programs for place-bound, multicultural populations with barriers to educational access; and graduate increasing numbers of well-prepared, competent, community minded students."

Like OLLU and Heritage, the West Hills Community College District seeks to serve a population that has been largely invisible to mainstream higher education. Located in an agricultural region on the west side of California's Central Valley, West Hills has had such success in serving students from this rural community that it was recently selected by the MetLife Foundation as the small rural community college in the country that best promotes "educational and economic advancement for underserved youths and adults" (*Hear Us Out*, 2003, p. *ii*).

This focus is written into West Hills' mission statement in a somewhat unusual way: "West Hills College provides a world-class learning environment to a diverse population in a down home friendly atmosphere. Mi escuela es su escuela! [My school is your school!]" (www.westhillscollege.com/district/about/mission_vision.asp). While "world-class learning environment" and "diverse population" could—and probably do—appear in hundreds of college mission statements, "a down home friendly atmosphere" moves beyond the language of the academy to strike a deliberately colloquial chord. The college's appropriation and transformation of the familiar Mexican saying *mi casa es su casa* (my house is your house) resonates in precisely the same way.

A series of action plans formulated by the college address the question of what specifically and concretely such welcoming phrases imply. Goal three, "Enhance

> **Example from the Field: A Community Mission**
>
> "Community engagement is vital to our mission at West Hills College. Many of the students we serve are first or second generation Americans and many come from farm worker families. The opportunity for them to experience a work environment beyond the fields is critical to their education. Beyond that, the communities benefit from the work they do—whether it is a clinical setting for a nursing student in an extended care facility or a heavy equipment student helping build a community sports complex, the students are helping improve their community. Everyone wins."
>
> West Hills Community College District Chancellor Frank Gornick

student life and involvement," includes in its action steps "Identify student needs at the campuses—what are they here for? Include student's family in needs assessment," and "Invite community members to 'adopt' a student for the school year." Family, community, partnerships, alliances—this is the vocabulary the college uses to think, plan, and act.

To a degree that is rare even among community colleges, West Hills sees itself as part of the community. As West Hills' director of marketing Frances Squire explained, the college's chief goal is to "develop and strengthen college and community interactions to improve our positive image in our community." During our site visit we found that people at the college use phrases like "community work," "community service," and "service-learning" largely interchangeably, primarily because at a very basic level academic work *is* community work. The community can only move forward through education, and education can only take place through the community.

Administrative and Academic Leadership

This conviction that the work of the campus and that of the community are basically one and the same varies in significance among HSIs, depending on the degree to which the campus sees itself as actually growing up out of the community. However, what does not vary significantly is the institutional resolve to *serve* the surrounding community. This resolve is largely due to the strength of this unit's second indicator, "Administrative and Academic Leadership." Again and again on our site visits we encountered presidents, provosts, and deans whose top priorities involved service to the community.

For example, Frank Gornick, chancellor of West Hills Community College District, and Anthony Tricoli, president of West Hills Community College Coalinga, were determined that the community be given every chance to shape the institution's strategic priorities. In leading a planning process called "Voices, Values and Vision," they convened a series of "town call" meetings where community residents could help identify where the college should go next. As President Tricoli explained ("A Vision for West Hills: Voices and Values from Its Communities," p.1),

> Our vision is the creation of a future for the college that is built on a solid foundation of collaboration, trust, and understanding. Together, we will develop activities where all people (students, faculty, staff, and local residents) provide input into the processes of planning our college's future.

A similarly democratic impulse informs the leadership of Heritage University President Kathleen Ross. President Ross, together with two local Native American leaders, founded Heritage a little more than 20 years ago. When Ross, then academic vice president at Fort Wright College, brought the news to the Yakama Valley that Fort Wright would have to close its branch campus there, Martha Yallup and Violet Rau, community leaders of the Yakama Nation, suggested that the branch campus be converted into a new institution. In an age in which most new private institutions reflect the interests of a corporation or wealthy donor, Heritage was created in the image of the community. As President Ross noted in one of our interviews, the community's image is still unmistakable:

> First and foremost, at Heritage College,[1] the student body is the community voice. The average age of students at Heritage is 31, with a very wide variance, 18-70. These people have families, have jobs, and care about their community. Furthermore, most of the faculty and administrators live in the community, and are very active in the community. Second, the Heritage College Board of Directors/Trustees is made up completely of community members; there are no internal Heritage College members.

Ross herself sits on a number of community boards and is an active presence in the local community. In addition, she has been pivotal in making Heritage the home of the Community Outreach Partnership Center, which reaches out to economically disadvantaged members of the local community.

Although it starts at the highest level, exemplary leadership is not limited to the very top of the administrative hierarchy. At Our Lady of the Lake, Provost Maria Shelton has instituted as a regular feature of her weekly Provost's Council a practice called "Share the positives," where community-related work is shared in detail with all of the department chairs and deans. At St. Edward's, University in Austin, Texas, one of the university's deans, Brother John Paige, CSC, has helped make the School of Education an outstanding example of community engagement. According to Paige, commitment to the university's outreach mission is deliberate and systematic. As one reflection of this "lived ethos," he has seen to it that education majors are placed only in schools with high social need and has made helping both public and parochial schools that serve underresourced populations one of his division's priorities.

At Heritage, other academic and administrative leaders have joined President Ross in her commitment to the local community. Like the president, they serve on the

---

1. At this time of this interview, Heritage had not yet changed its name from Heritage College to Heritage University.

boards of local service groups, such as school boards, religious organizations, and Hispanic and Native American organizations. They also conduct research on economic development issues and share what they have learned with local schools. In addition, they run a variety of partnerships, such as the Circle of Success program, in which students visit local parents of preschool children to share information on children's health and development.

Curriculum and Pedagogy

Best Practices

- Create academic programming in response to community needs.
- Offer a wide range of service-learning courses.
- Require service-learning courses.
- Commit the institution to experiential learning and innovative pedagogies.
- Focus on cultural diversity as part of the college or university's teaching and learning strategy.

Departments, Disciplines, and Interdisciplinary Work

Since all of the HSIs we visited are primarily teaching institutions, it is to be expected that their commitment to civic and community engagement should be embodied in their teaching activities. However, this embodiment takes several different forms. Our first indicator of engagement involving academic programs asks to what extent such engagement has become a part of the way in which academic units across the curriculum do their work.

"Departments, Disciplines, and Interdisciplinary Work" finds expression in both depth and breadth of initiatives. A good example of depth is Carlos Abizu University, a Florida school specializing in culturally sensitive mental health practice, serving Puerto Rican students. Through its community program, the university has donated more than 500,000 hours of mental health consulting for local residents. St. Edward's School of Education, discussed above, is another example, as is St. Edward's School of Business, which not only has its own service-learning coordinator but also has made service-learning a required feature of one of its core courses.

Breadth can also be found at St. Edward's, where, according to Provost Sister Donna Jurick, every discipline has at least one course or program that involves community work. Glendale Community College in Arizona boasts service-learning courses in biology, child/family studies, communications, English, ESL, and math. At Heritage, President Ross estimated that over 50% of the college's courses "have some form of community involvement that provides services and benefits to the local community."

Some of these programs are designed specifically to meet workplace needs. For example, Heritage's board of directors has established a Community Partnership Committee that seeks input from and works with local businesses, nonprofit organizations, government agencies, and community leaders to identify educational needs. The committee also works with academic department heads and the board's own academic committee to create new programs to address those needs. A similar situation exists at West Hills, where much of the academic programming has been created in response to the community's workplace requirements. Naturally, this programming often includes some kind of community-based "practicum."

At other HSIs, pre-professional or vocational responsiveness is not what anchors community engagement in the curriculum. At California State University (CSU)–Stanislaus, for example, the university has not only created many academic programs in response to local socioeconomic needs, it has also created a university-wide service-learning program that helps incorporate community-based work even in those disciplinary areas where such work serves no immediate pre-professional purpose. According to the university's Office of Service-Learning, during the 2002–2003 academic year, 37 faculty members taught 42 service-

---

**Example from the Field:
Service-Learning Courses at CSU–Stanislaus, 2004**

COURSE (DEPARTMENT)

Human Development: Childhood (Child Development)

Early Intervention High-Risk Children (Child Development)

Chem in Elem School Classroom (Chemistry)

Biochemistry I (Chemistry)

Public Relations Campaigns (Communication Studies)

Intercultural Communication (Communication Studies)

Mathematical Methods (Multidisciplinary)

Science & Health (Multidisciplinary)

Restorative Human Ecology (Geography)

Community and Diversity (Liberal Studies)

Liberal Studies Deans' Team (Liberal Studies)

Seminar in Community Learning (Multidisciplinary)

Service-Learning in American Government (Politics & Public Administration)

Hunger, Homelessness, & Social Policy (Sociology)

Intercultural Communication (Teacher Education)

Introduction to Multilingual Education (Multidisciplinary)

Human Ecology (Geography)

American Government (Politics & Public Administration)

Community and Diversity (Liberal Studies)

Human Development II: Adolescent (Child Development)

Persuasive Messages (Communication Studies)

Leadership for Communication (Communication Studies)

Cooperative Education (Communication Studies)

Individual Study (Communication Studies)

Permaculture Application in Diverse Environments (Geography)

Beginning Field Experience (Liberal Studies)

Intermediate Field Experience (Liberal Studies)

Liberal Studies Peer Advising (Liberal Studies)

learning courses in disciplines ranging from liberal studies to economics to chemistry.

Our Lady of the Lake University has adopted a different but equally promising curricular strategy. In the spring of 2003, OLLU's Faculty Assembly approved a new general education curriculum that includes two required service-learning courses. Thus, "Service-Learning Across the Curriculum" has assumed an importance in the school's educational design comparable to "Writing Across the Curriculum," "Technology and Information Literacy Across the Curriculum," and "Critical Thinking Across the Curriculum"—that is, it has become a core institutional competency. In making this move, the faculty also took an important step toward establishing an institution-wide understanding of what does (and does not) constitute academically legitimate service-learning practice.

Teaching and Learning

Whatever variation exists among HSIs with regard to the extent and the nature of their community-related courses and programs, there can be no doubt that all recognize the importance of opening up the educational process to new approaches to "Teaching and Learning," the second indicator in this unit. As President Ross of Heritage University has remarked: "So many people in the changing demography of America are not prepared for a preconceived educational mold."

In response to this recognition of the demonstrable limitations of "preconceived" educational strategies, Heritage has made a deliberate effort to move its faculty to embrace pedagogical innovation as a core value. A university document titled "Key Characteristics of Highly Effective Faculty and Measures of Faculty Success" notes that "The effective educator understands human development and utilizes teaching strategies which best meet students' developmental stages and learning styles." Such attention to different ways of knowing has borne fruit. Although the national graduation rate from entry to six years for low-income students and students of color is only about 10%, a recent Heritage class had a graduation rate of 55%.

At St. Edward's, the university is "committed to all forms of experiential learning—whether in the classroom, workplace, student life, student activities, campus ministry, or community." Its reasons for doing so include "help[ing] students become more motivated and empowered as learners and as members of society" (www.stedwards.edu/cte/ServiceLearning/index.htm).

The structures within which HSIs promote engaged teaching and learning vary widely. At St. Edward's, the Center for Teaching Effectiveness supports the university's commitment to engaged learning. CSU–Stanislaus has a similar center, the Faculty Center for Excellence in Teaching and Learning. One of the most important and visible of the university's recent investments, the center seeks, according to its brochure, to provide "practical advice on the integration of **innovative pedagogies** designed to improve instruction" [original emphasis]. Thus, the center also houses the university's Office of Service Learning. Less formal structures can also be effective. At Glendale Community College, a looser structure gives faculty complete freedom in how they connect service and community-based work to their courses.

A review of faculty documents from Our Lady of the Lake University reveals a similar emphasis on the importance of pedagogical flexibility and innovation. The university's Faculty Manual notes that "OLLU faculty are distinguished by their exceptional willingness to accommodate the special needs of their students through personalized attention, extra availability and approachability, and adaptive and often innovative teaching methods." One especially innovative teaching method in which the university has invested is the utilization of what it calls "Barrio Professors." These are described in the Faculty Manual as "non-credentialed academic personnel who provide for university students the practical benefit of their own life and work experience in barrio or ghetto settings."

OLLU's Barrio Professors introduce another feature of "Teaching and Learning" common at engaged HSIs: an intensive focus on cultural diversity. This makes sense given that HSIs—unlike some HBCUs and most TCUs—work with a very racially and culturally mixed student population. From more traditional comprehensives like St. Edward's and CSU–Stanislaus with a minority Hispanic population to schools like OLLU, Heritage (Toppenish campus), and West Hills, where Hispanic students are in the majority, teaching individuals to understand and respect a variety of cultural traditions is a necessity. As one St. Edward's faculty member remarked, "Race, class, and gender are dealt with in every course." For example, once course in the required "Cultural Foundations" sequence includes a "roots" paper assignment designed to help students learn to appreciate both their own family backgrounds and those of their classmates (www.stedwards.edu/unpg/culf1320/about.html).

In short, there may be no other group of higher education institutions that makes diversity such deliberate a part of their teaching and learning strategy. And because active learning, multiple learning styles, alternative pedagogies, cultural pluralism, and community-based work naturally complement each other, any investment in one is likely to also strengthen the others. The final three sentences of

---

Example from the Field: The Importance of Cultural Diversity

"Heritage believes that vital to the economic and cultural future of our region and state, and even the world, is the reversal of the historical underrepresentation in higher education of some cultural groups. Each student, faculty, and staff's cultural background is viewed as an asset. We strive to build community in a deliberately pluralistic setting."

Heritage University President Kathleen Ross, in a welcome letter to students and others

Heritage's vision statement could, with some modification, be taken to speak to the vision of all engaged HSIs we looked at:

> To develop community and concern for the common good, Heritage University seeks to provide leadership in supporting cultural pluralism within our own and other communities. Cultural pluralism creates a climate of respect and appreciation by fostering "learning about us" in an interdependent and connected world. Heritage University acts to make its curriculum, staffing, teaching, and other college activities reflect this learning (www.heritage.edu/about/vision.htm).

Faculty Culture

Best Practices

- Support engaged faculty work through tenure and promotion guidelines.
- Implement informal structures to reward faculty who participate in service-learning and other engaged pedagogies.
- Support faculty development through events, on-campus trainings, grants, and project development stipends.
- Establish an office to support faculty involvement in service-learning.

Like the indicators that comprise "Curriculum and Pedagogy," those that comprise "Faculty Culture" point to an institution's ability to put its engaged mission into practice through its academic programs. Here, however, the focus is on the concrete *professional* support given to those charged with delivering those programs.

Faculty Roles and Rewards

Institutional support for engaged faculty work—as measured by a willingness to see such work as worthy of promotion, tenure, and other forms of recognition—varied little among the schools we visited, regardless of institutional type. Most faculty we talked with saw such work not just as an available option but as an institutional expectation. For example, St. Edward's Faculty Manual, revised in 2002, states:

> In the spirit of the Mission Statement, faculty may also be reasonably expected to render service to the larger community, i.e., from neighborhood to international service. This generally excludes service in the faculty member's area of study, which is covered in Professional Development

The manual identifies examples of service, including volunteering at community service organizations, participating in service related to religious organizations, working with political organizations, and serving the educational system. Service within a faculty member's discipline, covered under professional development, includes "training for and/or implementation of service-learning programs." In addition, a section of the annual faculty report requires faculty to identify community-related work. As one faculty member put it, such work is simply "part of what's expected if one wants to stay here."

OLLU's faculty manual proffers closely related sentiments:

> The impact of an educational institution upon the community in which it exists depends in great part upon the contribution the faculty makes to its total environment.... Each is expected, without detriment to the on-campus program, to exert, in whatever sphere he or she can best function, an educational or professional influence on the community outside the University.

Reinforcing this position, the university's faculty assembly recently passed a resolution identifying a commitment to community service as one of its top values. Passed as part of the new general education curriculum, the resolution reads, in part:

**Example from the Field:
Expectations for Engaged Faculty Work**

The university mission statement holds that "a caring faculty" should "encourage individuals to confront the critical issues of society and to seek justice and peace," as well as "to understand themselves, clarify their personal values, and recognize their responsibility to the world community." The university itself serves as the role model for this commitment to service. In this spirit, the faculty at St. Edward's University shall be evaluated in the area of service.

At St. Edward's University the faculty is expected to render service. This may include service within and/or outside of the university community. Both of these categories are evaluated according to two criteria. The first criterion considers what service is rendered, i.e., responsibility, while the second considers the spirit in which it is rendered, i.e., collegial relations. Both are considered important aspects of service and must be included as part of the evaluation.

SOURCE: St. Edward's Faculty Manual (www.stedwards.edu/academic/faculty_manual.htm).

> The General Education program will embody the mission and values of the University as these are derived from the values of the Congregation of Divine Providence. Such values include social justice, service to others, care of the environment, and commitment to the advancement of the disadvantaged, minorities, and women.

The faculty's decision to make two service-learning courses part of the school's core general education requirement is in keeping with this priority. The same is true of the faculty manual's explicit identification of service-learning as one of the university's priorities for faculty development. This focus on faculty engagement dovetails another goal of the general education curriculum: to prepare students "to participate in service to their civic, national, and global communities."

According to Larry Petry, the president's assistant for community outreach at Heritage University, faculty public service is also "a strong part of the evaluation process" at Heritage. Such service typically includes volunteering at local high schools and serving on nonprofit boards. One faculty member observed, "Heritage faculty themselves interact with the community more than at any other place any of us knows about." Corroborating this view, one of the school's community partners noted, "The faculty really volunteer and are active in the community and on boards, bringing in so much information and sharing so many resources. They are significantly more active than average faculty or even the best faculty at other institutions."

Reinforcing this spirit of engagement, the college explicitly identifies as "Key Characteristics of Highly Effective Faculty" items like "Models giving service in the local communities," "Functions comfortably and effectively in other cultural contexts, including communities served by Heritage College," and "Connects discipline content to authentic, real life applications and current issues."

Pride in faculty contributions to the local community was one of the most consistent sentiments we found among all constituencies at engaged HSIs. Whether such service is required or a preferred option, whether it primarily takes the form of engaged academic work or of more generic public service, it plays a central role in the way in which faculty roles are conceptualized. Thus, at CSU–Stanislaus, although community-based work is not required, Provost David Dauwalder noted that:

> The passion and the excitement of faculty in the community are outstanding. A strong core of passionate people here has ignited the rest of the folks. The community involvement keeps growing each year. Each year this work is more accepted as a strong methodology that can be utilized to help students learn.... With regard to faculty retention, tenure, and promotion processes, if the faculty identify service-learning in their activity files, I notice. It is important to attend to the service work in order to be on track.

To encourage faculty to stay "on track," Diana Demetrulias, vice provost for academic affairs and dean of the CSU–Stanislaus Graduate School, has identified several unit goals that seek to promote and support faculty in "ongoing service projects and the development of service-learning coursework." The university has also instituted an Outstanding Professor Award in the area of community service.

Of course, there are also other, less formal ways to recognize and reward faculty who contribute to the community. At Heritage University, for example, the provost honors one or more faculty members for leadership and community service at an annual Academic Convocation. Service projects spearheaded by faculty are among the projects showcased by the university's faculty lecture series. Even at the university's monthly academic affairs meetings, the provost identifies faculty members involved in new community service projects.

At OLLU, a ceremony at the end of each academic year recognizes and honors outstanding faculty members in six categories, one of which is excellence in service-learning. Faculty, students, and community partners are all encouraged to nominate exemplary instructors for this award. Prior to the final selection, faculty members who agree to be nominated must showcase their service-learning efforts at a faculty development workshop. In addition, the OLLU newspaper plans to begin a regular series called "Spotlight on Service-Learning," which will highlight faculty members and students who are involved in service-learning.

Faculty Development

At CSU–Stanislaus, another way in which the university signals its support for engaged faculty work is through its investment in the indicator we call "Faculty Development." Unlike "Faculty Roles and Rewards," this indicator shows considerable variation among the schools we visited, largely because of the schools' widely varying financial situations. Unfortunately, like many other minority-serving institutions, some HSIs simply cannot afford costs not directly related to basic service delivery. Hence, while they encourage—or even require—community-based activities, they must rely largely on individual faculty initiative to acquire the skills and resources needed to undertake those activities.

Clearly this is not the case at CSU–Stanislaus, which has been able to promote and support faculty development as a major institutional priority. By housing its Office of Service Learning in its new Faculty Development Center, the school has sent a visible signal to faculty that quality community-based programs are in everyone's best interests. Repaying the trust placed in it, the service-learning office has become a hive of faculty development activities, offering both regularly scheduled group trainings and special developmental opportunities.

Of the latter, perhaps the most innovative is the Community Agency Bus Tour. Organized by the office's director, Julie Fox, and hosted by a representative of the city's Chamber of Commerce, the tour brings together a group of faculty, administrators, students, nonprofit leaders, and government officials to visit some of the school's partners. At each site, the partner discusses its mission and needs, and distributes relevant handout materials. According to Fox, many on the first tour in 2003 had never been inside the social service agencies visited, which included the Salvation Army and the United Samaritans.

Events and on-campus trainings are, however, only one dimension of the office's faculty development strategy. In recent years it has also been able to provide mini-grants to supplement project development stipends already offered by individual academic departments and has helped faculty access service-learning resources made available by the chancellor's office of the California State University system. Through a rich combination of group and individual opportunities, the office has helped an ever-larger number of faculty not only become acquainted with community-based work but also advance along a progression designed to achieve both enhanced program quality and greater faculty independence.

Other CSU campuses have similar structures in place. CSU–Bakersfield's Community Service Programs (CSP) office provides faculty with support and resources for developing and sustaining service-learning and other community-based activities. Because the office is located within academic affairs and reports to the dean of undergraduate studies, the office is easily accessible for faculty. The CSP has also established a relationship with the Faculty Teaching and Learning Center, which supports service-learning roundtables and workshops. The CSP office has developed relationships with many individual academic departments and campus centers to ensure the best possible support for faculty service-learning efforts.

At CSU–Monterey Bay, the Service Learning Institute is the main campus resource for community-based work. The institute tracks all service-learning partnerships online and is currently implementing a risk-management system. An introduction to service-learning is part of all new faculty orientations, where the Service Learning Institute is identified as the hub of community partnership work for the campus.

CSU–Northridge has set aside considerable funding for faculty development, specifically in service-learning. For the past five years, more than $20,000 a year has been allocated for this use. Departments have received additional funds for service-learning coordinators, mentoring programs, interdisciplinary planning, and travel to present on service-learning research at disciplinary conferences. Funding has also been made available for specific training initiatives such Campus Compact's Engaged Department Institutes. In addition, faculty interests and course content are matched with an aggressive pursuit of grants to add to the budget the university already provides.

OLLU also provides centralized faculty development resources. Since the faculty recently made service-learning part of the school's general education requirement, the administration has allocated $100,025 over five years through a grant received from the Lilly Endowment to support training for this initiative. These monies have been used to develop a Service-Learning Faculty Fellows Seminar, a 35-hour intensive faculty training offered each summer, as well as other faculty development opportunities. Thus far, 14 full-time faculty members have graduated from the seminar, which culminates in the redesign of courses to integrate service-learning. These and other community-related faculty development opportunities are facilitated by the school's service-learning office, called the Center for Service Learning and Volunteerism (CSLV). In drafting a document titled "Values and

Skills Across the Curriculum: Guidelines for Course Validations" (available online at www.ollusa. edu/catalogs/undergrad/2003-2005/undergrad_info.asp#5), which took effect in fall 2004, the faculty explicitly recommended that the administration channel relevant development resources through the CSLV, which already has responsibility for approving courses given a service-learning designation in the university's course schedule.

Although schools with less funding cannot support faculty development in the same way, many have effective development initiatives to train, motivate, and provide logistical support for faculty working with the community. For example, Florida International University, which serves many Cuban American students, offers a variety of services to faculty members to encourage them to incorporate service into their classes, including making contacts with relevant community partners—particularly in the Cuban American community—and supporting professional development opportunities.

Mechanisms and Resources

Best Practices

- Have the office responsible for faculty development in service-learning assist with the administrative work related to engagement in order to relieve faculty workloads.

- Use outside grants or programs to support enabling infrastructures.

- Create a center to serve all institutional constituencies and bridge curricular and non-curricular community engagement.

- Make sure this central office has sufficient resources, is funded with hard money, and is centrally located and accessible to all.

- Develop students to become future community leaders by encouraging them to be involved on major institutional committees, developing a strong student government, and encouraging civic and political engagement.

One of the most interesting things we discovered in researching the indicators that comprise this unit—"Support Structures and Resources," "Internal Budget and Resource Allocation," "Coordination of Community-Based Activities," and "Student Voice"—is that the internal coherence they have shown at other kinds of institutions was often not present to the same extent in this group of schools. One notable exception is Center for Civic Engagement at the University of Texas at Brownsville and Texas Southmost College. The center has a comprehensive website dedicated to civic engagement (www.civicengagement.com).

There seem to be several reasons for the more diverging approaches here, including different ways of understanding what the indicators include or imply, significantly different institutional contexts and self-definitions, and the specific role played by Hispanic programs. As a result, the findings here are somewhat less generalizable than are many other practices identified in this chapter. In one sense this is fortuitous: it allows us to explore a range of structures and approaches, which together should create a selection with broad applicability for HSIs as well as other institutions.

Support Structures and Resources

Among the schools we looked at, those with strong faculty development programs also tended to be those with the kinds of practical/logistical resources that facilitate faculty practice. In the case of CSU–Stanislaus, for example, the Office of Service Learning offers both academic and practical support.

To facilitate this "soup to nuts" approach to faculty support, the office publishes its own Faculty Handbook. Here faculty find a range of information, including specific responsibilities the office is willing to assume on their behalf and scholarly journals that may be interested in publishing the results of their work. The handbook also includes many of the forms that can clarify and expedite their arrangements with students and community partners. As the office's director, Julie Fox, said during our site visit:

> We try to have a menu plan where faculty can be involved as much as they want to be involved. This menu approach calls for a progressive role: as the first-time faculty think about service-learning, they want tons of support from the Office of Service Learning, and then after that they take more and more initiative.

Example from the Field:
Role of an Exemplary Service-Learning Office

CSU–Stanislaus' Office of Service Learning moves seamlessly between academic and practical support. While helping faculty achieve greater professional competence in community-based work, it also relieves them of many of the non-academic tasks that attend such work: on the one hand, it will assist faculty with "syllabus generation/curricular development" while making available academic resources and publications; on the other hand, it will help faculty develop concrete community partnerships and assist with such things as "site coordination and student orientations."

SOURCE: CSU–Stanislaus Office of Service Learning fact sheet.

A similar relationship between faculty development and support structures can be found at the University of Texas at El Paso. The university's Center for Civic Engagement offers sample syllabi and tries to address the extra labor objection sometimes associated with service-learning, even offering to help co-teach courses. In return, the center asks participating faculty members to document their service-learning projects and to file a syllabus with the center so it can build a library of service-related courses.

OLLU's Center for Service-Learning and Volunteerism also provides a range of services although, as its name suggests, its focus is less exclusively academic. In addition to service-learning, the CSLV coordinates two active non-academic service initiatives, "OLLU Serves" and the "vOLLUnteer Unity Council." During our visit, several different constituencies stressed—without intending in any way to downplay the importance of academic engagement—that community service activities outweigh service-learning in creating the intensely service-oriented culture that defines the university.

The fact that the CSLV houses key student-run programs as well as academic programs may help explain why, in addition to the many kinds of assistance it provides to faculty, it puts considerable emphasis on student preparation for, and development through, service-learning courses. If faculty approve, the center will work with students in areas like coordinating meetings, risk assessment, midterm assessment, project evaluation, and partner etiquette. Indeed, OLLU's overall approach to service-learning seems to point toward a progressive student development model. This was confirmed by the students we interviewed, who noted that while most lower-level community projects were defined for them, they worked much more collaboratively with faculty to design upper-level projects.

Housing engaged student and faculty work through the same office can create synergies, both for funding and for the work itself. For example, the grant from the Lilly Endowment mentioned earlier also funds two student positions, a service-learning graduate assistant and a service-learning administrative clerk. Both positions provide support to faculty members who teach service-learning courses.

Still another kind of support structure can be found at St. Edward's, where a Kellogg-funded Engaging Latino Communities for Education (ENLACE) program runs parallel to the school's other service-learning initiatives. Like academic community-based work in general, ENLACE, according to its brochure, seeks both to strengthen HSIs "to serve as catalysts and models for educational and community change" and to support "the creation or adoption of educational models based on best practices" that improve student success. ENLACE seeks to achieve these and other goals largely through the formation of partnerships. Thus, the program at St. Edward's also includes Austin Community College, the Austin Independent School District, the Austin Interfaith coalition, the Austin Latino Alliance, and members of the Montopolis neighborhood community.

One important part of St. Edward's ENLACE program is a special service-learning program "designed to place students in profit and nonprofit organizations dedicated to supporting the success of the Latino and Montopolis communities." Students participating in any of the program's community-based initiatives are required to take a one-credit seminar taught by the program's service-learning coordinator. Here they are both prepared for their service work and helped to reflect on that work from multiple perspectives. With its deeply reciprocal relationship with the community, St. Edward's ENLACE service-learning program can be seen as a model of what is possible with this approach in a specifically Hispanic context.

Coordination of Community-Based Activities

OLLU's Center for Service Learning and Volunteerism is an excellent example of "Coordination of Community-Based Activities," since it serves all institutional constituencies while at the same time acting as a bridge between curricular and non-curricular community-based programming. With its combination of academic and non-academic responsibilities and resources, the center is able to provide a level of support and coordination to non-curricular programs that is unusual in its thoroughness and professionalism. From the standpoint of the university's community partners, the fact that the center commands such a broad overview of OLLU's outreach activities helps to make the school's internal operations and procedures more transparent while also making it easier to mount and coordinate multi-faceted initiatives.

A similar situation exists at CSU–Stanislaus. Since the university has no non-curricular volunteer office, the Office of Service-Learning coordinates both curricular and non-curricular service. The service-learning website keeps updated lists of local volunteer opportunities, providing students with agencies, contact information, and a brief description of the types of service opportunities offered at each site. Thus, all students who are involved in volunteer work have a common base for resources and support.

A very different kind of coordinating arrangement can be found at Heritage University. Although Heritage does not have the same kind of formal infrastructure as OLLU or CSU–Stanislaus, the president's office has emerged as a central organizing point for campus-community relations. Given the pivotal role the president herself has played in the college's founding as a community-based institution, this is hardly surprising. The college as a whole plays such a central role in the life of the community—"continually mapping needs and resources with just about everything they do," as one community partner put it—that the school itself can be seen as "in many ways the clearinghouse of information for all community partners' needs."

Strongly supporting this view is the fact that the director of the university's Office of External Affairs also serves on the board of directors' Community Partnership Committee and several local community boards. The Partnership Committee often discusses and addresses community needs identified at these local board meetings. This director reports to the provost and also sits on the president's cabinet, which gives the Office of External Affairs direct access to the president.

Internal Budget and Resource Allocations

Typically, this indicator points to a willingness to internalize funding for a central office, such as OLLU's Center for Service Learning and Volunteerism and CSU–Stanislaus' Office of Service Learning; to locate that office in a central, accessible place; and to allocate sufficient resources for all constituencies—students, faculty, and staff—to do their work effectively and without undue self-sacrifice.

Most of the schools we visited make such resources available, to a greater or lesser extent. At OLLU, a modest budget for the central office is supplemented by faculty funding for the center's director, positions supported by outside grants, and the provost's special allocation for service-learning course development. Similarly, at CSU–Stanislaus, base-level funding from the university is supplemented by assistance from the chancellor's office, extramural funding for specific faculty-driven programs, and partnerships with local organizations. One partnership designed to encourage literacy development involved the Office of Service-Learning, a psychology professor, the local nonprofit Parent Resource Center, and the Stanislaus County Office of Education. This collaboration with several diverse partners allows the office to undertake projects of broader scope and impact than could be achieved with university funding alone.

The University of Texas at Brownsville offers a good example of how specifically allocated resources can have a major impact. During the spring of 2004, the university offered eight $1,000 student civic engagement scholarships through the university's Center for Civic Engagement. Students used this funding to design a project that required 10 hours of community work a week per student for 12 to 14 weeks. The eight students chose to renovate the local Boys & Girls Club and succeeded in convincing nearly 100 of their peers to participate.

Not all schools approach this indicator in the typical way. Because of its closeness to the community, Heritage, for example, has a different approach. Rather than earmarking specific resources for external allocation, the college supports community-based work through its intrinsic operations. This position is best expressed by President Ross: since everything the college does is with and for the community, separating resources into those that support community-based work and those that do not makes little sense. As another member of the administration pointed out, at least half of all the college's employees would identify community work as a significant part of their job.

Student Voice

Like its predecessors, the final indicator for this unit, "Student Voice," takes on a different meaning depending on the kind of institution in question. Despite such variations, it seems clear that empowering students to articulate their concerns and to play an active, shaping role in the engagement process is a matter of considerable importance to all the HSIs visited as part of this project. At CSU–Stanislaus, one of the most impressive indications of student voice is the role students are invited to play on all major institutional committees. According to Provost David Dauwalder,

> Students are members on all of our strategic planning committees, our graduate counsels, our Assessment of Student Learning Committee, and all of our educational policy committees, and two of our students are voting members of our Academic Faculty Senate. The incoming president of the student senate is invited to participate in our annual top-layer administrative retreat.

At St. Edward's University, students also participate in nearly every aspect of the university's work. Not only does the president of the Student Government Association have an ex-officio seat on the Board of Trustees, but students also sit on most internal standing committees, such as the Academic Council, the Athletics Council, and student activity operation committees. Perhaps most remarkable is student involvement in the hiring process for almost all academic and student life positions as well as senior administrative positions. St. Edward's students even serve on the search committee for the institution's president.

Many other schools make similar efforts to let students be heard. St. Peter's College in New Jersey offers a variety of forums for student voice, including membership on board committees as well as formal student leadership programs and President and Cabinet Forums hosted by student groups. At Occidental College in Los Angeles, the faculty committee of the Community Based Learning Office has two student members as well as a community representative. Students have also taken it upon themselves to press the administration about campus services and other issues and to plan dialogues about civic engagement in the dorms. Dialogue also features heavily at the University of Miami, where President Donna Shalala started the President Lecture series, which informs students about issues and fosters dialogue between students and the speakers on these issues. In addition, the campus has a "free-speech platform" where students can inform each other about social issues and discuss their opinions.

At OLLU, student voice is very much bound up with the outreach work of student-run organizations such as the vOLLUnteer Unity Council (VUC) and OLLU Serves. Both are recognized as highly effective organizing bodies. The Texas Coordinating Board has identified OLLU Serves as a model program. The VUC has helped create a comprehensive framework and support system for the community-based work of student organizations. OLLU students, who work an average of 50 hours per academic year in student-led service projects, regard the VUC as a powerful expression of their voice. Faculty, administrators, and community partners agree.

At many HSIs, the students literally *are* the local community; hence, in a very real sense, student voice and community voice are more or less indistinguishable. This is particularly true at Heritage University and West Hills Community College District. At Heritage, a Presidential Fellows Program grooms a small number of specially selected students each year to become future community leaders. The program puts the students in direct contact with current community leaders who introduce them to issues and provide guidance as the students begin to design their own responses to these issues. At both Heritage and West Hills, students also see the power of their voice reflected in the growing coherence of student government as embodied in the Associated Student Board.

Many of the schools we visited encourage student voice not just on campus but through civic and political engagement. One West Hills faculty member noted that "Everything we do in class must be relevant to our community, our state, and our country" and suggested that his students "are probably the most informed people in Kings County." To make sure his students make the connection between local issues and politics, and to help them develop the kind of voice that will make itself heard in state government, this professor regularly brings his students with him to the state capitol in Sacramento. There they sit in on legislative sessions and committee meetings and share the results of their engaged work with local and state legislators. Students at Heritage make a similar trip to their state capitol in Olympia.

Overall, civic engagement—not just community engagement—seems to be an important concern at engaged HSIs. Perhaps the bond between Hispanic students and Hispanic communities makes students aware of the importance of political and economic power in achieving sustainable results. At St. Edward's, minority students suggested that, compared with their non-minority peers, they were disproportionately involved in activities and issues that sought to address contemporary social problems; for example, it was clear that the Hispanic students involved in ENLACE were not just providing services, they were also being groomed to become effective community leaders.

Other examples abound. At OLLU, one of the VUC's member organizations is the Civic Education Team—a group that has participated in Campus Compact's "Raise Your Voice" campaign and has lobbied state legislators person to person. One of the most impressive events with which CSU–Stanislaus' Office of Service Learning has been recently involved is a two-day Civic Mission of Education conference that brought together college and high school students and their teachers to discuss ways to promote civic responsibility in the community. The conference was followed by a more local forum on civic education hosted by the Office of Service Learning.

Finally, the interest of all these schools in helping students not just work in the community but become effective in their community work can be seen in their willingness to train students to do such work. We noted above how such preparation is a key part of St. Edward's ENLACE program. It is also a key aspect of all the service work at OLLU. As one community partner observed of her experience with service-learning students, "The training and organization skills of the students are excellent. The key elements of these trainings are that they teach the students how to learn with and through service-learning." She concluded that when the students come to the agency, "the system is working perfectly, effectively, smoothly, efficiently."

Such praise is particularly meaningful given that one of the most common complaints community partners have about service-learning in general is that students haven't been adequately prepared for work in the community. To take student training seriously is not only to act responsibly but also to show respect both for students and for the community partners with whom they work.

Community-Campus Exchange

Best Practices

- Hold town meetings with community members to hear their input on the college's plans and to identify and meet community needs.
- Pursue grants in conjunction with the community and use grant funds to develop community-based programs.
- Provide resources, programs, or other support structures directly to the community.
- Share the institution's physical resources with the community.

Although engaged HSIs have many strengths, there is perhaps no area in which they excel more than in their community relationships. Again and again we found a genuine willingness to invite and respond to community input and to invest in the community in a variety of ways. Thus, the indicators in this unit—"Community Voice," "Forums for Fostering Public Dialogue," and "External Resource Allocations"—are particularly strong. They can also be closely connected, as West Hills' "Voices, Values and Visions" planning process makes evident: through a series of public forums the college sought to capture the priorities of the local community in order to mobilize resources to address those priorities.

Community Voice

The planning process at West Hills, in which administrative and academic leaders held a series of town hall meetings for community residents to help identify where the college should go next, puts community voice at the forefront of the institution's priorities. In addition to these and regional meetings, community partners are included on West Hills' board of trustees. This deliberate seeking out of community input points to a very special kind of reciprocity. As one of the college's community partners put it:

> What makes West Hills different is that they are constantly in contact with each of their partners all of the time about needs, resources, vision, opportunities. We are one big vibrant family helping each other. We say, "By the way, we need…can you help? Or "Do you want to come along with us on this idea or project?" All the time, we're talking to each other.

Communication of this kind differs in nature from the more formal, contractual arrangements that characterize most campus-community partnerships. While it is clearly important to include the community's voice in specific activities such as service-learning course design, program evaluation, and the work of relevant institutional committees, such community input can quickly become one consideration among many. In the case of schools like West Hills, community input is not merely influential; it is elemental. This approach to community voice is a distinctive feature at many engaged HSIs.

Heritage University is another example. According to Larry Petry, the president's assistant for community outreach, most of Heritage's projects, programs, and courses represent a direct response to community interests and concerns. The goal of the Education Division, for example, is to create programs that serve school districts, "rather than the other way around." From "listening closely" to the community's voice, the division has developed many specific initiatives to meet community needs, including a program to help paraprofessionals in particular school districts become qualified teachers, an English as a second language (ESL) master's program, a counseling certification program, and a principles of leadership academy. Since the college's student body is virtually indistinguishable from the local community, even the college's commitment to addressing student issues like the need for daycare and special scheduling can be seen as part of a larger commitment to designing education on a community foundation.

Many other examples point in the same general direction—namely, to an understanding of the local community and its voice not as an inconsequential or secondary factor but as a significant feature of the educational experience. Among those we found are the fact that CSU–Stanislaus has made a serious effort to match community demographics, with 9 of its 22 teacher education professors bilingual and bicultural; St. Edward's commitment both to ENLACE and to the College Assistance Migrant Program (CAMP); CSU–San Bernardino's inclusion of community partners on their Service-Learning Cabinet; and OLLU's multi-layered ties to West San Antonio as well as its explicit emphasis on the "Hispanic heritage" of its region. Without becoming parochial or provincial, engaged HSIs see full community engagement as a new educational model.

Forums for Fostering Public Dialogue

Just as unusually open campus-community communication can lead to a new understanding of the possibilities of "Community Voice," so it can lead to a new understanding of the ways in which "Forums for Fostering Public Dialogue" can serve the community-building process.

CSU–San Bernardino's Office of Community-University Partnerships (CUP) uses a forum called Dialogue for Vital Communities, followed by a neighborhood revitalization game, to bring community residents together to discuss common challenges and to to identify and prioritize community improvement efforts. These efforts, in turn, are linked to campus-based community engagement and service-learning opportunities. About 15 local neighborhoods around the campus have participated in this process. The neighborhood revitalization game also provides an opportunity for local neighborhoods to come together to address more regional challenges and to envision their ideal community. In this way it illustrates the concrete results that public dialogue can achieve. Forum participants identify the real-life problems that challenge the envisioned ideal and develop strategies to resolve these challenges. The campus is committed to using these strategies in its work with neighborhoods.

At CSU–Fresno, a number of forums foster and support public dialogue. One is the Kenneth L. Maddy Institute of Public Affairs, which presents talks with current and former elected officials and an annual lecture by a professor at the institute. The institute also supports research and publications on central California issues, as well as symposia and extension courses on politics, policy, and public administration. (In addition to fostering public dialogue, the institute offers a range of other community benefits, including practical training for local officials and civic leaders, recognition for public officials who serve the community, and government and nonprofit internships for CSU–Fresno students.) Another university program, the Fresno Central Valley Health Policy Institute, facilitates an interactive regional process to identify, monitor, and analyze emerging health policy issues that influence the health of people living in central California.

A more unusual forum for public dialogue is the Service-Learning Community Partner-Faculty Mixer at OLLU. The mixer began as the inaugural event for the Service-Learning Community Council, which is made up of more than 80 community representatives who participated in a half-day service-learning workshop. During the first mixer, which took place in fall 2004, community members received a guide to faculty members based on pre-submitted service-learning proposals. They then circulated to meet faculty whose work coincided with theirs to discuss potential collaborations. Cynthia Median, an assistant professor and the director of the Center for Service-Learning and Volunteerism, notes:

> This reaped a high degree of non-stop interaction that exceeded the 90 minutes scheduled for this event. Faculty members reported being exhausted from attentively listening to community members describe needs. But more importantly, they stated they left with a rich list of ideas that were well suited to service-learning within their disciplines.

In the weeks following the mixer, the Service-Learning Community Council and the Service-Learning Faculty Council met to discuss the event and to provide feedback to the Center for Service-Learning and Volunteerism.

External Resource Allocations

What initiatives like this suggest is that many of the schools we looked at function not simply as local higher education institutions but as institutions central to the future of their communities. This alternative self-understanding shapes the very meaning of a concept like "external" resource allocation.

The pursuit of grants is a good example. In many cases, campus grant applications now require a community partner to be competitive. More often than not, however, these grants still disproportionately benefit campus-based constituencies. When an institution like West Hills pursues grants, it is because those monies are essential for the community's well being. Over the past several years, West Hills grant writers have brought in more than $40 million for programs of direct benefit to the local community, such as workforce development and encouraging underserved youth to attend college. Grant writing for the community's benefit is also central to the agenda at Heritage. Not only does the university have the knowledge and skills needed to pursue grants successfully; it also can offer in-kind services to cover any required match and can team up with other higher education institutions, like the University of Washington, to extend external resources still further.

One especially important focus of many grants of this type is local families. Since family units play a powerful structural role in Hispanic communities, working successfully with them is often a pre-condition for other kinds of success. At West Hills, this family focus has led to the creation of five early education child care centers where students in the college's childhood development and teacher preparation programs are essential resources. Through the work of these centers, adults develop new-parenting skills and receive the kind of practical assistance they need to be able to return to school. At the same time, the idea of higher education is introduced as a natural and achievable family expectation.

> **Example from the Field: Partnering to Extend Resources**
>
> With the help of a $534,000 grant from the U.S. Department of Housing and Urban Development (HUD), a coalition that includes Heritage University and the University of Washington has teamed to create the Community Outreach Partnership Center, based at Heritage. (The grant went to the University of Washington's Office of Educational Partnerships and Learning Technologies, Heritage University, the city of Toppenish, the Northwest Communities Education Center/Radio KDNA, and the Yakama Nation.) The new center facilitates collaboration among community members, faculty, and students to improve living and working conditions in Toppenish. Grant monies are used to develop small businesses and to revitalize neighborhoods while enabling faculty and students from both universities to provide information technology training for members of the Yakama Nation. According to Heritage University President Kathleen Ross (quoted in Ozuna, 2002),
>
>> This grant provides more resources for Heritage to pursue its long-standing service to the Yakama Nation and the residents of Toppenish, and it increases once again the level of collaboration between Heritage and the UW. These partnerships are so important for truly successful community education in central Washington.

To help defray student costs and ensure that this expectation really is achievable, the college has begun participating in the same College Assistance Migrant Program (CAMP) in which St. Edward's participates. At St. Edward's, 40 students each year are awarded grants to cover tuition, room and board, books and supplies, transportation, health insurance, and living expenses, and they also receive a range of academic, career, and health care counseling services.

In West San Antonio, an Annie E. Casey grant to strengthen families in that community works in part through OLLU's Center for Women. Partnering with a variety of community organizations, the center focuses in part on family economic success, offering workshops on managing personal finances, budgeting, cash management, and building a good credit record. OLLU's commitment to families in West San Antonio is in some ways parallel to St. Edward's commitment to Austin's Montopolis community. Social consciousness-raising, organizing, advocacy, and education in a specifically Hispanic cultural context seek to reverse years of neglect and discrimination.

Such a combination of activities points to another way in which engaged HSIs typically provide external resources: they help their communities mobilize to meet their needs. When the only rural health provider in the area, Coalinga State Hospital, was forced into bankruptcy because of costs related to an earthquake, West Hills helped the hospital develop a new long-term vision as well as powerful new partnerships to help that vision succeed. Similarly, in the Yakama Valley, Heritage laid the foundation for the Exemplary Multicultural Practices in Rural Education (EMPIRE) consortium program. In return for a $1,000 consortium fee,

Heritage provides teams from local K-12 schools with a long list of resources related to multicultural programming, including:

- Access to $1,000 mini-grants for K-12 multicultural programs.
- Participation in Heritage's fall planning retreat.
- Participation in Heritage's annual spring multicultural fair.
- Free site visits and consultant services.
- Subscriptions to the university's newsletters, resource lists, and multicultural consortium library.
- Access to other library resources.
- Participation in collaborative projects (such as the InterValley Ambassadors Program).
- Help in aligning projects with the Washington State Essential Learning Program.

As some of these items suggest, sharing an institution's physical resources is still another way in which engaged HSIs provide external resources. White Hills Community College District built the library on its Lemoore campus in partnership with the local school district. It is the largest library in Kings County, and all of its facilities and resources are open to the public. Heritage is in the process of developing a community chemistry laboratory in conjunction with the Yakama tribe. By design, most of Heritage's buildings are shared-use facilities: if there is an empty room, community organizations are welcome to use it. Similarly, Palo Alto College has opened its facilities, including its state-of-the-art library and Olympic-sized pool, to local schools and the general community. At the other end of the country, Bronx Community College not only provides free space to a local planning board but also houses on campus a public high school, with which it shares some programming.

Finally, as is true of engaged institutions of all kinds, sharing of external resources includes—perhaps first and foremost—the people associated with these schools. These are the legions of students involved in service efforts, the faculty who bring their professional expertise to local issues and who serve on local boards, the administrators and trustees who use their leadership positions and skills to advocate for community interests, forge effective alliances, and influence decision makers. We have already alluded to so many instances of such activities that it would be redundant to cite examples here. However, in the case of engaged HSIs, one aspect of this people-to-people commitment deserves special emphasis, as it reflects the special nature of the campus-community relationship that often prevails among these schools; namely, that when individuals and groups from the campus "give back" to the community, they are often giving to their own community.

Such "self help" is part of the logic behind the service-learning component of St. Edward's ENLACE program. It is also a central to the thinking behind community engagement at OLLU. Because so many OLLU students are first-generation college students who receive financial aid, they feel a deep indebtedness for the special opportunities given to them. By making it not just possible but easy for them to contribute to the neighborhoods they come from, OLLU allows them to accept financial aid with less internal conflict. In several of the K-12 partnerships set up by schools like Heritage and West Hills, student service involvement—both higher education and K-12—is a central structural feature.

Like their students, a significant number of faculty at many of these engaged HSIs are either from or have chosen to live in the local community. For them, too, "giving back" has a special internal logic. For example, Robert Azura, executive director of the Community Outreach Partnership Center housed at Heritage University, was a member of Heritage's first graduating class.

In the end, the operative concept for so much of what happens at engaged HSIs is a concept we have already invoked on several occasions: family. Family here refers not only to the deliberate cultivation of an open, supportive, relationship-oriented campus environment; it also means having a deep appreciation of the need to attend to the families of both traditional-aged students and adult students with their own children. It also means seeing the family as the social key to the community's future. Hence, whether or not a given program or activity is explicitly Hispanic, Hispanic cultural values can be said to inform the environment that produced it and that gives it meaning.

HSI Profiles

California State University–Stanislaus

Located 70 miles south of Sacramento, CSU–Stanislaus is a public institution whose educational mission includes developing community partnerships aimed at increasing the region's cultural and economic development. The university was formed in the 1960s, and has since grown to more than 8,000 students at two campuses in the diverse cities of Turlock and Stockton. The fact that three-fourths of the faculty at CSU–Stanislaus are actively involved in community work (service-learning, internships, and cooperative education) is evidence that the university has put its mission into action. Each semester, more than 25% of the university's full-time students register for service-learning courses in the disciplines of social work, nursing, public administration, liberal studies, mathematics, child development, business, and communication studies. In addition, a large majority of the student body participates in a variety of co-curricular community engagement projects and campus outreach programs.

A Culture of Engagement

Three factors contribute to the success of civic engagement at CSU–Stanislaus. First, the university's top administrators have created a culture that makes civic engagement both exciting and expected. Contributing to this culture is their ability to delivering a consistent message and to develop key partnerships with community organizations and institutions. Administrators have also focused consciously on recruiting and developing faculty who have community-based values and passion.

Second, the university has created both formal and informal structures to solicit input from students—most of whom are lifelong community members—in designing and delivering community-based programs. Student government representatives serve as voting members on all university strategic planning committees, graduate counsels, assessment committees, and policy committees, as well as the academic faculty senate. In addition, the president of the student senate is invited each year to participate in the university's annual retreat for top administrators. More informally, CSU–Stanislaus has a tradition called "Wednesdays in the Quad," where the students publicly present community issues that they would like the university to help resolve. The inclusion of students' voices has helped the student body take ownership of the university's community work.

Third, CSU–Stanislaus has strategically housed the service-learning center in a brand-new faculty development building, highlighting the university's commitment to faculty as lead players in community initiatives. Peter DeCaro, a communications professor, describes the teaching culture this way: "We do community work because it is important to do, and because the community needs us." The service-learning center and its dynamic director, Julie Fox, provide a vast menu of state-of-the-art support for faculty and community organizations interested in developing community-engaged courses and projects. In addition to acting as a clearinghouse for information, the center provides mini-grants, course release time, training, and service awards to help faculty develop effective engagement practices. The office regularly schedules networking and mentoring opportunities for faculty members and community partners to meet and discuss community needs and service-learning projects.

Innovation Across Disciplines

Interdisciplinary community work is common at CSU–Stanislaus. For example, teacher education and mathematics majors work together to tutor schoolchildren in service-learning programs that have received the highest praise from the school districts. In additional, family development, accounting, and honors students work together with local banks, the Immigration and Naturalization Service, and the Internal Revenue Service in an innovative Volunteer Income Tax Assistance (VITA) program.

In another program, honor students at the university lead focus groups and facilitate discussions with area high school students about what they want out of their school experience. These events culminate in presentations about school issues such as course content, racism, bullying, and school facilities at an annual conference called the Civic Mission of Education. A high-level panel that includes the university president, city mayors, other elected officials, the superintendent of Modesto city schools, and school principals hears and responds to the students' presentations. Significant improvements have resulted at the high schools.

The combination of administrative leadership, support for faculty development, and inclusion of student voice has resulted in a culture that embraces the diverse student body and the needs of local communities. One of the most innovative events at CSU–Stanislaus is the Community Agency Bus Tour. The university rents a bus, and faculty, community members, students, and administrators spend the day traveling to community agencies to hear about the agencies' missions, services, and most pressing needs. Then a local leader, such as the president of the Chamber of Commerce, leads a discussion about opportunities for partnering with the agencies. This multi-stakeholder approach to community problem solving has been extremely effective, leading to a range of successful partnerships.

Heritage University

Founded as Holy Names College in Spokane, Washington, in 1907, Heritage was purchased, restructured and renamed in 1981 as Heritage College (and more recently Heritage University). Heritage is an independent, nonprofit, nondenominational institution with 1,300 students. The university's mission is to develop students who value diverse cultures, whether geographic, ethnic, religious, or economic, and who are trained in grassroots community involvement and community development. Heritage focuses on traditionally underserved college populations; students are primarily non-Caucasian (82%) and female (75%), with an average age of 31 years. Most of the students are from the area, already have families of their own, work while they take classes, and care deeply about the economic and cultural future of their communities.

Developing Leaders

Heritage has adopted a developmental model for its service-learning courses. Students are first required to register for a freshman seminar designed to teach them how to succeed with community-based projects and research. Pre-planned community projects in the seminar are designed to develop five key responsibilities: 1) knowledge—knowing why you should be civically engaged; 2) insight—knowing what you need to do; 3) skills—knowing how to do it; 4) engaging yourself—knowing how to recognize a real and important community need; and 5) partnering—knowing how to build partnerships to get the job done properly. Students are also required to take a junior-level course where they take primary responsibility for identifying a community need and developing a sustainable community project. Complementing this approach is the Heritage Presidential Leadership Council, where students work closely with community mentors on specific projects and on leadership training. In 2004, more than 50% of Heritage courses involved service-learning projects.

This culture of civic engagement and leadership development is fueled by the decision to fill the university's board of directors and departmental advisory boards exclusively with community leaders. Members of these boards report that the majority of their work involves providing ideas and resources for Heritage-driven community projects, such as needs assessments, asset mapping, logistical solutions, grant writing, and program assessment evaluations. In an informal return on this investment, Heritage faculty serve on more than 80 community organization boards. This "cross-seeding" of academic and community board members has proven to be extremely effective in developing long-term partnerships and sustainable community projects.

These partnerships have resulted in many shared resources and facilities. Heritage classrooms, library, and computer labs are designed for use by a wide variety of community members. Through a partnership with the University of Washington, Heritage has built many homes for migrant workers, several computer labs, and a small business assistance center. Heritage supports these facilities by providing neighborhood revitalization programs, computer lab management, and job skills training programs for community members.

A Spectrum of Service Programs

Heritage has developed numerous multi-stakeholder community programs, including K-12 programs, college access initiatives, diversity training, and the Enterprise Institute, a business idea generator and concept incubator. Heritage has also developed a bid management training program for local farmers; research programs aimed at transforming grape waste into paper, soap, grape oils, fuel, and brandy; nursing programs to address the shortage of Spanish-speaking nurses in the valley; and a drug and rehabilitation center. In a uniquely reciprocal program with the Yakama Tribe, Heritage teaches Yakama students the science of wetlands care and preservation, and a Yakama elder teaches Heritage students tribal uses of the wetlands plant *tilia* (bulrush), believed to have spiritual energy.

Heritage's numerous co-curricular civic engagement programs complement its academic community programs. The Students in Free Enterprise (SIFE) club teaches at-risk eighth graders about ethics, economics, and global markets. The Social Work Club paints walls in retirement communities. The Computer Science Club helps maintain various computer labs in the community. The student government prepares food and gift baskets for needy families. The Circle of Success, Early Parents Support, and Success by Six programs reach out to teen mothers and families with young children. These programs are all part of the university's plan to train future community leaders by helping to improve the community today.

Our Lady of the Lake University

Our Lady of the Lake University (OLLU), founded in 1895, is a private Catholic liberal arts institution located in West San Antonio, Texas, a city recently rated as the 11th poorest in the United States. Currently, OLLU has 3,300 students, 60% of whom are Hispanic.

OLLU has made a university-wide commitment to improving the quality of life for the families in West San Antonio. The university's mission is to develop effective multicultural leaders who are committed to community service, social and economic justice, and peaceful approaches to improving society through authentic partnerships. The administrators, faculty, staff, and students at OLLU possess a deep moral commitment to social justice and community service. The power of this collective value system is central to the success of OLLU's civic engagement practices.

High Standards for Service

While OLLU supports a variety of centers that serve community needs, the Center for Service-Learning and Volunteerism, directed by Cynthia Medina, has emerged as the central clearinghouse of resources for OLLU's community work. The center sets high standards for both curricular and co-curricular community work. To support those standards, the center has developed a range of resources, training programs, and tools for faculty, students, and community partners. The center maintains a large community partner database, develops relationships with partners, and manages an active community partner advisory board. Center staff train new community partners and match them with courses, student clubs, and volunteer events. Student training includes training for both curricular and co-curricular service. Students learn effective community strategies, how to manage required activities (e.g., background checks, assessments, time logs), and community partner relationship skills. In 2003, the center was one of 50 agencies around the country selected as a "lead agency" for the Annual National Youth Service Day.

Students' commitment to the community is best evidenced by the quantity and quality of their co-curricular community work. The Volunteer Unity Council, a student government body, leads, develops, and manages these programs. Four student officers manage the university's intensive alternative spring break programs, marketing for community service opportunities and programs, community partner development, and project evaluations and reflections. Recently, OLLU students joined together and as a university voted to become a Meals on Wheels site. In a remarkable display of solidarity, the faculty and staff committed to covering meal deliveries whenever the students were on semester and holiday breaks, providing year-round coverage for the housebound elderly of West San Antonio.

Encouraging Engagement

OLLU's administration encourages and supports this commitment to civic engagement through a variety of mechanisms. First, the faculty code requires faculty to share quality educational and professional resources with the community. Whenever needed, OLLU faculty can apply for curriculum development grants for new community-engaged courses. Second, the administration has developed a variety of innovative teaching appointments to support its commitment to community partnerships. These appointments include "demonstration teachers" who supervise OLLU students serving in the local school districts, "clinical instructors" who supervise students providing clinical services, and "Barrio professors" who support and supervise students who serve in challenged neighborhoods.

Faculty members have considerable freedom in selecting innovative community-based learning methodologies, and as a result, many service-learning courses have been developed in each discipline. In 2004, the faculty senate voted to adopt a two-course service-learning requirement for the general education curriculum that includes a lower-division service-learning project that has bee pre-structured as well as a higher-division course where the students take more of a leadership role in selecting and formulating projects. Furthermore, many of the dozens of majors at OLLU have upper-level service-learning requirements for their students. Each year, OLLU honors and recognizes several students and faculty with outstanding community service awards.

OLLU has partnered with many community agencies and other local universities to improve the quality of life in West San Antonio. The "Making Connections" Annie E. Casey Foundation grant focuses on improving the economics, education, health, welfare, and careers of the families of West San Antonio; OLLU is participating by providing volunteer income tax assistance and personal finance instruction, and by developing and training neighborhood leaders. With another grant from the Kauffman Foundation, students are building a Web store called "Mucho San Antonio," designed to support and encourage development of local small businesses by providing a cost-free Internet channel for the sale of their products. These and other programs are designed to help prepare the future leaders of West San Antonio and beyond.

St. Edward's University

Established in 1885, St. Edward's University is a private, Catholic, liberal arts institution in Austin, Texas, that offers bachelor's and master's degrees in numerous fields. Thirty-six percent of its 4,400 students are minority students, mostly Latino. The university demonstrates its commitment to its Hispanic students in many ways, including implementing a bilingual education program, ensuring ethnic diversity in the literature curriculum, and putting programs like Engaging Latino Communities for Education (ENLACE) into practice.

A Community Mission

The university's Catholic mission plays an essential role in its operation, and is a major driving force behind its incorporation of service-learning and civic engagement. These programs are also supported by the university's focus on student needs, diversity, and social justice. Furthermore, support for community-based efforts by administrators and faculty is endorsed as part of the school's promotion of excellence and is perceived to be embodied in the pedagogies the school values, as well as in its plans for new interdisciplinary majors. Thus, service-learning courses are spread across the curriculum.

Because community involvement and student development are key institutional goals, St. Edward's takes a holistic approach to teaching and learning, and every discipline has at least one course or program involving community work. The School of Education is committed to multiple forms of engagement, with the dean prioritizing help for both parochial and public schools that serve underresourced populations. The School of Business requires its students to take a gateway service-learning course, and it has its own service-learning coordinator. The Psychology Department requires a service-learning internship. Up to 30% of the faculty is involved with community-based work, and the university's publications regularly feature engaged faculty work. All faculty candidates are aware of the school's community commitments.

A New Era of Civic Engagement

St. Edward's ENLACE program, supported by a grant from the Kellogg Foundation, provides a deep, reciprocal partnership with the Latino community, partly because it provides training both for St. Edward's students and for community members. Components of the program include literacy programs for pre-kindergarten students; college outreach to elementary and middle-school students; increased college awareness and community- and school-based academic preparation; increased university applications and admissions of Latino students; community leadership development; and efforts to build on an interfaith church-school alliance program to increase parental involvement and advocacy.

Programs like ENLACE, which has been lauded by the university's community partners, can serve as vehicles to promote and expand campus-community relationships. Emphasizing or building on strengths like these and establishing a coordinating center for all community-related activities have led to a new era of civic engagement at St. Edward's; they also help the university prepare students to live in a diverse democracy.

West Hills Community College District

West Hills Community College District is located on the west side of California's San Joachim Valley, the largest and poorest farming community in the United States. Starting out as a small extension site for Fresno State University in 1932, West Hills is now a state-of-the-art rural public community college system with three campuses in Coalinga, Lemoore, and Firebaugh. In 2002, the MetLife Foundation selected West Hills Community College as the best small college in the nation that serves the needs of a diverse student body.

Mentoring and Motivating Students

"Once you go here, you can go anywhere" and "Students don't care how much you know until they know how much you care" are more than just tag lines at West Hills. These slogans capture the college's dedication to mentoring and motivating all students to achieve recognized leadership in their career and community. Administrators, staff, students, and faculty all view West Hills as integrated with the community rather than as a separate and distinct institution. Academic work, by West Hills' definition, must improve the quality of life in the valley, or it simply has no value. West Hills first identifies top community needs and then translates those needs into relevant student programs. Because most students have a local history and a deep commitment to community improvement, both curricular and co-curricular community work abounds at West Hills. During 2003, students provided 2,200 direct outreach hours and 15,700 indirect outreach hours for the community.

West Hills' trademark is its ability to establish authentic partnerships with its communities' leaders and members. Through ongoing dialogues that have unified the college's "Voices, Values and Vision" planning process, West Hills has positioned itself as an incubator and catalyst for local community initiatives by providing vision, project management, grant writing, and survey and research skills. As a result, sizable investments are being made in otherwise underresourced local agriculture projects. Since 1999, West Hills has been awarded more than $40 million in federal, state, and local grants. It has used this funding to increase economic capacity in its communities, build shared facilities, develop a systematic family-focused infrastructure to support students who are also parents, and develop a variety of accredited programs in health care, construction, and farming techniques and research.

Learning in the Community

West Hills in Coalinga has helped parents return to school by building neighborhood day care centers and developing accredited programs for early childhood education and parental training. During the day, students do academic service-learning as part of their coursework in the day care centers. In the evenings and on weekends, students run co-curricular parent training programs, community events, and youth activity programs. Reflection activities highlight the importance of successful social skills, parental skills, civic responsibility, financial responsibility, and self-confidence.

Partnering with the Lemoore school district, the Lemoore campus has built a charter school on its property to support local children's educational training and college goal setting. West Hills students work at the school in a service-learning program as part of their teacher education curriculum. West Hills also has a special training program for developing teachers certified to work with severely disabled students.

Civic engagement at West Hills is a mode of operation, not a pedagogical "add-on." Students build local parks, sports fields, and irrigation systems for their communities. They tutor local children and serve in local hospitals, convalescent centers, and prisons. They run community events such as blood drives, youth summer camps, fundraisers, and cultural celebrations. This type of community work is simply the West Hills way to study and learn.

Engagement at Tribal Colleges and Universities

Tribal colleges and universities (TCUs), which see themselves as guardians of their tribe's culture, key preservers of its language, and advocates for its children's educational success and spiritual health, obviously model engagement in a very powerful way. And yet, the ways in which they do so cannot always be adequately captured through an analytic tool like the indicators of engagement, which separates engagement into discrete categories. This separation does not exist at many TCUs, which see themselves as simultaneously serving the needs of their students, their communities, and their tribes.

This is not to deny that some of the indicators—"Mission and Purpose," for example—help point up exemplary practices at these schools. It is only to suggest that building an understanding of engagement by examining each indicator for approaches that are "more" or "less" engaged is often inappropriate in the case of TCUs. The challenge, then, is not to miss the forest for the trees. Our hope is that the indicators, when used with care and sensitivity, can help those not immediately familiar with TCUs better understand some of the general strengths and challenges that characterize engagement efforts at these institutions. Such a process, in turn, can lead educators and policymakers to appreciate the importance of those efforts, learn from them, and lend them assistance.

TCUs and Reservation Communities

An earlier chapter discussed some of the important ways in which minority-serving institutions differ. Beyond those general differences, however, TCUs embody another difference of special significance. As noted in the earlier discussion, fundamental to the identity of TCUs is the fact that they belong to and serve sovereign nations other than the United States. Hence, in a way that is not true of HBCUs and HSIs, they are really places apart—legally, geographically, and economically. Native Americans have sometimes been called "America's forgotten minority," and when it comes to the work of TCUs, this being apart has profound consequences.

Consider, for example, the economic circumstances that define Native American communities and their colleges. With the poverty rate in reservation areas at "60.3%, three times the national average" (Ambler, 2003, p. 8), it is estimated that "85% of Tribal college students live at or below poverty levels" (Fann, 2002, p. 2). Such poverty is, of course, accompanied by a host of social problems:

> A survey by the Institute of American Indian Arts (IAIA) in Santa Fe found that 33% of the respondents had a family history of substance abuse; 48% had a family history of violence; and 28% had considered attempting suicide.
>
> American Indian youth have the highest suicide rates of all ethnic groups and are twice as likely to die from alcohol or other substance abuse as other racial groups in the United States (Ambler, 2003, p. 8).

Unfortunately, the educational funding available to meet the needs of this population is also far below average. In the late 1990s mainstream nonresident community colleges operated at $7,000 per full-time enrolled student; the funding per full-time enrolled Indian student was $2,900 (Fann, 2002, p. 2). While the average two-year school with academic ranks paid its faculty $50,832 in 2003–2004, the average Tribal college faculty salary, reported by respondents to a 2002–2003 survey, was $34,951 (Voorhees, 2003). Although "infrastructure and facilities needs average $9 million per school," until recently funding has been "at a rate of $12 million over five years for all schools" (Goetz, 2001, p. 45).

A needs and resources picture like this does not simply affect engagement activities at TCUs—it fundamentally defines them. This is especially true when one considers that economic survival is not even the most pressing issue. For many Native American communities, cultural survival is even more important. Perhaps no other American minority has come under such relentless pressure to abandon its racial/ethnic identity, including pressure exerted through education systems. As Boyer (1989, p. 4) points out,

> Advocating complete submersion in white culture, every effort was made to separate students from their own heritage, even their language. At Carlisle Indian Institute, one of the first Indian boarding schools, use of English was mandatory at all times and violators were punished. Traditional dress was, of course, not acceptable and long hair on men was to be cut. Any evidence of continued attachment to their own culture was viewed by administrators as an act of defiance.

TCUs must struggle against this history in striving to preserve tribal culture. Indeed, during one of our focus groups with TCUs, one Native American educator noted that even today many of her students report never having heard a positive reference to their own culture before they enrolled in the Tribal college.

It is therefore readily understandable why cultural engagement and community validation are among the most important and overt goals of tribal higher education. While other minority-serving institutions must find an appropriate balance between minority cultural affirmation and mainstream opportunities, TCUs have also had to deal with sovereignty and national survival as contemporary community issues.

The Unique Nature of Engagement at TCUs

In examining the ways in which TCUs have attempted to deal with their communities' unique circumstances, needs, and potential, it is clear that these schools play a pivotal role in helping to bolster the spiritual, cultural, and economic health of those communities. Their work in this regard has a threefold emphasis:

1. A curriculum that draws upon native culture, wisdom, and ways of thinking.

2. An approach to teaching and learning that empowers tribal learners.

3. Programs that directly address the community's most pressing social needs.

To some degree, all three of these emphases can also be found at non-tribal MSIs. What makes the efforts of TCUs in this regard especially noteworthy is what is at stake in their success. In many instances, either the colleges will deliver what is needed or some fundamental need simply will not be met. There are, in short, few backups either on or off the reservation.

Take, for example, TCUs' commitment to celebrating and renewing Indian cultures. On some reservations, the college is almost all that stands in the way of the extinction of the tribe's language—hence the widespread TCU requirement that all students take at least several semesters of the tribal language, as well as the outreach to K-12 tribal education. At Fort Belknap College, the Speaking White Clay Project matches Gros Ventre-speaking tribal elders with young adults. The college also provides space and personnel to make possible an after-school program that brings a group of young children to the college five days a week for an hour of linguistic immersion: "students mainly learn their ancestors' tongue through 'total physical response,' or learning through action" (Selden, 2004, p. 22).

Perhaps less dramatic but no less important are the many TCU courses and programs aimed at helping students both understand and embody the tribe's cultural values. Diné College, the oldest Tribal college, is typical in this regard, requiring that all students take a course in Diné/Navajo studies. Like many of its sister institutions, Diné College also requires faculty to become conversant with Navajo culture. As an educator at another Tribal college noted, the purpose of such a requirement is less to make all faculty directly teach the culture than to ensure that all faculty can teach *through* the culture, thus making it a lens that affects all aspects of a student's education.

Such an objective has at least as much to do with student success as it does with cultural preservation and transmission. Just as TCUs are often the only institutions standing in the way of the permanent loss of a tribe's language, so they are often the only institutions standing in the way of a huge loss of potential among a tribe's youths. Many young Native Americans find their futures jeopardized by educational experiences that deny them both identity and self-respect. In 1970, the attrition rate for Native Americans in mainstream higher education was estimated to be 75%. At many individual colleges and universities, it was 90% or higher (Boyer, 1997, p. 25).

Given the almost total absence of any culturally validating experiences for many Indian youth at the K-12 level, such dropout rates are hardly surprising. It is impressive that any "miracle survivors" (HeavyRunner & Marshall, 2003, p. 15) do make it through the system. One Native American educator we interviewed spoke sadly of the "whitening of the classroom" in high schools near her reservation as each year more and more Indian students simply stopped attending. Lacking role models, culturally sensitive courses, and alternative employment opportunities, many Indian youths had nowhere to turn before the founding of Tribal colleges.

Although the data on students at TCUs remains limited, what data we do have is remarkably positive. Despite the fact that such students often "bring with them a long list of special needs" (Boyer, 1997, p. 2) such as reliable daycare and transportation, retention rates are high. In addition, according to the American Indian College Fund (AICF), "one year after graduating, 91% of Tribal college students are working or pursuing a higher degree" (AICF fact sheet, www.collegefund.org). By all accounts, Tribal colleges are successful in awakening in their students a new sense of purpose and self-worth. According to a Carnegie Foundation study, Tribal colleges offer a very different experience for Native students than they receive at other institutions: "Rather than being a disorienting experience for students, college represents a reinforcement of values inherent in the tribal community" (Carnegie Foundation for the Advancement of Teaching, 1989, p. 56).

Finally, engagement in a Tribal college context is characterized by attempts to bring to the community concrete resources in a number of key social areas. When the American Indian Higher Education Consortium (AIHEC) and the Institute for Higher Education Policy (IHEP) published *Building Strong Communities: Tribal Colleges as Engaged Institutions* (Cunningham & Redmond, 2001), the engagement they had in mind was of a decidedly practical nature. In addition to chapters on "Cultural Development and Preservation" and "The Special Role of Faculty" in serving as role models for Indian youth, the publication focused on

"Involvement in Pre-school and K-12 Education," "Participation in Health and Nutrition Activities" and "Agriculture and Natural Resource Management." In other words, programs that address early education, health, and land-based business enterprises are of special concern. Here, as in the area of cultural preservation, the work of the college extends beyond the education of enrolled students to have a direct impact on the community's quality of life.

Applying the Indicators

Given the special circumstances that define both the purposes of and the challenges facing TCUs, our application of the indicators in this chapter necessarily takes a somewhat different form than in material examining other types of institutions. For example, service-learning generally does not exist as a distinct program at TCUs. On the whole, terms such as "service-learning" and "civic engagement" do not resonate in a tribal context, where community engagement is so much a part of everyday operations that it is difficult to draw a line between school and community life.

In order to understand better how TCU engagement compares with engagement as practiced in other sectors of higher education, as well as those areas where TCUs need significant additional resources if they are to fulfill their potential, we have divided Campus Compact's original list of 13 indicators into three groups:

1. *Indicators that resonate at TCUs, and where TCU practice is exemplary by any standard.* Indicators in this group include "Mission and Purpose," "Administrative and Academic Leadership," "Departments, Disciplines, and Interdisciplinary Work," "Teaching and Learning," "Community Voice," "External Resource Allocations," and "Forums for Fostering Public Dialogue."

2. *Indicators where TCU practice is severely constrained by lack of resources.* These indicators include "Faculty Development," "Faculty Roles and Rewards," "Support Structures and Resources," and "Internal Budget and Resource Allocation."

3. *Indicators that must be understood in a somewhat different way when applied in a tribal context.* "Coordination of Community-based Activities" and "Student Voice" fall into this group.

Because TCUs are among the country's newest higher education institutions (all are less than 40 years old), are often quite small in size, and serve their sponsoring tribes in analogous ways, we have decided to address their practices as a group. In this way, we are able to draw upon a richer store of examples while at the same time reflecting the spirit of engagement that informs this sector as a whole.

However, as is the case in other sections of this monograph, specific institutional vignettes have been included to complement this general review.

Indicators That Resonate at TCUs

Mission and Purpose

"Mission and Purpose" is by far the most impressive of all the indicators as practiced by TCUs. At these schools, everything else flows directly from the stated mission and purpose of the institution. Unlike the situation at many mainstream schools, where the more engaged dimensions of the mission statement find little embodiment in programs and policies, TCU mission statements are actively guiding documents. Take, for example, the mission statement of Diné College (www.dinecollege.edu/aboutdc/mission.php):

> Diné College is a public institution of higher education chartered by the Navajo Nation. The mission of Diné College is to apply the Sa'ah Naagháí Bik'eh Hózhóón principles to advance quality student learning:
>
> - Through Notsáhákees (Thinking), Nahatá (Planning), Iiná (Living) and Sihasin (Assurance).
>
> - In study of the Diné language, history and culture.
>
> - In preparation for further studies and employment in a multi-cultural and technological world.
>
> - In fostering social responsibility, community service and scholarly research that contribute to the social, economic and cultural well-being of the Navajo Nation.

Appropriately, the statement begins and ends with the community and its interests. (It is also followed by a list of "activities to implement the mission," including Diné studies and on-site outreach programs.) Navajo culture is acknowledged both as an end in itself and as a primary vehicle of student development. It allows students not only to advance their individual careers but also to contribute to the "well-being of the Navajo Nation as a whole." Almost every aspect of the college's organization, operations, budgeting, planning, and programming reflects this vision. There is no disjunction between the institution as it imagines and presents itself and the way in which it actually functions; moreover, this congruence is a result not of individual inclination but of formal policy.

Except for a number of faith-based institutions and some community and technical colleges, it would be hard to find a comparable degree of coherence at most non-MSI institutions. For the many of these schools, the mission statement serves more as a rhetorical ideal to be invoked on important occasions than as a document that helps to determine what happens on a day-to-day basis. For Diné

College, however, engagement with the community and its values is precisely what the college is about. The relationship between college and community is so transparent that even the word "engagement" is misleading: the college is not so much "engaged" with its community as it is an embodiment of that community.

This close relationship among mission, programming, and community is more representative of TCUs as a group than it is exceptional. Although not all Tribal colleges so explicitly identify the way in which the community's concepts and values ground the educational process or so directly require all students and faculty to understand and apply those concepts and values, they point in a similar direction. (This may in part be because as the first Tribal college, Diné established precedents that its sister institutions have followed.) For example, Oglala Lakota College in South Dakota takes as its motto "Wolakolkiciyapi: Learning Lakota ways of life in community." The college states its mission this way (see www.olc.edu/college_info/mission.htm):

> Oglala Lakota College is chartered by the Oglala Sioux Tribe. Its mission is to provide educational opportunities that enhance Lakota life. These opportunities include community service, certificates, GED, associate, bachelor, and graduate degrees. Oglala Lakota College provides a framework of excellence for student knowledge, skills, and values toward Piya Wiconi—a new beginning for harmony in fulfillment of aspirations and dreams. Oglala Lakota College is committed to continuous improvement and is creating Oglala Lakota University through outstanding teaching, research, community services and assessment.

Fort Peck Community College (FPCC) in Montana echoes this theme of community-college interdependence in its mission statement, which describes both the goals and the methods of the college's programs as being uniquely tribal (see www.fpcc.edu/about.htm):

> FPCC serves the people of the Fort Peck Reservation and northeastern Montana as a medium of Indian awareness, enabling increased self-awareness.... The College serves the people by initiating and supporting community activities and organizations based on the needs and wishes of community members.

In the same vein, Sinte Gleska University's mission statement calls for both inputs and outcomes that reflect its Lakota identity (see www.sinte.edu/catalog/SGUctlg011.html):

> The mission of Sinte Gleska University is to plan, design, implement, and assess post-secondary programs and other educational resources uniquely appropriate to the Lakota people in order to facilitate individual development and tribal autonomy.

Other mission statements include phrases like "education grounded in the Anishaabe language and culture of the Red Lake Band of Ojibwe" (Red Lake Nation College brochure) and "an academic environment in which the culture

Examples from the Field: Mission Statements with Civic Emphasis

FROM WHITE EARTH TRIBAL AND COMMUNITY COLLEGE:

College Mission Statement

White Earth Tribal and Community College [WETCC], a tribally controlled institution of higher education, is dedicated to providing a culturally relevant curriculum and environment through partnerships with students, staff, community, and industry.

Goals and Intentions

WETCC publicly declares its goals and intentions by providing:

- A learning environment emphasizing the application of academic concepts to real life situations.

- An awareness that academic learning is a lifelong process.

- Teaching and learning grounded in the intellectual disciplines and traditions of the White Earth Nation.

- Classroom opportunities to discover the nature of Indian society, its history, variation, and current and future needs.

- An opportunity for students and faculty to serve as contributing members of the community.

- The highest quality of institutional programs that meet the challenges and needs of its people.

- An Associate of Arts (A.A.) and Associate of Science (A.S.) degree, as well as certificate programs of study to qualified students.

SOURCE: White Earth Tribal and Community College Student Handbook, www.wetcc.org/stu/Hndbk.htm.

FROM SALISH KOOTENAI COLLEGE:

Mission Statement

The mission of Salish Kootenai College is to provide quality postsecondary educational opportunities for Native Americans, locally and from throughout the United States. The College will strive to provide opportunities for individual self-improvement to promote and help maintain the cultures of the Confederated Tribes of the Flathead Indian Nation.

Vision

The vision of Salish Kootenai College is to foster curricula and vocational certification, and associates and bachelors degree programs that meet the unique needs of the Native American population. While the college encourages diversity, its primary purpose is to serve the needs of Native American People.

Goals

The Salish Kootenai College Board of Directors has adopted the following goals. These were formulated to provide further specificity to the Mission Statement.

1. To assist with the preservation of the cultures, languages, histories, and natural environment of the Salish, Pend d'Oreille, and Kootenai people.

2. To provide postsecondary education opportunities for Native Americans in the following areas: degree programs, vocational training, college transfer programs, community service, Native American culture and history, and adult education.

3. To provide a learning environment in which students develop skills in effective communication, critical thinking, cultural understanding, and citizenship.

4. To provide comprehensive student services.

5. To provide lifelong, continuing education opportunities for both personal and professional development through a variety of instructional formats offered on and off campus.

6. To provide assistance to tribal entities and departments in staff preparation, planning, research, and services according to identified needs.

7. To assist the Indian community with economic development needs of the Flathead Indian Nation.

8. To provide adequate institutional support and financial resources.

SOURCE: Salish Kootenai College mission statement, available at www.skc.edu/about/missionvision.html.

and social heritage of the Turtle Mountain Band of Chippewa is brought to bear" (Turtle Mountain Community College website, www.turtle-mountain.cc.nd.us). These statements all suggest an inextricable link between TCUs' educational programs and their support for and dependence upon the tribal community—the defining characteristics of civic engagement at these institutions.

Furthermore, the community focus of such mission statements is often reinforced by a variety of other, complementary statements. Commenting on her school's mission, Helen Klassen, former president of White Earth Tribal and Community College, has noted that its mission is to "positively impact the future of all members of the White Earth Reservation and the surrounding communities" (Robbins, 2002, p. 76). Similarly, President Elden Lawrence of Sisseton Wahpeton Community College in South Dakota has emphasized that his institution "does not exist in a vacuum":

> '[I]t exists through community and political efforts that reach beyond the institution's administrative process. The college responds to the priorities set forth by the tribal council that are focused on the needs of the tribal community' (quoted in Robbins, 2002, p. 62).

Administrative and Academic Leadership

Another indicator of engagement through which TCUs have much to teach American higher education is "Administrative and Academic Leadership." For the most part, tribal administrators, unlike many faculty members, are themselves Native American, and in many ways function as the "personnel equivalents" of their mission statements. This is especially true of Tribal college presidents. However, to understand the role of administrative leaders, one must first understand the way in which "leadership" is understood in many Native American communities.

Perhaps the closest non-Indian equivalent would be John Greenleaf's concept of "servant leadership" (Greenleaf, 1998, p. 16): "the great leader is seen as servant first, and that simple fact is the key to his greatness." Like Greenleaf's servant leaders, TCU leaders have little interest in promoting their own stature; their task is to make sure their institutions flourish, or at least survive. Leadership is not marked by perks and power but by a willingness to do whatever needs to be done. Hence, as one TCU president told us, at the end of the day she may not be able to leave until she has first mopped the hall floor.

Unlike Greenleaf's servant leaders, however, TCU administrators often do not assume their positions because they have heard a call or had some important insight about what needs to be done. Instead, they are chosen by the community itself. One administrator explained that within the Tribal college community, leadership is not something you seek; it is something to which you are appointed

ONE WITH THE COMMUNITY

> **Example from the Field: Administrative Leadership**
>
> **AIHEC HONORS TRIBAL COLLEGE FOUNDERS**
>
> The American Indian Higher Education Consortium (AIHEC) took time out from a busy meeting with the W.K. Kellogg Foundation in Albuquerque last spring to honor some of the Tribal colleges' founders. The Navajo Nation in 1968 chartered the first tribal college. "When I was growing up, the BIA (Bureau of Indian Affairs) had total control. When you went to BIA schools, they wouldn't let you in to see what your children were being taught," Guy Gorman told the crowd of administrators and faculty from tribal colleges and mainstream schools assembled for the Kellogg meeting. "I was on the education committee of the Navajo Nation, and we started talking about it. We asked the parents, 'How do you want your schools?' That was the day something happened," he said.
>
> Navajo Community College (NCC, now Diné College) could have killed the fledgling consortium of Tribal colleges, according to Wayne Stein, Ed.D., author of *Tribally Controlled Colleges: Making Good Medicine*, who served as master of ceremonies in Albuquerque. Instead, the Navajo college supported the birth of other Tribal colleges and their organization in many ways. NCC sponsored the first grant to start AIHEC. Tom Atcitty, president of NCC, served as the first president of AIHEC. Jim Hena, a Tesuque Pueblo man employed by NCC, taught AIHEC's first executive director, David Gipp, the ways of the hill. Today Gipp is president of AIHEC as well as United Tribes Technical College, and he is widely acknowledged as one of the colleges' best advocates in Congress.
>
> One of the most moving moments of the emotional reunion came when Lionel Bordeaux credited Dr. Bob Roessel for inspiring him over 40 years ago. Bordeaux attended a South Dakota Indian youth council meeting, and Roessel gave a speech entitled, "If it is to be, it's up to me." Bordeaux took those words to heart; he has been president of Sinte Gleska University for 28 years. Roessel and his Navajo wife, Ruth, were instrumental in changing the face of education on the Navajo Reservation at Navajo Community College and Rough Rock Community School. Bordeaux also credited Dave Risling, then president of D-Q University in California. "We couldn't even get an appointment with the BIA. Dave taught us to fight," he said.
>
> Louis LaRose, a founder of Nebraska Indian Community College, said, "We came in from Nebraska because we saw the vision and wanted to be a part of it.... Later, when I opened the Sioux Falls newspaper and saw that Congress had passed the Tribally Controlled Community Colleges Act, I cried. The vision was reality." That 1978 law provided the first federal funding for Tribal colleges.
>
> AIHEC and the American Indian College Fund presented gifts to the NCC founders; Bordeaux; Gerald One Feather, a founder of Oglala Lakota College; Risling; Gipp; and LaRose. They honored several founders who had died and supporters who were not present, including Helen Scheirbeck and Gerald Brown. They also presented gifts to several people from the Kellogg Foundation.
>
> SOURCE: *Tribal College Journal of American Indian Higher Education*, 12(1) 2000.
>
> Reprinted with permission from *Tribal College Journal of American Indian Higher Education*, a quarterly magazine published at P.O. Box 720, Mancos, CO 81328. For information call (888) 899-6693, e-mail info@tribalcollegejournal.org, or see the website at www.tribalcollegejournal.org.

because the community has recognized that you are best able to meet a certain need at a certain time. As Elden Lawrence, president of Sisseton Wahpeton Community College, has observed:

> '[Traditional] leaders were not campaigners or political appointees. The people observed them for years and looked at how they made decisions, how they treated people, and how they showed concern for the people and their village. They were not wealthy or prestigious. They were there to help. They led through influence and respect and trust of the people. They caused people to want to do things' (quoted in Archambault & Allen, 2002, p. 16).

Such a concept of leadership is inherently non-hierarchical, and this fact has had important consequences for TCU leaders, especially presidents. To begin with, the respect leaders are accorded is based on what they actually do, not on the position they occupy. If the president truly is subordinate to the college's—and the community's—needs, mopping a floor or providing transportation for a student whose car has broken down is not an extraordinary act; it is simply what the job demands at that moment.

Embracing such a non-hierarchical understanding of leadership may well lead to conflicts with non-Indian cultural norms. If true authority is reflected in one's ability to contribute, the college must be free to draw upon the wisdom of traditional tribal elders and the expertise of those who lack the kind of accreditation mainstream higher education takes for granted. Boyer (1995, p. 14) notes that one college president even "took criticism from her college's accrediting agency for not having a clearly hierarchical administration and instituting a flat salary scale for all employees."

In short, TCU leaders are as closely tied to their community and its culture as are their colleges' mission statements. In a wide variety of ways, their agenda is the community's agenda—whether that involves finding ways to help more students succeed; using the college's resources to archive and promote the tribe's history, culture, and language; defending the college's distinctive identity and indigenous credentialing standards; bringing in programs and funding that promote the community's physical and economic well-being; or lobbying Washington to live up to its treaty obligations. In contrast to many of their mainstream colleagues, they resist putting their own interests, their college's interests, and the community's interests into separate categories.

Renee Gurneau, president of Red Lake Nation College, is a good example. In the fall of 2003, the tribal council of the Red Lake reservation in Northern Minnesota asked Gurneau to step in as the first tribal president of the college. Gurneau, a former Kellogg Fellow who studied liberation theology in Chiapas and served as director of the first tribal AmeriCorps program, immediately began providing strong, visionary leadership for both the college and the community. Within months, she and her team had collaborated with the tribal council, the housing agency, and local community agencies to renovate the college building, which now serves as a hub of community activity. They also worked to establish programs that operate within the walls of the college at all hours of the day—programs like the elder nutrition program, which offers free lunch for elders. Finally, they launched a variety of free computer, language, and culture classes open to everyone in the community, regardless of their formal ties to the college.

As President Gurneau explained, her strategy has been first to establish the college's commitment to the community as a whole, with academic programming following naturally from that relationship. To implement this strategy, she has made leading the college a 24-hour-a-day, 7-day-a-week commitment.

Joe McDonald, president of Salish Kootenai College, is another case in point. A powerful advocate for community service as essential to the life of the campus community, he devotes a great deal of personal time to the community and to tribal affairs. He has established an annual campus-wide painting project that brings together students, faculty, staff, and administrators to paint schools, barns, and other community facilities, as well as a community trash pickup that also involves the entire campus. As a committed and regular participant in community events, he dances at powwows, attends all tribal weddings and funerals, and plays with the local traditional drumming group. The fact that he is in his 70s doesn't seem to slow him in the least.

Departments, Disciplines, and Interdisciplinary Work

A third indicator of engagement in which many TCUs excel is "Departments, Disciplines, and Interdisciplinary Work." In many ways this excellence can be seen as completing a triad of major engaged factors. If "Mission and Purpose" enshrines engagement in the very purpose of the college, and "Administrative and Academic Leadership" enlists the college's leaders as stewards of that purpose, "Departments, Disciplines, and Interdisciplinary Work" represents the specific set of academic activities that move the community's values and interests into the working heart of the institution: the curriculum itself.

What makes the manifestation of this indicator at TCUs exceptional is its relative scarcity elsewhere. Although few college mission statements are as community-grounded as those of TCUs, mission statements by their nature tend to include public ideals and references to the common good. Mainstream administrative leaders who personally support engagement as an institutional priority are far less numerous but by no means impossible to find. What is truly rare in American higher education is the recognition that without engagement *in and through the curriculum*, engagement must remain peripheral to what an institution actually stands for. What Conti and Fellenz (1991, p. 18) have remarked of Tribal colleges is in fact true for every kind of non-proprietary college and university:

> The mission of the Tribal college must be reflected in the curriculum. The content that is included in the curriculum, the way the curriculum is formulated, and the roles of the students and teachers in this educational transition are the primary ways for the Tribal colleges to fulfill their mission and communicate it to the community.

Claiming engagement through mission and administrative leadership without involvement of the curriculum is like a having map and a driver without a car.

TCUs employ several different strategies to ensure that their mission statements and their curricula are cut from the same cloth. We have already noted that most schools put courses on tribal culture and language at the heart of their general education requirements. However, equally important is their attempt to link courses across the entire curriculum to the community's cultural traditions and to Native American ways of thinking. At D-Q University in California, "introductory science courses begin not with Western theorists, but with an examination of the sophisticated Aztec calendar" (Boyer, 1989, p. 6).

In the same vein, the science department at Sisseton Wahpeton College has used grant funding to "examine ways to infuse Dakota concepts into classes" (Wynia, 2003, p. 33). One new class involves Dakota elders in field trips that teach students to identify local plants. At Leech Lake Tribal College, students can take an integrated biology course called Ethnobiology, which focuses on both Western scientific analysis and the Anishinaabe perspective in understanding the natural world. According to the college's course catalog:

> Laboratory and empirical analysis will be integrated with cultural values, traditions, and techniques to deliver a holistic and intimate knowledge of the natural world. This course will explore the cycles of the natural world and how all living things are related and maintain balance in their respective communities. (See www.lltc.org/academics/course_list/course_descriptions.shtml.)

In fact, most of the biology courses at Leech Lake explore Western and indigenous views in tandem. Another part of the biology course description reads, "This course examines two worldviews of understanding the natural world: Western scientific analysis and the Anishinaabe perspective." The same is true of science courses at many other TCUs.

In some cases, even the business curriculum is being recast to accommodate community values and traditions. The First Nations Development Institute has created an entire Building Native Communities curriculum; drawing upon Native traditions and values, it "uses stories, visual aids, activities, and references to demystify personal finances" (Phillips, 2004, p. 28). At Oglala Lakota College, a Manager as Warrior curriculum attempts to "reconcile the discipline of business management with traditional values…[by identifying] seven key Lakota values and [matching] them with the values of the modern business world" (Boyer, 1995, p.16). Like D-Q University's use of the Aztec calendar or Leech Lake College's approach to biology, making such a connection helps show students that, as Boyer (1995, p.16) notes, "the qualities inherent in [their] culture already allow for success."

At the same time they incorporate tribal cultural beliefs and values into the curriculum, TCUs strive to help Native American students access and utilize the power of non-Native ways of knowing. Hence, as fundamental as Navajo cultural beliefs are for Diné College, one of the college's instructors described her work as preparing Navajo students to compete in business with non-Navajos. Similarly, a dean from Southwestern Indian Polytechnic Institute noted that her school's students needed to learn traditional political science because they were citizens of both the United States and their tribes, and understanding the former was essential to serving the latter.

As one administrator noted, TCUs strive to be "culturally responsive," indicating that their curricula respect the integrity of indigenous culture, serve the community, enhance students' sense of place, and enable students to thrive within any culture. As the administrator put it, "Being able to thrive amidst any culture means that we know who we are as Native/indigenous people, but also that we respect all people and cultures." These goals epitomize the recognition by academic and administrative leaders that all learning at a Tribal college is "service-learning" on behalf of the tribal community.

Despite this recognition, TCUs generally do not refer to such practices as instances of service-learning. Although this term is becoming more common at many TCUs, "experiential" or "hands-on" learning is still the expression of choice. Given that community relevance and a tribal cultural context are as established a part of TCU educational practice as lectures are of practice at most other higher education institutions, this difference in nomenclature is not surprising. Tribal schools have little need to import non-Native terminology for what they do naturally—except when seeking outside funding.

Teaching and Learning
Infusion of community concepts and values into courses across the curriculum is closely related to the indicator "Teaching and Learning." In developing and exploring its indicators of engagement, Campus Compact has naturally stressed the importance of civic and community engagement through formal academic programs for the simple reason that those programs constitute the core of the credentialing process: students receive their degree through what they achieve in and

Matching TCU Curricula with Local Needs

TRIBAL COLLEGE OR UNIVERSITY	SELECTED MAJOR INDUSTRIES/EMPLOYERS	EXAMPLES OF PROGRAMS OFFERED (2004–2005)
Bay Mills Community College (MI)	Local government; tobacco sales	Human Services; Corrections; Great Lakes Native American Studies
Blackfeet Community College (MT)	Construction; agriculture/livestock; tourism	Construction Technology; Hospitality Operations Management; Natural Resources Management
Candeska Cikana Community College (ND)	Land leases; manufacturing	Office Techology; Tribal Administration
Chief Dull Knife College (MT)	Small business	Business; Entrepreneurship
College of the Menominee Nation (WI)	Lumber; sawmill; hospitality and tourism	Natural Resources; Sustainable Development; Business Administration
Diné College (AZ)	Agriculture/livestock; forestry; mining	Environmental Sciences; Pre-Engineering
Fond du Lac Tribal and Community College (MN)	Local government	Tribal Business Management; Law Enforcement
Fort Belknap College (MT)	Agriculture; land leases	Natural Resources
Fort Berthold Community College (ND)	Gaming; construction	Accounting/Business Administration; Construction Technology
Fort Peck Community College (MT)	Livestock; defense manufacturing	Environment Sciences; Electronics Technology
Keweena Bay Ojibwa Community College (MI)	Tourism; forestry; fisheries	Business; Environmental Science
Lac Courte Oreilles Ojibwa Community College (WI)	Local government; logging; cranberry farming	Community Health Education; Agriculture and Natural Resource Management
Leech Lake Tribal College (MN)	Fishing; retail trade	Woodlands Wisdom Nutrition; Business Management

CONTINUED ON NEXT PAGE

Matching TCU Curricula with Local Needs (continued from previous page)

TRIBAL COLLEGE OR UNIVERSITY	SELECTED MAJOR INDUSTRIES/EMPLOYERS	EXAMPLES OF PROGRAMS OFFERED (2004–2005)
Little Big Horn College (MT)	Mineral resource leases; federal government	Pre-Engineering; Natural Resources; Community Health
Little Priest Tribal College (NE)	Agriculture	Environment
Nebraska Indian Community College (NE)	Goverment; agriculture	Human Services/Social Work; Horiculture
Northwest Indian College (WA)	Fishing; seafood processing	Tribal Environmental & Natural Resource Management
Oglala Lakota College (SD)	Agriculture; small businesses	Natural Resources Management; Business Administration
Saginaw Chippewa Tribal College (MI)	Gaming; tourism	Business
Salish Kootenai College (MT)	Lumber; construction	Environmental Science; Highway Contruction
Si Tanka College (SD)	Agriculture and livestock	Agriculture Management
Sinte Gleska University (SD)	Livestock; jewelry	Tribal Lands Management & Environmental Science; Lakota Arts
Sisseton Wahpeton Community College (SD)	Agriculture (leases); livestock; manufacturing	Interdisciplinary Environmental; Business Administration
Sitting Bull College (ND)	Land leases; gaming	Farm/Ranch Management; Business Administration/Tribal Management
Stone Child College (MT)	Lumber	Natural Resources
Tohono O'odham Community College (AZ)	Land leases; mining; foreign trade	Agriculture and Natural Resource Management; Business
Turtle Mountain Community College (ND)	Manufacturing; data entry	Engineering Studies
White Earth Tribal and Community College (MN)	Local government; retail trade; manufacturing	Management Information Systems; Tribal Business Administration

NOTE: The Tribal colleges listed are all reservation based members of the American Indian Higher Education Consortium (AIHEC). Excluded are the five non–reservation-based Tribal colleges within AIHEC. SOURCE: American Indian Higher Education Consortium (2005). "Matching Reservation-Based Tribal College Curricula with Local Needs." From the AIHEC website, www.aihec.org. Used by permission.

through faculty-sponsored courses. Tribal educators echo this emphasis, recognizing the curriculum as perhaps the single most important tool they have to realize their mission.

While many in mainstream higher education are discovering the power of "alternative pedagogies" for the first time, Tribal college educators can draw upon a repertoire of active learning techniques resonant of core Native American educational practice. Learning by doing, learning through mentoring and apprenticeship, field experiences, place-based knowledge and research, and interactive group processing all enjoy special favor precisely because they are known to work.

At many schools, "talking circles"—a form of what is now called "collaborative learning"—have long overshadowed lecture as the favored classroom strategy. At Salish Kootenai College, an experimental program allows students to learn "not in the classroom or through formal instruction but by working directly with an elder in the community" (Boyer, 1997, p. 66). When a group of students at White Earth Tribal and Community College were asked about "hands-on" learning outside the classroom, they were able to identify faculty from across the curriculum who regularly gave such assignments. (Confirming the difference in prevalent terminology, only two of these students knew the term "service-learning" in this context.)

Lending even greater significance to this commitment to engaged teaching practices is that these practices often play a decisive part in a strategy of fostering students' "cultural resilience." As HeavyRunner and Marshall (2003, p. 15) explain:

> For the 200 years before the Navajo Nation opened the first Tribal college in 1968, higher education was an Anglo institution with compulsory Western methods of learning that attempted to eradicate tribal culture. As a result, American Indian students left mainstream institutions at high rates without graduating. When tribes built their colleges and universities, they wanted institutions that could strengthen reservation economies and tribal culture without forcing assimilation. With programs built from an indigenous framework, the colleges naturally promote student resilience.

Example from the Field: Service and Learning at Little Big Horn College

SERVICE
Little Big Horn's service ranges far and wide. Some of their activities include tutoring Head Start and other K-12 students, self-defense courses, community gardening, AIDS awareness, leadership training, and environmental water testing. Their service-learning program also targets such social problems as literacy, health and safety, youth development, substance abuse, environmental issues, and other community concerns of the Crow Indian community.

LEARNING
Little Big Horn mainly incorporates service into the curriculum through the school's Writing Across the Curriculum requirement. Students do written assignments relating to their service experiences that incorporate not only learning but appropriate reflection as well.

SOURCE: Dawson, Calvin T. and Lauren G. Grayson, *Native American Service-Learning: Learning to Serve, Serving to Learn.* Washington, DC: Learn and Serve America (Corporation for National Service), 2001, pp. 34–35.

For HeavyRunner and Marshall, "Resilience is the natural, human capacity to navigate life well" (p. 15). But for this concept to work most effectively in a Native American context, traditional "resilience" research must be extended to identify and include "cultural factors that nurture, encourage, and support Indian students, families, and communities" (p. 16).

In addition to building cultural resilience, the pedagogical practices of TCUs, like the integration of cultural references into the curriculum, are intended to help Indian students achieve a higher rate of academic success than they have historically achieved at mainstream institutions. And in fact the use of culturally appropriate pedagogical strategies is an important factor contributing to students' success at these schools. Native American educators we interviewed at TCUs spoke of students saying that in many subject areas they now "got it" for the first time. Statistics bear out this success: 56% of Tribal college graduates go on to complete a 4-year degree at another college or university (AICF fact sheet, www.collegefund.org), compared with only 22% of community college graduates in general (The National Committee of Inquiry into Higher Education, 1997).

What make such successes especially important are the subjects most tribal students choose to major in. At Salish Kootenai College in Montana, for example, health care, K-12 education, and business are the most popular fields of concentration (Boyer, 1997). When one also takes into account the fact that the vast majority of TCU graduates choose to remain with their home communities, one can see how their personal academic success quickly translates into much-need public resources.

Regardless of the specific terms used to characterize the teaching and learning process—e.g., hands-on learning, experiential learning, service-learning—the fact is that most programs offered in a Tribal college context both value direct experience and directly benefit the larger community. As Jerry Reynolds, a staff member at the First Nations Development Institute, points out, even the concept of entrepreneurship must be understood in a special way:

> '…the whole notion of entrepreneurialism is different. You are not an individual entrepreneur on the Donald Trump model. You are a person who knows how to do a few things that benefit *the whole community*, and yourself in the process' (quoted in Boyer, 1997, p. 48).

"Community" Indicators

For all its importance, the curriculum is only one of many tools, especially in the case of institutions where the student body and the surrounding community are largely indistinguishable. In such circumstances, the blurry line between students and community members may result not only in a broader understanding of the college's constituency but also in a wide range of critically needed programs outside the core, credit-bearing curriculum. Certificate programs, vocational skills courses, GED preparation, and off-campus educational outreach all play a significant role in allowing such colleges to fulfill their mission to "reach" as well as to "teach" (Zlotkowski et al., 2004).

This is particularly true at Tribal colleges, where—even in comparison with many other "community" colleges—there really is "no clear distinction between the college community and the community-at-large" (Webster, 2003, p. 4). This merging of communities is intensified by the relative isolation of many reservations, their general lack of resources, and their consequent dependence on the college for services that elsewhere might be handled by other kinds of institutions. The 1994 designation of Tribal colleges as land-grant institutions officially recognized TCUs' sponsorship of a broad community agenda.

What all this means with regard to the indicators of engagement is that, in the case of TCUs, the non-academic indicators play an especially prominent role. "Community Voice," "External Resource Allocations," and "Forums for Fostering Public Dialogue" together form a "community indicator index" in which tribal practice is often qualitatively different from what one finds at the vast majority of mainstream institutions. Given that TCUs are actually chartered by their tribes to meet their needs, this is not surprising. In a very real sense, a tribe's governing council and its college are simply different manifestations of the same community, the same culture, the same "extended family."

Sometimes the relationship between a Tribal college and tribal interests as represented on the college's board are so close as to be in some ways counterproductive. As Phyllis Howard, director of the Association of North Dakota Tribal Colleges and herself a former Tribal college president, has pointed out: "Sometimes board members do not understand what Tribal colleges have to go through to operate. They don't know the financial situation, the external mandates, and the vision. They try to make them a tribal program, and this cannot work" (quoted in Archambault & Allen, 2002, p. 16). Thus, while most American higher education institutions must make a special effort to connect to the off-campus community, TCUs must sometimes make a special effort to assert their distinctive identity and function.

It would be difficult to identify all the ways in which TCUs serve their communities beyond the formal curriculum. They are as varied as the needs and interests of the tribal communities they serve. Many TCUs serve as broad community service agencies, providing tutoring, counseling, health care, and hunger relief, among other services. Resource sharing and hosting of community meetings, celebrations, and other events are also common.

One innovative activity hosted by Red Lake Nation College is a public gallery of community members who have served in the armed forces. The gallery provides a forum for the tribe to coalesce around these "warriors" in pride and solidarity. In this way, "External Resource Allocations" shades into both "Community Voice" and "Forums for Fostering Public Dialogue." The college's "Recovering from Columbus" celebration and Chiefs' Day (instead of Presidents' Day) in February provide similar opportunities to meet multiple needs. Storytelling, spiritual healing, and recognition of esteemed ancestors all come together to create a distinctively Native American cultural resource.

Facility sharing is also common. Some TCUs have created college libraries that also serve as the community's library; others use their libraries to maintain and extend tribal archives. Red Lake Nation College provides space for local programs for elders, including a nutrition program and computer classes. In addition, Red Lake's president has created administrative positions intended specifically to support Anishaabe culture and language instruction, filling them with tribal elders with deep roots in the local community. These leaders bought and renovated a college building, which is used to host a nutrition program, computer classes for community members, and other community programs and events.

At White Earth Tribal and Community College, a partnership with the Circle of Life School and the University of Minnesota Extension Office offers summer pro-

---

Examples from the Field: Community Services Provided by TCUs

FORT PECK COMMUNITY COLLEGE (FPCC)

'Quality lifelong learning is the mission of [FPCC's] community services.... The department of community services is committed to improving employee proficiency within local businesses, schools, industries, and local government agencies, and in the teaching of Native American studies, particularly the Assiniboine and Dakota/Nakota arts, language, and traditional teachings.

Community service activities are central to FPCC and include a wide array of offerings that serve the community in ways conventional course offerings do not:

- The Center for Family and Community Development
- The Community Business Assistance Center
- Family literacy and parenting
- Agriculture and ranching
- Distance learning
- The Center for Community Health and Wellness

TURTLE MOUNTAIN COMMUNITY COLLEGE (TMCC)

Community and civic service is a major component of the college's mission. TMCC provides service through its Center for New Growth and Economic Development. Job creation and local tribal business development take place in the center. Several programs target extreme poverty issues such as welfare to work, GED, job skill preparation, and family wellness.

SOURCE: Excerpted from Robbins, Rebecca L. *Tribal College and University Profiles.* Pablo, MT: Salish Kootenai College, 2002, pp. 33–34, 72.

grams for community members. Students receive hands-on experience in cultural and environmental education. The partnership is leading the way for the development of a new environmental center, called Nibi (water). The science department at White Earth also offers classes to the community in permaculture, holistic management, and medicinal plants, all of which will be offered at the center.

Many TCUs serve as a primary source of programs that promote the community's health. Turtle Mountain Community College in North Dakota has developed the Anishinaubag Wellness Center "to enable the Ojibwa people to return to their original healthy way of life" (Office of Community Partnerships, 2003, p. 5). Another Ojibwa college, Leech Lake in Minnesota, has developed a community gardening project that "encourages tribal members to improve their health" by growing indigenous crops (Boyer, 1997, p. 70). According to the American Indian Higher Education Consortium, approximately 40% of TCUs currently offer nutrition and health services (Cunningham & Redmond, 2001, p. 19). Many college health programs place a special emphasis on combating alcoholism and diabetes, two diseases that disproportionately affect Native populations.

As TCUs take on the challenge of improving their community's well-being, their work necessarily includes a wide variety of programs related to economic development. These include, first and foremost, programs related to land use: "technical assistance…, training opportunities, and other forms of knowledge dissemination" (Cunningham & Redmond, 2001, p. 34). Thanks to their status as land-grant institutions, many TCUs are now eligible for competitive grants awarded through Land Grant Extension Programs. Without the colleges' ability to apply for such grants, tribal communities would be cut off from an important source of funding.

In addition to natural resources, TCUs have begun to support small business centers and revolving loan funds that assist tribal start-up companies that banks consider too risky. Northwest Indian College, Salish Kootenai College, Fort Belknap College, Sinte Gleska University, Little Big Horn College, and Turtle Mountain Community College are just some of the schools that have focused special attention on supporting tribal entrepreneurship. By soliciting grants from a number of foundations—most notably the Theodore R. & Vivian M. Johnson Scholarship Foundation—TCUs have been able to support student entrepreneurs and small-business start-ups that enhance the local economy. Salish Kootenai College received an initial grant from the Johnson Foundation to establish the SKC Tribal Business Assistance Center in 1995, which subsequently served as a model and source of financial support for business centers at other TCUs.

When one adds to all these forms of community outreach a host of special programs directed at pre-school and K-12 education, which virtually every Tribal college offers, one can begin to appreciate just how powerful the "community indicator index" is at TCUs. Indeed, it would be hard to identify any other category of schools that delivers so much in the way of "External Resource Allocations." With the prevalence of structures and programs that encourage "Community Voice" and "Forums for Fostering Public Dialogue," one can only marvel at how TCUs manage to accomplish so much, especially given their limited resources.

Indicators Affected by Financial Constraints

Faculty Indicators

Although data on TCUs is scarce, several surveys over the past decade—including surveys of TCU students (1995), graduates (2000), and faculty (2003)—have found faculty quality to be a major strength. According to Boyer (1997, p. 3),

> One of the clearest, most important, findings of the Carnegie Foundation survey was the high regard held by students for their teachers and the quality of instruction. For example, over 94% believed their professors were accessible outside the classroom, and 96% said their professors appeared to enjoy teaching. In these and related questions, truly dissatisfied students represented no more than 1% of the responses.

Survey results were so positive that Boyer concludes that faculty members appear "not merely dedicated; they emerge as heroic figures" (p. 3). The more recent survey of tribal graduates points in the same direction, with 87% "satisfied" or "very satisfied" with the level of overall instruction (Cunningham & Redd, 2000, p. 14).

The 2003 TCU faculty survey uncovered several complementary findings. For both Indian and non-Indian faculty members, by far the single most important factor motivating them to teach at a Tribal college is a desire to "make a difference in the lives of others" (78.6% and 64.1%). Both groups also welcome the "challenge" of teaching at such an institution (42.9% and 45.6%), while Indian faculty also express a very strong interest in teaching Indian students (73.2%) (Voorhees, 2003, p. 5). Clearly the intrinsic, teaching-oriented motivation of TCU faculty makes itself felt in the extremely high levels of student and graduate satisfaction the other two surveys reflect.

It is therefore ironic that two of the least well developed indicators in a TCU context are "Faculty Development" and "Faculty Roles and Rewards." To be sure, faculty development is a high institutional priority if it is taken to include the efforts TCUs make to help all faculty appreciate and teach through the tribal culture. Furthermore, from a civic and community engagement perspective, faculty development of this kind is of primary importance since it creates the cultural awareness that makes much of that engagement possible in the first place. Nonetheless, when faculty development is considered in a broader sense, taking it to include all those on- and off-campus opportunities faculty typically expect as part of their professional development (e.g., release time, pedagogical and disciplinary workshops, travel money to attend national and regional conferences, funds for technological and print resources), TCUs are caught in a financial bind.

An additional consequence of this bind is that it often prevents faculty members at TCUs from pursuing research or advanced degrees. Most TCU faculty members teach overloads, "often in excess of 20 credits per term" (Clayton & Born, 1998, p. 4), either because the college expects it or because they need to do so for financial reasons. These overloads leave little time for other professionally nurturing academic activities. When economic constraints and the geographical remoteness of many TCUs are added to the picture, one can begin to appreciate just how difficult it is for faculty to become involved in research collectives or to pursue advanced degrees at other institutions.

Fortunately, in recent years, some notable efforts have been made to counter these limitations by funding faculty enrollment in distance-learning ventures and low-residency programs, among other types of programs. Haskell Indian Nations University in Kansas recently received a Title III grant that allows a limited number of faculty to take sabbaticals to finish their doctorates and to develop a "research and service agenda" for the university (Tippeconnic & McKinney, 2003, p. 250). Such opportunities are scarce, however, and they remain dependent on the vagaries of external funding.

Although the lack of professional development opportunities does not seem to result in overt job dissatisfaction, Cunningham and Redmond (2001, p. 28) note that "retention of high-quality faculty is made difficult with no viable options for professional development." Even among Native faculty, with their strong dedication specifically to Native American students, the sense of mobility is high; these faculty members are twice as likely as other 2-year college faculty to "indicate that it is somewhat or very likely they will accept full-time work outside of a postsecondary institution within three years and are also more likely to indicate they will find full-time work in other postsecondary institutions" (Voorhees, 2003, p. 7).

Lack of faculty development opportunities is not necessarily the motive when faculty members decide to leave a Tribal college. Nonetheless, this factor was sufficiently worrisome to lead the Carnegie Foundation to highlight "the need for a comprehensive program of faculty development at tribal colleges" (Boyer 1997, p. 91) as one of its primary recommendations.

Even more troublesome than the lack of resources to provide adequate faculty development opportunities is the lack of funds to offer competitive faculty salaries. Normally, if "Faculty Roles and Rewards" is a weak indicator of civic engagement, it means that the institution in question does not truly value engaged faculty work—as demonstrated by a failure to link such work to tangible forms of recognition such as promotion and tenure. In the case of TCUs, however, this is clearly not at issue. Rather than failing to recognize the value of engaged work, TCUs often require it; nonetheless, they often cannot reward it explicitly. In other words, the weakness of this indicator in this instance has nothing to do with ideology and everything to do with finances.

As noted earlier, the average TCU faculty salary reported for 2002-2003 was $34,951; thus, "current annual salaries at mainstream, public 2-year colleges are likely to exceed [TCU faculty] salaries by almost $10,000" (Voorhees, 2003, pp. 2-3). Hence, although other survey data "strongly suggest American Indian faculty are motivated less by dollars than by altruism" (Voorhees, 2003, p. 6), the fact that the majority of TCU faculty are *not* Native American lends support to the conclusion that low salaries have a major impact:

> Contributing to high faculty turnover rates at many of the Tribal colleges are inadequate resources and low salaries.... Clearly, faculty at many of the colleges do not remain long on the job before moving on to other employment, presumably out of personal financial necessity.... An outcome of low salaries is that faculty tenure is not a viable option for most Tribal colleges due to the high cost of implementing a tenure system (Cunningham & Redmond, 2001, p. 27).

Needless to say, absence of tenure and other extrinsic rewards cannot simply be translated into lack of faculty loyalty. At Salish Kootenai College, for example, there is no tenure system, and annual "step raises" are not always possible. Nonetheless, our research found strong loyalty to the college among faculty members, many of whom noted the intrinsic rewards of teaching at TCUs.

"Enabling" Indicators

Indicators related to faculty support represent the first broad area in which a lack of resources weakens the ability of TCUs to advance their engagement agenda as effectively as they would like. A second broad area has to do with infrastructure and other "enabling mechanisms" (Walshok, 1995). Lack of funding means that indicators in this category—"Support Structures and Resources" and "Internal Budget and Resource Allocation"—are underdeveloped at TCUs. Specific indices used to measure these enabling mechanisms in the Indicators of Engagement Project include a full range of forms and procedures; a centralized office committed to community-based teaching and learning; adequate funding to support, enhance, and deepen community involvement; and sufficient long-term staffing. These are all areas in which finances play a major role.

If there is any area in which TCUs are weak by their own reckoning, it is in the area of instructional and program-related "nonessentials." TCUs must relay on core functions and personnel to accomplish what most other kinds of institutions do only with the help of specially dedicated staff, offices, and line items. In our conversations with tribal educators, lack of adequate support staff came up constantly as one of the most challenging and exhausting aspects of their work. Some exceptions exist; at Red Lake Nation College, for example, many functions have been covered by temporary staff assigned to the college as part of New Beginnings, a welfare-to-work program. Most other TCUs do not have access to this resource, however.

Administrators simply working harder and in more diverse roles cannot adequately address this problem. When it comes to skill-specific jobs, in particular, the need in question must often go unmet. For example, an inability to offer competitive salaries to computer technicians—on average, TCUs offer only half the industry rate—has hindered many Tribal colleges' access to computer technology and resources (United States Congress, 2003).

To this lack of adequate staff we can add a lack of adequate "physical" support such as technology and lab equipment, facilities, and buildings. We noted above how appreciative tribal students are of faculty efforts and how satisfied they are with the quality of the education they receive. Their judgment on the concrete resources available to them and their instructors is very different, however. As Boyer (1997, p. 3) summarizes:

> Tribal college students believe people are the great strength of their institutions. They uniformly praise faculty, administrators, staff, and fellow students. But when asked about campus facilities and equipment, the mood turns sour. In sharp contrast to the high level of satisfaction found elsewhere in the survey, students found fault with nearly every aspect of their college's buildings, grounds, and equipment: classrooms, computers, recreation facilities, desks, water fountains—everything.

Clearly, TCUs succeed in their work of engagement *despite* limitations in infrastructure support and other enabling mechanisms. They can do so in part because of the willingness of faculty and administrators to go the extra mile; in part because everything about their operation relates immediately back to their core mission and vision as engaged institutions; and in part because of the fundamentally holistic nature of the Native American worldview.

Indicators Requiring Special Interpretation

This holistic worldview best explains the special way in which TCUs embody the remaining two indicators. In these cases, the indicators are embodied not so much by specific actions or structures but by the institutions' overall priorities, as driven by Native American belief systems.

In an article entitled "The Indigenous Worldview as a Prerequisite for Effective Civic Learning in Higher Education" (2001), Don Trent Jacobs, dean of education at Oglala Lakota College, suggests that

> Until we courageously investigate and challenge some of our assumptions about our most basic institutions, we may be fooling ourselves about the potential for colleges to become models for civic learning, moral development, and authentic democratic engagement (p. 2).

He goes on to identify a set of beliefs and priorities that he feels are far more encoded in the Native American worldview than in the Western worldview that dominates most of American higher education. Many of these priorities have to do with inclusiveness, interdependence, and intrinsic motivation. Jacobs maintains that when an educational institution embraces these characteristics, it is far better positioned to develop qualities of personal integrity and civic engagement than when those goals are at odds with the priorities an institution's structures, practices, and programs inherently suggest. In the first case, moral and civic development is part and parcel of everything the institution does. In the second, it is dependent upon discrete interventions that can never, in the end, fully succeed—precisely because they contradict what the rest of the educational experience implies.

When it comes to "Coordination of Community-Based Activities" as an indicator of engagement, not surprisingly, TCUs have little to show by way of specially designed offices, mechanisms, and procedures, yet their engagement efforts can hardly be considered disjointed or dysfunctional in any critical way. Their small size (ranging from approximately 2,000 students at Diné College to schools with fewer than 300 students), the relative homogeneity of their on- and off-campus communities, and their prioritization of the needs of those (often identical) communities make it easier to avoid the kind of fragmentation that besets American higher education as a whole. In addition, the fundamentally holistic thrust of the Native American worldview is an important contributing factor to the coherence of their engagement agenda. After all, if even entrepreneurship, itself a touchstone of Western individualism, is seen largely as a community good in the Native American context, how can more intrinsically social fields not be seen as integrative undertakings?

Less obvious but no less important is the way in which our final indicator, "Student Voice," takes on a different meaning thanks to the integrative impulse that informs TCUs. Typically, student voice is meant to identify concrete mechanisms for integrating students into a school's decision-making process, thus ensuring that the engagement process does not happen *to* them but *with* and *through* them. In a Tribal college context, however, the ties between students, faculty, administration, and the off-campus community are so strong, the resources of the college are so uniquely committed to student success, and student success is so closely bound up with the well-being of the whole community that much of the logic behind formal mechanisms intended to facilitate student voice in other educational contexts is less compelling here.

A sequence of events at White Earth Tribal and Community College uncovered in our research illustrates this point. According to a cohort of second-year students, academic engagement and general student development were being inhibited by a number of faculty members who seemed unwilling or unable to move beyond traditional lecturing. The administration encouraged students to identify the kind of teaching they needed in order to succeed. As a result, the school made a deliberate—and successful—effort to move in the direction of more genuinely interactive instruction. Several of the old guard either left or were let go, and more student-oriented instructors were hired in their place.

In this case, there was no formal mechanism for student voice, but students not only felt heard, they felt empowered to claim for themselves a concrete role in shaping the college's academic culture. Although most members of this student group had major family commitments and had to drive great distances to attend class, all were completely committed to the college. They felt quite certain they would have difficulty finding a comparable kind of institutional responsiveness elsewhere. For them, White Earth was, without qualification, *the* school of choice.

Such informal receptivity to student voice does not mean students are not also able to draw on more formal arrangements, such as student representation on college governing boards. At Sisseton Wahpeton College, for example, the student senate president also serves as a representative to the board of trustees.

**Example from the Field:
Coordination of Community-based Activities**
From Salish-Kootenai College

Salish Kootenai College coordinates all of the following community programs and activities:

- SKC-TV is a low-power public television station serving the Flathead Indian Reservation with local and PBS programming.

- The D'Arcy McNickle Library with 55,000 volumes, including an extensive collection on Salish and Kootenai history and culture, is open to the public.

- The Human Services Department offers special services for disabled Indian and non-Indian residents of the Flathead Reservation.

- The Bilingual Education Program is working with the Flathead Culture Committee and the Kootenai Culture Committee to develop instructional materials and dictionaries in the Salish and Kootenai languages.

- The Dental Assistant Program provides dental care to Indian Health Service patients on the Flathead Reservation.

- The Tribal Business Assistance Center provides a range of management and technical assistance to the Indian-owned small businesses on the Flathead Reservation.

With this unique relationship to the board, he/she can keep the student senate closely informed about key issues affecting the college's students. What makes this situation unusual is that students need to penetrate relatively few layers of bureaucracy to make their voice heard.

One of the more striking ways in which student voice functions as an essential and integral part of the Tribal college approach to civic and community engagement is discussed in an article on the research potential of TCUs (Mortensen, Nelson, & Strauss, 2001). Basing their findings on both an Internet-based search of Tribal college research and interviews with 25 faculty members from 19 TCUs, the authors conclude that

> Students are considered 'integral' to the research process at Tribal colleges, according to all but four survey respondents. One respondent remarked that '[students are] the central cog in research at Tribal colleges.' Students were described as 'partners,' 'aides,' 'translators,' and 'research assistants,' doing work such as gathering data in the field, entering information on the computer, and presenting results at formal meetings....
>
> These interviews portrayed how research experiences open new opportunities for a student's future; how research is incorporated into a classroom activity; how the particular research project is enriched by student involvement; and how student involvement ultimately works toward the greater good of the entire community and the future of Tribal colleges (p. 3).

The importance of this finding is highlighted by the role of research in assisting tribal communities—specifically, how little traditional academic research has benefited these communities and how critical relevant research is in helping them obtain the resources they need to begin addressing their most important issues. Another aspect of this study that bears notice is the respect that faculty members pay students. Where else in American higher education one can find this kind of significance attached to the work of students at undergraduate institutions, particularly two-year institutions? Despite their limited physical resources, TCUs have not failed to recognize that the full participation of one's students may be the single most important resource of all.

TCU Profiles

Red Lake Nation College

Red Lake Nation College in Red Lake, Minnesota, was chartered in 2001 by the tribal council of the Red Lake Band of Ojibwe. Institutional development was fairly slow until September 2003, when the council appointed Renee Gurneau president of the college. Gurneau, a former Kellogg Fellow who has studied liberation theology and directed the first tribal AmeriCorps program, provides strong, visionary leadership.

Able to select college board members herself, Gurneau purposefully selected elders and others immersed in Anishinaabe language and culture. Three additional leadership positions (academic dean, administrative assistant, and language instructor) are supported by the tribal council and are filled by women and men with deep local roots and commitments. Adjunct faculty member Mary Ringhand, who has a doctorate in law and is also an education outreach liaison with the Get Ready! college access program, is another important team member.

Institutional History and Culture

Gurneau and her colleagues understand education as a sovereignty issue. Red Lake is somewhat isolated geographically, and it conducts political affairs separately from other Anishinaabe tribes in Minnesota. There is great pride in the fact that Red Lake is one of only two closed reservations in the United States, meaning all 800,000 acres are held in common by tribal members.

The college's mission and identity are grounded in the health and well-being of the community, and awareness of community needs and strengths is pervasive. The community faces many challenges. A range of government policies and church practices—including pillaging of the forest, criminalization of native language and religious practices, imposition of foreign governance structures, and deliberate destruction of family and culture through boarding schools—have had a devastating and lasting effect. (Added to that is continuing discrimination, which is bad enough to have caused the American Civil Liberties Union to open an office in Bemidji.) These practices have led to economic isolation, high unemployment, significant internalized oppression, and the need to heal from the multifaceted effects of colonization.

Addressing community needs is an important function of Red Lake Nation College. When the college held its first orientation ceremony in January 2004, it offered classes in Anishinaabe studies, Ojibwe language, moccasin making, mathematics, writing, computer science, and casino management. In response to a need for college preparatory classes, the college also sponsored a summer institute focused on basic reading, writing, math, and typing skills. A computer class for elders is so popular that it has a waiting list. A range of other courses and programs to meet the needs of students as community members as well as the needs of the rest of the community are either in place or in development (see below).

Curriculum Approaches

A poster reminds visitors to the college that "unless a child learns about the forces which shaped him, the history of his people, their values, their customs, their language, he will never really know himself or his potential." Gurneau cites Paulo Freire as one of her primary educational influences. Yet rather than mandate a particular pedagogy, the college empowers instructors to use the methods they consider most appropriate and effective. Lecture, media, talking circles, hands-on experiential learning, and facilitated discussion are all used to enhance knowledge and critical thinking skills. Gurneau and her colleagues seek to foster self-knowledge and appreciation of indigenous ways of learning that stress active observation and participation.

For students, gaining practical, useful, and inclusive skills provides for a meaningful educational experience. For example, Mary Ringhand has students in her writing class seek out elder wisdom and stories for the college newsletter. In addition, classes clearly and deliberately connect students' life experiences to Anishinaabe history as well as to the reality of modern Anishinaabe life. For many students, this is first such experience they have in school. Renee Gurneau's Anishinaabe history class often yields powerful emotions; anger and grief are common reactions as students wonder why they do not already know about their tribal history.

Teaching the traditions of the Anishinaabe extends beyond formal history classes. As it seeks to provide a comprehensive tribal history, the college draws not only on local archives, but also on traditional singers, elders, storytellers, and fluent Ojibwe speakers. The college requires all full-time students to enroll in both Ojibwe language classes and Anishinaabe studies courses. In addition, the college promotes traditional arts and seasonal customs, providing instruction in birch bark basketry, moccasin making, and other activities. As the college continues to grow, more classes will be added; new courses are being planned in Red Lake history and oral traditions as well as in advanced writing and language studies.

Gurneau and other institutional leaders believe strongly in the value of their curriculum content and approach. They have a mentoring relationship with Bemidji State University (BSU), in which BSU faculty review syllabi and visit classrooms. This relationship ensures that credits from the college are transferable to other higher education institutions. This strategy reflects the administration's conviction that education can go in both directions; students at BSU and other non-Native institutions can benefit from Red Lake classes just as much as Red Lake students can benefit from classes taught elsewhere.

Community Building

In pursuing its central mission of education and empowerment, the college does not restrict itself to formal academic classes. Students and other community members all benefit. For example, as part of its goal of revitalizing tribal culture and identity, the college hosts a daily Anishinaabe language table, which is facilitated by the language instructor but is open to students and community members alike.

Among other efforts, Red Lake Nation College is working in partnership with local veterans' groups and color guard on an "Ogichidaag (Warriors) Wall of Honor" project to honor Red Lake's veterans. The computer lab has become a popular place where families bring photos to be scanned, enlarged, and sometimes repaired, then placed on the wall. This ongoing celebration of the warrior spirit has become an important part of the college's efforts to empower Anishinaabe people.

The college also works to enhance community interaction by building relationships and partnerships with many programs and organizations in the area. It has started a student newsletter that it distributes to schools and other locations in the community. The newsletter functions as a visibility enhancer for the college and as an important education and communication tool. In addition to enhancing community ties, students can gain useful experience doing interviews, writing and editing articles, sharing event information, and conducting historical research.

Local economic development is another college priority. The tribal council's higher education program pays for the tuition and books of tribal members, meaning money that previously might have gone to distant institutions now stays on the reservation. Through an ongoing partnership with a welfare-to-work program called New Beginnings, program participants have covered many staff functions at the college. Although such assignments are temporary, the experience has increased many participants' interest in attending college, and one early participant stayed on as the college's administrative assistant. The tribal council has also instituted a policy that allows any tribal employee to attend up to five hours of classes per week.

As the college grows, many more opportunities to support the community will arise. The college leadership continues to seek additional ways of serving community needs by hosting training seminars and workshops. By developing programs to serve in crucially needed areas such as science, technology, and the monitoring of natural resources, the college can strengthen the community.

Resources

Red Lake Nation College plans to seek accreditation, which will give students access to federal and state financial aid. Red Lake has articulation agreements with Turtle Lake Tribal College and Fond du Lac Tribal and Community College and is applying for membership in the American Indian Higher Education Consortium. Although still a very young institution, Red Lake Nation College operates with clear and community-oriented vision and a set of strong traditional values to guide it.

Salish Kootenai College

Salish Kootenai College on Montana's Flathead Reservation, home to the Salish and Kootenai tribes, is one of seven TCUs in Montana (each of the seven Indian reservations in Montana has a college). Like the other six TCUs, Salish Kootenai College is accredited and has received land-grant college status from Congress, a designation that allows for enhanced federal funding. The college currently offers four bachelor's degrees, 14 associate degrees, and seven certificate programs. There are 49 full-time and 60 part-time faculty members and more than 500 full-time students.

In many respects, Salish Kootenai College is a model campus for community engagement. It has several committed faculty members who use service-learning as a teaching and learning method; a committed staff and administration; an active and engaged student body, including a strong student council; and robust and sustained campus-community partnerships. Students take an active role on campus, serving on all campus committees, including the hiring and academic curriculum committees.

Learning Philosophy

Service is an integral part of the learning philosophy at Salish Kootenai College. Joe McDonald, president of the college, was a founding member of Montana Campus Compact, which has helped promote the use of service as a viable and important pedagogy. Furthermore, under the direction of the academic vice president, all academic programs have added a one-credit service-learning component to their mandatory courses.

Partly because of this requirement, nursing students at the college provide health care services to schoolchildren, the elderly, and low-income families. In addition, early childhood education students tutor and mentor preschoolers, and environmental science students test wells for contaminants for area residents. These three departments—nursing, early childhood education, and environmental science—stand out for teaching strategies that involve service to the community. Students appreciate both the service orientation and the focus on the practical applications of coursework. They have come to expect that most of a course will be taught "on location," and look forward to getting out of the classroom.

Institutional Values

The sense of service also resonates with the faculty and the staff. Everyone works to make the college sustainable; for instance, a faculty member may participate in a project to repaint a community building even if he or she is not paid for it. Although no one is compensated for everything he or she does, there are very few complaints. Loyalty to the school runs deep.

The inclusion of service in the curriculum appears to be in full alignment with the college's institutional mission and goals. Certainly, the concept of service-learning is consistent with tribal values related to the importance of caring for community and environment. Students are expected to be engaged as part of their tribal identity. Perhaps more important, service-learning offers an opportunity for the college and the community to interact in a reciprocal way to influence the development of the reservation's future leaders.

Making a Difference

Salish Kootenai has a range of community partnerships, including several focusing on K-12 education. The college's Gear Up Program, to help middle school children prepare for college, serves more than 300 students a year at the Ronan Middle School and Two Eagle River School. Program components include installation of educational software, implementation of a new science curriculum, tutoring, mentoring, and a reading program, as well as solicitation of parental involvement. Another program, Upward Bound, served 75 families and students from across the reservation last year. The program includes tutoring, mentoring, and college visits, leading to higher grade point average attainment.

A particularly successful partnership is "Making a Difference," a collaboration between the college and the Confederated Salish and Kootenai Tribes' Early Childhood Services Program. The partnership is geared toward easing a severe teacher shortage by increasing the number of qualified early childhood education teachers on the Flathead Reservation. This partnership was selected as a finalist for the 2004 Montana Carter Partnership Award for Campus-Community Collaboration.

White Earth Tribal and Community College

White Earth Tribal and Community College (WETCC) in Mahnomen, Minnesota, was established by the White Earth Reservation Tribal Council in 1997. Helen Klassen, who had grown up on the reservation, took a leave from her tenured professorship at Moorhead State University (now Minnesota State University, Moorhead) to serve as the founding president.

Concerned that the native population on the White Earth Reservation could not support a college alone, Klassen and other leaders identified the institution as an intercultural one that served all residents even as it strived to develop programs that, "as appropriate, express the Anishinaabe language, values, customs, beliefs, traditions, spirituality, and family structure," and preserve the Anishinaabe people's "concepts of sovereignty and nationhood." With support from Senator Paul Wellstone, who put a rider on the 2002 farm bill, the college achieved land-grant status. It thus became eligible for additional federal funds—an important step given that three-quarters of the institution's budget comes from grants.

The college has actively pursued full accreditation since early in its history, and in May 2004 a visiting team from the Higher Learning Commission of the North Central Association recommended the college for initial candidacy. Meanwhile, articulation agreements exist under which several regional colleges and universities accept credits from WETCC. Through an agreement with Minnesota State University, Moorhead, WETCC faculty members have a Moorhead faculty member who reviews their syllabi and visits classes. WETCC faculty recognize the value of the program to their students; half of the graduates of the para-education program, for instance, have transferred to work toward four-year special education degrees.

Hands-on Learning

WETCC leaders know that experiential learning— often the combination of observing, practicing, and asking questions—is traditional in native communities, and cite Suellen Reed's research on learning styles as confirmation. Many faculty members at the college use hands-on methods, and some programs include service components. The college's Environmental Science program, for instance, makes frequent use of field trips and active projects. The Associate of Arts degree in para-education—the largest program currently offered by the college, enrolling approximately 50 of 80 full-time students—has a service requirement.

When considering ways in which the college embodies and promotes community engagement, the structure of educational opportunities and the broader context communicated to students are as important as pedagogy. The early childhood education and para-education programs explicitly aim to prepare students to work effectively in multicultural settings, something the majority of professionals may be ill prepared to do. Part of the environmental science curriculum is the traditional practitioners curriculum, "developed and presented by local individuals with knowledge of the traditional natural resource management practices of the Anishinaabe." Including practitioners as part-time faculty is part of the college's governing philosophy. Each of the academic programs mentioned here also receives guidance from a committee of local elders.

Community members are seen as potential learners as well as teachers. The college opened an Extension Office in 2003 with non-credit courses and other offerings focused on holistic land management, permaculture, and native plant knowledge. It is preparing to launch an initiative to award indigenous gardener certificates to community members who meet on Saturdays over two years to learn traditional methods and some Western science related to planting, preserving heritage seeds, gathering wild plants, and other agricultural activities. Participants in this certificate program will also be required to do some community service within their chosen area of specialization. Recognizing the variety of ways in which learning and teaching happen seems to be a crucial element of the college's efforts to promote cultural preservation and self-determination.

Engaging the Community

WETCC seeks to support the tribe's well-being—including its "holistic social and economic development"—by responding to a variety of interests and needs. Gaming has been a major economic growth industry for the White Earth Reservation, contributing to a decline in the unemployment rate for residents from 80% to 55%, though most are low-paying jobs. The casino management requested training that might reduce staff turnover, and partly as a result the college offers a degree in Tribal Business Administration and Entrepreneurship. A degree program in nutrition aims to address chronic health problems in part by enhancing students' understanding of traditional food systems and educating the broader community about related issues.

Encouraging community members to stay and succeed in school is another high priority. Faculty members from WETCC partner with faculty from the University of Minnesota Extension Service on a summer math and science program geared toward increasing students' skill and interest in these areas. The program engages young students with a variety of experiential learning opportunities and connections to Anishinaabe culture. Another initiative, the Nandagikendan "Seek to Know" Even Start Family Literacy Program, provides a wide range of culturally relevant programs for children and parents. Its Adult Basic Education program graduates more people than the nine surrounding school districts combined, and the location adjacent to one of the college buildings eases the transfer of graduates to the college.

Partnering for Excellence

WETCC officially identifies itself as an institution that is "dedicated to educational excellence through the provision of a culturally relevant curriculum, in partnership with students, staff, community, and industry." The assumption of partnership is evident in the programs described above and in numerous additional initiatives, with more planned in the future. For example, interest in creating a museum or heritage center may lead to such an organization being located within or near the college's future Nibi Center.

Creative partnerships have benefited the college and the community alike. When the college received a grant to build a greenhouse but found no appropriate space available by the college's buildings, it constructed the greenhouse on land belonging to a Catholic church. College faculty and students will be able to interact with children from the church, model sustainable growing practices, and undertake projects that benefit the larger community, such as growing and distributing starter plants.

Along with such local partnerships, WETCC is interested in working through questions and challenges unique to Tribal colleges with peer institutions in other communities. The college is a full voting member of the American Indian Higher Education Consortium and is clearly devoted to culturally relevant education and the well-being of the Anishinaabe people. As it continues to develop partnerships and programs, moves toward accreditation, and hires a new president, the college will likely engage its students, staff, faculty, and community in ongoing deliberation about how best to achieve its mission.

Conclusion

Minority-Serving Institutions as Models

It is ironic that colleges and universities that are sometimes regarded as being on the fringe of American higher education should, in many ways, be closer to one of its founding principles than are most of their mainstream peers. That principle is the belief that education for the common good is of fundamental importance, and that to be truly educated means to recognize and embrace one's social and civic responsibilities. From this perspective, the founding of TCUs, the establishment of an HSI designation, and the strong reassertion of service as central to the HBCU experience—all events of the past few decades—are educational phenomena of potentially great significance. As has happened so often in American history, minority leadership could well be one of the decisive factors that help all of us rediscover our core democratic ideals.

Such a rediscovery can take place only if the academic establishment recognizes and is willing to learn from these institutions. Facilitating this process was one of the primary goals Campus Compact set for itself in undertaking the project documented in this book. The best practices of minority-serving programs and institutions are not only worthy of acknowledgment; they have the capacity to teach all of higher education lessons we very much need to learn. Given the shifting demographics of the country, one could go even further and argue that a failure to learn from the engagement practices of MSIs could result in a civic crisis of serious proportions.

To be sure, not all the practices and strategies described here lend themselves to transfer. For example, much of the strength of Tribal institutions derives from their being grounded directly in reservation communities. For mainstream institutions, this is not an option. Similarly, many HBCUs are able to connect new students to a history and logic of engagement that speaks specifically to the African-American experience of self-improvement. Majority-white institutions obviously cannot draw upon this powerful source of motivation and pride. Still, a remarkably large number of practices can be adapted by institutional types across the spectrum of higher education—even if they can't simply be transferred intact. And even more practices can be used to inform campus programming to make it more effective for all participants, including minority students.

Lessons Learned

A Culture of Commitment

Perhaps the single most important lesson to be learned from MSIs is that it is possible to create and sustain within contemporary higher education a culture that regards service and engagement as normative rather than exceptional. The preceding chapters offer numerous examples of the ways many MSIs implement the "common good" dimension of their mission statement so that it actually guides institutional decision-making and academic programming. Academics at many mainstream institutions would be amazed to discover that at some schools top administrators mean what they say about the importance of service, and a faculty member's community-related work counts in the decisions that define academic success. At many MSIs, engagement is not only seen as academically "legitimate"; it is actually *required* for academic success.

Such a high degree of integrity—linking mission statement, guiding policies, and academic expectations—has a number of important implications. It means, for example, that "culture" can often compensate for a scarcity of resources. At many mainstream institutions, both a formal infrastructure to support engagement and concrete faculty incentives are necessary for community-based work to take root and sustain itself. At MSIs, on the other hand, a culture of community commitment carries everyone forward: those on campus make an exemplary effort, at least in part, because such an effort is seen as ordinary.

Another important implication of such integrity is that it strengthens the resolve of many MSIs to face the issue of political power. Unlike the majority of mainstream institutions, even those with strong service-learning programs, MSIs may well insist that service cannot be seen as an end in itself, but must be viewed in relation to larger issues of public resource allocation. Since many minority communities lack adequate resources because of political decisions and priorities, this broader focus makes minority students more likely to understand the systemic nature of contemporary social problems and to include advocacy in their service work.

This broader awareness does not imply a marginalization of direct service activities, however. At many mainstream institutions, engagement as an institutional value has been finessed through a combination of theory-based courses that deal with national and international issues and extracurricular volunteer activities that speak to more local concerns. Such an arrangement sends several counterproductive messages, one of the most unfortunate of which is that community-based service experiences are personally enriching but not necessary to understand policy and decision making.

At MSIs, institutional integrity dictates that community engagement be valued in all institutional venues: within the curriculum and outside it; as a pre-professional, discipline-specific experience and as a vehicle of personal development; as a complement to theory and as a test of theory. As a result, students at these schools are less likely to fall into the trap of seeing service as unrelated either to a career or to the formal processes of representative democracy. Surely it is not coincidental that MSIs graduate so many students who go into service professions.

Furthermore, the full spectrum of substantive service-related opportunities these schools support is itself complemented by a spectrum of institutional initiatives that have little to do directly with academic culture or student development in the narrow sense. MSIs sponsor or closely collaborate with Community Development Corporations, provide meals and health services for community members, provide assistance to the families of students or potential students, share their facilities and resources with community groups, and advocate for the community with a variety of power brokers. In some cases, the non-academic dimension of a school's outreach efforts overshadow the impact of its curricular offerings. MSIs are proud, not wary, of being seen as direct service providers; for this reason, few non-MSIs model the engaged campus in so many of its dimensions.

As a result, MSIs and the communities they serve often identify with each other to a degree that is unusual in American higher education. Among mainstream institutions, perhaps only a few dozen community colleges come close to a comparable blurring of the boundaries between campus and community, and in many instances, these schools are also MSIs, in fact if not in name. Perhaps one of the most important reasons for this is that at MSIs one is far less likely to experience a culture and an attitude derived from contemporary America's cult of individualism. Engagement at MSIs often suggests not just greater generosity, deeper charity, or more determined social activism; it suggests a fundamentally different approach to the relationship between the individual and the collective, with the former seen as a subset rather than the opposite of the latter. As Fort Peck Community College, a Tribal college in Montana, announces in a sign outside the school, the college is there to serve "individuals," "families," "community," and "tribes." All four are units deserving of the school's attention, resources, and respect.

The Community as Teacher

Given that the cultural philosophy informing MSIs differs in some fundamental ways from that informing most mainstream institutions, how can the latter learn from the former? Clearly, the kind of community solidarity MSIs demonstrate is not something one can simply orchestrate—it is too closely intertwined with a collectivist tradition that most of mainstream America does not reflect. But if practice can influence values just as values inform practice, are there ways of proceeding that can at least make greater solidarity more likely?

Two guiding principles may help in this endeavor. To begin with, any school that seeks to emulate the MSI record of community engagement should place the development of sustained personal relationships with all stakeholders close to the top of its agenda. This means an approach to engagement grounded not just in an abstract sense of obligation and social justice but also in a personal demonstration of interest and concern. The students, organizations, and community members you work with are not simply partners in a contractual arrangement or a cause; they are friends and neighbors, people with whom you wish to share a bond of trust and affection, people you know by name.

Such relationships should never be confused with "getting things done," however important it may be to get things done. Instead, they imply taking the time to cultivate feelings of familiarity and comfort. What sustains both student and community development is personal empowerment, and personal empowerment demands a profound personal investment. "Family" is an essential, if not necessarily explicit or literal, concept in this approach. No individual stands alone; each is embedded in an extended set of relationships that define who he or she is and what he or she can and should do. One cannot simply cut through this set of relationships to get to the heart of the matter: the defining nexus *is* the heart of the matter.

Partially for this reason, MSIs often stress a close connection between service or community engagement and character development. How a person develops, what he or she becomes, is the ultimate guarantor that that person stands for more than individual success. At many MSIs, service is also closely linked to some kind of spirituality. Spirit is invoked, acknowledged, and renewed as a matter of course. Hence, any mainstream service program that fails to recognize how affective, personal, and religious factors powerfully inform minority student engagement may well fail to draw significant minority student participation.

Related to this willingness to stress personal relationships and personal development is an analogous appreciation of the power of learning through experience. According to Charles Schroeder (1993), most people (apart from faculty) prefer what he calls a "sensing learning style"—that is, "the concrete, the practical, and the immediate" (p. 22). At this point, considerations related to academic engagement and conditions related to civic/community engagement begin to overlap: factors that allow MSIs to excel in promoting community development also allow them to excel in promoting their students' general academic development. Community empowerment leads to student empowerment, and student empowerment leads to community empowerment.

The fact that many minority traditions draw heavily on experience as a teaching and learning strategy reinforces the importance of resisting the temptation to equate effective instruction with lecture and discussion, or intelligence with traditional academic analysis. Roberto Ibarra's concept of "multicontextuality" (2001) and Robert Sternberg's concept of "successful intelligence" (1996) both help us understand the ways in which an overly narrow, insufficiently flexible framing of the learning process has undermined student academic engagement—especially among minority students.

In other words, campus-community partnerships not only need to be grounded in personal relationships built on deep mutual respect; they also need to acknowledge that the community is a *necessary* teacher, a powerful partner in the educational process. Students do not work in the community simply to "give back" but also because there is no better place for them to learn things fundamental to being an educated person. The "giving" clearly goes in both directions: the campus needs the community at least as much as the community needs the campus. Few mainstream institutions are willing to acknowledge such a deep level of interdependency, to discard the idea that they are really self-contained entities, providing all the "expertise" their students require.

Since, moreover, majority white-institutions have available physical and technical resources that most MSIs—and many non-campus communities—can only dream of, it is easy to understand why such institutions might see themselves as independent of local circumstances. Of what resource value is a poor Hispanic community when one already has a state-of-the art language lab and can tune in Madrid, Buenos Aires, and Mexico City at will? The very possibility of such technical self-sufficiency works to thwart the discovery of the fundamental educational importance of partnerships.

Of course, MSIs also need technical resources, and for these they generally depend not on their community partners but on umbrella organizations and outside funding. In an earlier chapter we reviewed the enormous contribution made to MSIs by associations like the United Negro College Fund, the American Indian Higher Education Consortium, and the Hispanic Association of Colleges and Universities. Private foundations and government programs like the U.S. Department of Housing and Urban Development's Community Outreach

Partnership Centers (COPC) program have also been invaluable in helping MSIs do some of the work they do best. Given the fiscal constraints so many of them must operate under, one can only marvel at what they have achieved.

Appendix I

Research Methodology

Evaluation Framework

Campus Compact's Indicators of Engagement Project (IOEP) has benefited from a consistent, ongoing process for developing and evaluating the research methodology since the first phase of work with community colleges began in 2002. In year two of the IOEP, the initial research framework continued to serve as an effective template for the project team's work with minority-serving institutions (MSIs), while incorporating modifications that reflect learning gleaned from the first year of the project.

The evaluation design was derived from the primary goal of the project: *To identify, document, and disseminate best practices of civic engagement that demonstrate successful strategies for each of the 13 indicators of engagement, using exemplars from minority-serving institutions.* The focus was evaluation of short-term impacts that were measurable within the one-year time frame of the phase of the project focusing on MSIs. While the overall project goal was to highlight exemplary practices, an important component of the evaluation design was to identify lessons learned and opportunities for improvement related to the indicators of engagement, as well as to cite areas of accomplishment. As a result, learning from the first year's work with community colleges (see findings in Zlotkowski et al., 2004) informed the second year's work with MSIs.

Evaluation of higher education programs, especially those that focus on community engagement, must be practical and defined within a reasonable scope (Gelmon et al., 2001). Thus, the evaluation design for this project involved a process common to community-based and higher education programs. That process included the following steps to create an evaluation matrix (Figure 1):

- Define key concepts for the evaluation that reflect the program and evaluation goals. (What do we want to know?)
- Determine specific measurable or observable indicators for each concept. (How will we know it through measurable or observable descriptors?)

- Develop unique instruments or adapt existing ones appropriate to the indicator. (What methods will we use to collect this evidence?)

The evaluation matrix is not specific to any one year of the project but was designed to guide each year's activities. Therefore, the matrix presented in Figure 1 is identical to the evaluation framework for the first year of the project, with the addition of one method (focus groups) under "Refinement of indicators of engagement."

The 13 indicators of engagement represent those characteristics that best align higher education resources with the needs of various communities to address social, civic, and economic problems (Boyer, 1996; Hollander, Saltmarsh, & Zlotkowski, 2001). From this theoretical basis, the project team devised a detailed evaluation process to determine which characteristics promote institutional effectiveness by bringing together civic education and local community concerns. It

Figure 1: Evaluation Matrix

Key Concepts What do we want to know?	Key Indicators How will we know it?	Methods/Sources What methods will we use to collect the evidence?
Identification of exemplary practices of service-learning and civic engagement	Documented evidence of: – Innovation – Sustainability – Replicability – Significance – Intentionality – Recognition – Institutionalization – Transformative effect	Web-based screening survey Telephone follow-up screening survey Site visit protocol Supplemental site visitor survey Documentation review Supplemental information collection
Refinement of indicators of engagement	Operationalized indicators Testing of indicators in different markets and geographic contexts Revisions to clarify indicators	Panel review Surveys Site visits Focus groups
Dissemination of findings	Awareness among MSIs Knowledge of policymakers Sharing of best practices Use and application in multiple institutions	Presentations Publications Web resources Policy, advocacy State Compact use

was not expected that any one campus would manifest all 13 indicators of engagement; therefore, the project team chose to evaluate each indicator separately rather than to focus on the colleges with the most indicators.

In addition, the team chose to examine the indicators within each of three types of MSIs—historically Black colleges and universities (HBCUs), Hispanic-serving institutions (HSIs), and Tribal colleges and universities (TCUs)—rather than to make generalizations across MSIs. This approach allowed the project team to develop greater insight into how the indicators are put into practice and the extent to which the indicators reflect institutional engagement within specific minority contexts and cultures.

Methods of Evaluation

Operationalizing the Indicators

The assessment of campus programs included an extensive process to develop and refine protocols and procedures and "operationalize" the indicators of engagement to translate them from their initial conceptual form into more specific measurable and/or observable language. This process included reviewing documents and other evidence that illustrated the variety of ways the indicators might be made evident, as well as posing key questions to elicit both evidence of the presence of the indicators and a context for how the indicators are demonstrated at a specific campus.

The project team used these same steps to modify the language of the indicators to ensure their relevance to MSIs. Information from the first year of the IOEP led to some refinements, including more descriptive titles for some indicators (for example, "Enabling Mechanisms" became "Support Structures and Resources"). Other changes were made to incorporate more culturally relevant language, reduce redundancy, and increase clarity. For example, the indicators now more consistently use the broader language of "civic engagement" and "community-building" in addition to "service-learning."

The team continued to use the same terms as in the previous year to define "exemplary practice," to ensure a common understanding among project staff and to standardize measurement and observation of particular indicators. The language developed to define "exemplary" included the following eight characteristics:

- Innovative: new, special, groundbreaking
- Sustainable: continued, results used
- Replicable: transferable elsewhere
- Significant: makes a difference in mission

- Intentional: deliberate, planned, systematic
- Recognized: acknowledged, understood
- Institutionalized: integrated, part of culture
- Transforming: improves life, moves toward goals

To observe and test the key indicators previously illustrated in Figure 1, the project team designed a mix of quantitative and qualitative methods. These methods included a range of data collection strategies, including surveys, interviews, focus groups, reflection activities, observations, documentation review, and data analysis. The following paragraphs describe the design and development of each method.

Survey of Exemplary Practices

In order to gain access to MSIs to gather information on their approaches to civic engagement, project staff created a database of HBCUs, HSIs, and TCUs. The database was compiled from a variety of sources, including the membership listings of three prominent online websites—the White House Initiative on Tribal Colleges and Universities, the Hispanic Association of Colleges and Universities, and HBCU Central—as well as from Campus Compact's own membership list and the U.S. Department of Education's roster of minority-serving institutions.

Project staff then mailed copies of the *Compact Current* article exploring the findings from the first year of the IOEP to the MSIs, along with a letter announcing the second year's focus on minority-serving institutions and encouraging recipients to identify the most appropriate person on their campus to complete the survey. Next the project team sent an email announcement of the IOEP's new web-based survey for MSIs to the schools in the database, to each of Campus Compact's 30 state offices, and to various listservs. The announcement, which was also posted on the Campus Compact website, asked for minimal descriptive information about the institution and then offered the opportunity to describe exemplary practices or approaches for as many of the indicators as each campus chose to identify.

While the survey was being conducted, the project team invited the Campus Compact Engaged Scholars, state Compact directors, and other experts in the field of higher education to recommend MSIs that were known to be actively engaged with their communities. Schools identified by these experts received emails and phone calls encouraging them to complete the survey.

Forty-five MSIs submitted completed surveys, including 14 HBCUs, 29 HSIs, and 2 TCUs. Although the findings chapters in this book focus on the schools that later received site visits, they also include models and approaches from all of the schools that completed the survey.

Initial Telephone Screening Interview Protocol

Once the survey was complete, project staff identified that most promising survey respondents for follow-up telephone interviews to gather additional information regarding the engaged practices identified in the survey. The telephone interview protocol contained seven questions related to the indicators of engagement, and was designed to aid project staff in selecting institutions that would subsequently receive in-depth site visits. These open-ended questions were intended to elicit a more comprehensive range of responses than was feasible in the initial survey. The protocol also allowed interviewers to seek clarification of responses to the survey and to probe whether the self-identified practices were truly "exemplary." The seven questions, which were identical for each self-identified indicator, were modified and expanded from the original five of the first year of the project to generate a complete picture of how the indicators were actualized on campus. The questions are as follows (the two bolded questions were added in the second year):

1. Please explain how this practice might be innovative or unique compared with other approaches you have tried before or to similar practices of which you may be aware. In other words, how is this practice especially significant?

2. Please give some concrete examples of what makes this indicator exemplary.

3. Was there a deliberate or intentional effort to implement this practice?

4. I'd like to hear more about the details of how the approach was established on your campus. I would also like you to tell me how well this approach has been accepted on campus. Is there widespread support for the practice among your colleagues and the administration [or students and the community, if applicable to this indicator]?

5. Do any efforts/initiatives related to this indicator occur off campus (e.g., in the local community development corporation, or through national, non–campus-based student organizations)? **If so, how does your work connect to these efforts?**

6. Please explain how your work related to this indicator might be a transforming mechanism in terms of helping to institutionalize civic engagement and related activities such as service-learning on your campus.

7. **In addition to the activities you have described for these indicators, other civic engagement activities may be occurring on your campus. For example, there may be activities in the minority fraternities/sororities,**

or in the minority advocacy office around campus. Are there any other forms of student civic engagement at your campus that you wish to share with me? Please describe them.

The Campus Compact Engaged Scholars and Senior Faculty Fellow, as well as other members of the project staff, conducted the telephone interviews. The Engaged Scholar most familiar with each group of respondents led the interview process for that group. When a particular member of the project team had in-depth knowledge of a school's activities, he or she conducted that interview. The results of the interviews were used in the selection of sites to be visited (described in the next section), as well as in the findings chapters, as appropriate.

Selection of Institutions to Receive Site Visits

The project team selected sites to visit on the basis of several predefined parameters. The first consideration was to examine the institutions within the context of their particular ethnic identities and cultures. Information gathered from the surveys and the telephone screening interviews supported existing evidence that findings from HBCUs, HSIs, and TCUs could not be generalized in a way that would presume common themes and attributes across all minority institutions. It was determined, therefore, that the site visits would be clustered by institutional type, and that findings from each group would be written as separate reports. To ensure the broadest applicability of results within each institutional group, it was important to promote campus diversity across the sites. This presented an especially challenging goal since resource and time constraints for the project limited the number of site visits to five HBCUs and five HSIs. (The plan for how to best represent Tribal schools in the project given the very low rate of survey respondents is detailed later in this chapter.)

Among the factors the project team considered in selecting the schools were campus size, whether it was public or private, and the demographic context (i.e., urban or rural setting). While the geographic region of the schools visited was noted, it was not a determining factor in selecting sites because of the preponderance of HBCUs in southern states and of HSIs in western and south-central states. A primary concern was to ensure consistency in the number of indicators assessed both at each site visit and across visits within each cluster of institutional types. For this reason, and to ensure that there was adequate time to explore key practices in depth, the project team decided to maintain the first year's practice of addressing no more than three indicators at each site.

Following each telephone interview, the interviewer identified three to four potentially exemplary indicators for that campus. A decision matrix developed by the evaluation team aided in the selection process. The matrix helped the project team match the prospective sites by indicator and account for demographic and other factors. The project team then selected 10 sites to receive visits, representing a diversity of minority institutions based on institutional type (i.e., HBCU or HSI), size, and other descriptive factors (Figure 2).

In most cases, the project team was able to assess only one example of each indicator within a given institutional type. For example, Johnson C. Smith University was the only school among the HBCUs where the indicator "Teaching and Learning" was examined. To allow comparison of indicators within institutional types, investigators identified "shadow," or alternative, indicators for schools where they could identify a strong area in addition to the three indicators already identified for that site (see Figure 2). When time permitted, the site visitors examined these shadow indicators as well, to ensure that they were able to highlight a range of models of best practice for every indicator.

Site Visit Interview Protocol

The site visit interview protocol included sets of standardized questions for each of the 13 indicators, for five stakeholder groups: academic and administrative leaders, faculty, students, community service/service-learning directors, and community partners. Based on evaluative findings and site visitor experiences from the first year of the IOEP, project staff modified the interview protocol for each of the indicators to increase clarity, tighten the focus of the questions, and use language that would have more meaning for specific groups (in particular, students and community representatives). In addition, staff added a set of unique questions for each indicator for community service directors to gain a better perspective of their point of view.

In order to test the revised protocol, each of the three site visitors provided feedback on the content and application of the site visit protocol before and after their first site visit. The revisions required multiple iterations to incorporate all of the desired modifications while ensuring that the instrument remained valid and questions continued to reflect the original language of the indicators. The careful consideration of revisions by the project and evaluation teams helped ensure that the instrument provided the site visitors with clear direction on the areas of emphasis for each indicator and each stakeholder group.

Site Visit Supplementary Survey

The project team was also interested in obtaining an overall assessment from the site visitors that would reflect their perceptions of each campus they visited. Site visitors used a supplementary survey developed by evaluators during the first year of the project to judge the degree to which an indicator was exemplary. Using the descriptors developed to define "exemplary practice" (presented previously), the supplemental survey incorporated a Likert–scale-type format to rate eight

Figure 2: Schools and Indicators Selected for Site Visits

Institution	Rural/Urban	Size	Region	Public/Private	1	2	3	4	5	6	7	8	9	10	11	12	13
HBCUs																	
Benedict College	Urban	3,000	SE	Private		x						s				x	x
Johnson C. Smith University	Urban	1,595	SE	Private		s		x			x	x					
LeMoyne-Owen College	Urban	770	SE	Private	s	x				x			x				
North Carolina Central University	Urban	8,000	SE	Public	s		x		x								x
Xavier University of Louisiana	Urban	3,912	S/Central	Private	x									x			x
HSIs																	
CSU–Stanislaus	Suburb.	7,850	West	Public						x		x		s		x	s
Heritage University	Rural	1,276	NW	Private								s	x	x			x
Our Lady of the Lake University	Urban	3,324	S/Central	Private					x					x	x		
St. Edward's University	Urban	3,608	S/Central	Private	x			x	x								
West Hills Community College District	Rural	4,104	West	Public		x								x	x		

X=primary indicator; s=shadow/alternative indicator

Indicator Code:
1. Mission and Purpose
2. Administrative and Academic Leadership
3. Departments, Disciplines, and Interdisciplinary Work
4. Teaching and Learning
5. Faculty Development
6. Faculty Roles and Rewards
7. Support Structures and Resources
8. Internal Budget and Resource Allocation
9. Community Voice
10. External Resource Allocations
11. Coordination of Community-Based Activities
12. Forums for Fostering Public Dialogue
13. Student Voice

descriptors. At the end of each visit, the site visitor completed the survey for each of the three indicators selected for the campus.

Synthesis and Reporting of Site Visit Findings

The site visitors used the descriptions for each indicator of engagement developed by Hollander, Saltmarsh, and Zlotkowski (2001)—modified as described previously—as the framework for capturing the various aspects of each exemplary practice. This process involved synthesizing all material, including interview transcripts and notes, the site visitors' narrative reflections, and the supplemental surveys of best practices, to create a site visit report. These reports served as the basis for the narrative chapters of this monograph.

Using the indicator descriptions as the basis for synthesis allowed the project team to focus on areas of best practice that converged or were unique among the schools visited for each indicator under review. This approach offered substantial insight into how each school interpreted and expressed its civic commitment. The descriptions helped to show the context for engagement, which included whether and to what extent a practice had become entrenched at an institution, the degree of dissemination of the engaged practices within the institution and the community at large, and support for the principles of engagement among all (or some) stakeholder groups, leading to a sense of ownership of the best practices.

Working with Tribal Institutions

Project team members and associates of Campus Compact who have worked with tribal groups in the past helped to develop a different approach for including TCUs in the project after the methodology described earlier in this chapter failed to elicit a substantial response. Associates with a history of working with TCUs emphasized that it was necessary to have established a rapport over time with the schools of interest and that impersonal methods of communication and data gathering such as email or surveys posed a challenge in this regard. As a result, the project team identified individuals who had established relationships with various tribal groups and asked them to help organize focus groups with representatives of TCUs for the purpose of conducting guided conversations about the IOEP.

Focus Groups

To select focus group sites, the project team identified team members who had already established a rapport with potential focus group participants in a particular area. In order to gain multiple perspectives from a variety of traditions, the project team then selected diverse geographic areas with a high concentration of TCUs. Three sites met both criteria: Albuquerque, NM; Brainerd, MN; and Billings, MT.

The Albuquerque site was chosen because Campus Compact has an ongoing relationship with the University of New Mexico (UNM), which has ties to Native American students and cultural studies, although it is not a designated tribal institution. The university enrolls several thousand Native American students, and administrators in the UNM Native American Studies program have long-established relationships with TCUs in the Southwest. Through these network relationships, Diné College, the largest and oldest of the TCUs, agreed to participate, as did Southwest Indian Polytechnic Institute.

For the second focus group, a former staff member of Minnesota Campus Compact with ties to local tribes helped secure the participation of four TCUs in the Brainerd, MN, area: White Earth Tribal and Community College, Leech Lake Tribal College, Red Lake Nation College, and Bemidji State College. Bemidji has a significant Native American student population but has only recently pursued building relationships with the three Tribal schools, from which it is equidistant.

The final focus group location selected was Billings, MT, the site of an upcoming meeting of the American Indian Higher Education Consortium (AIHEC). The project team decided to schedule a focus group session at that event because the executive director of Montana Campus Compact had a long-term relationship with many of the consortium attendees. Additionally, the geographic location, coupled with the number of TCUs available to participate, appeared to produce the ideal environment. Unfortunately, this turned out not to be the case. The session drew few participants, possibly because conference attendees did not have enough information about the focus group session or about the project itself.

To explore the relevance of the indicators of engagement for TCUs at the Albuquerque and Brainerd focus groups, project staff modified and condensed the site visit protocol. They wrote one primary question, with a series of follow-up questions, for each indicator. They also combined some similar indicators (e.g., faculty development with faculty roles and rewards) to limit the number of questions and better conform to a focus group protocol format. Nonetheless, the focus group participants did not appear comfortable responding to this linear stream of questions. Therefore, the group facilitator chose a more culturally relevant approach that allowed the tribal administrators to talk about their institutions by telling stories about the histories, cultures, rituals, and practices that occur on campus.

Although the language of the IOEP did not always correspond with the language used by the TCU representatives, the focus group facilitator was able to glean information about community engagement at these institutions that corresponded to the following four questions:

- What are some innovative approaches that TCUs are using to engage with their communities?

- Do the indicators accurately reflect the engaged work of TCUs? What is missing? What is most relevant?

- How is tribal knowledge integrated into the curriculum and the co-curricular work of the institution?

- What can the ways that TCUs work with their communities teach the rest of higher education? How can this lead to future partnerships among tribal and majority institutions?

Site Visits

The focus groups underscored important differences between TCUs and other institutions of higher education, including other MSIs. The ways in which tribal schools respond to their communities and address community needs cannot necessarily be well understood in terms of the 13 indicators of engagement without concrete experience. Therefore, the project team scheduled site visits to Red Lake Nation College and White Earth Tribal and Community College in Minnesota, and to Salish Kootenai College in Montana, all of which had participated in the Campus Compact focus groups or the AIHEC conference.

The site visit process differed somewhat from that of other IOEP site visits, including those at the HBCUs and HSIs. For example, site visitors and representatives from the TCUs had already become familiar with one another through meetings, social events, and previous campus visits before the site visits occurred. The visits themselves were conducted informally; in the case of White Earth, the visit extended over the course of several days and included participation in a powwow. While the site visit protocol served as a useful guide for discussion, "interviews" occurred in the same storytelling style used in the focus group sessions. Finally, project staff committed to honoring the reciprocity requested from participants in the tribal focus groups. For example, two senior faculty project members conducting training sessions or spoke with key campus constituents by invitation.

Methodological Concerns and Limitations

The ongoing project evaluation and assessment process was essential in gaining an understanding of the implications and use of the indicators of engagement. Assessment is recognized as a critical tool that enables researchers to articulate what they are learning during the course of their work and to make incremental adjustments in methodology, leading to more valid findings (Gelmon, 2000). Assessment is especially useful in qualitative studies, as theory and findings often emerge throughout the course of the work.

This project, in particular, was conducive to a more reflective approach as the indicators were tested and refined and as new knowledge emerged about the nature of civic engagement at different types of MSIs. The evaluation component was therefore integrated throughout the entire project as part of a continuous cycle of learning through the steps of program development, delivery, and improvement. As a result, the evaluative component of this project enabled several timely modifications that improved strategies on behalf of the project goal.

Site visitors and project evaluators utilized the methodological instruments described to complete comprehensive site visit reports that discussed the prevalence of the indicators on each campus. While the variety of methods employed ensured that the resulting data were reliable, some limitations should be kept in mind in interpreting the findings. These include: a) variability in style and approach among site visitors; b) limited number of site visits and time at each location, which may have restricted the scope of information collected; c) limited number of responses to the initial survey, especially from TCUs; and d) the ability to generalize from a small number of observations within each institutional type.

Projects with multiple site visitors face concerns that each individual site visitor might use a standardized protocol quite differently, with some following it very attentively and others using it as a general guide but letting the conversation in each interview flow in a less structured way. The project team addressed this concern in several ways. First, the evaluators encouraged a single approach to interviewing to ensure that the site visitors obtained responses to all questions, regardless of the specific approach they used to get that information. Second, the site visitors received face-to-face training to ensure consistency in interviewing and reporting. Third, the evaluators provided a template developed in the first year of the project to guide the reporting process. In addition, an independent observer from the project team attended the first site visit with each visitor to observe and document interview procedures and recommend steps to standardize the site visitors' approach.

An additional concern was limiting variation among site visitors in their assessment of exemplary practices, since what one person deems exemplary another person may consider ordinary. Such variations were addressed through multiple conversations and exchanges of documentation among the project team and by careful adherence to the established definitions and characteristics of exemplary practice.

Scheduling constraints posed another challenge, since only one day on campus was available for each site visit. To ensure that they were able to ask all questions related to a particular indicator and that they reached all stakeholder groups, site visitors confirmed the list of interviewees and their schedules prior to arrival on campus. Although interviewers cited the ongoing challenge of interviewing five different stakeholder groups on three separate indicators in the space of a one-day visit, they were successful in gathering information on all of their questions from each stakeholder group.

There was also some concern about the limited number of responses to the initial survey from each of the three MSI institutional types, especially TCUs. Although the survey process revealed many exemplary practices, it is possible that other practices were not identified and remain unknown. Staff worked to increase survey responses by identifying the most appropriate individual on a campus to respond, reducing the burden of survey completion through design and format changes, and increasing awareness of the survey among the target respondent group. These efforts resulted in twice the total number of survey responses than were received in the first year of the project. However, the number of responses from each institutional type was actually less than in the prior year of the project, which focused on only one type of school (community colleges) rather than three. In the case of TCUs, the two survey responses were not complete enough to be useful as a tool for selecting institutions for consideration in the project, which resulted in the need to devise a new method to garner their participation.

Finally, the limited number of institutions at which each indicator could be observed made comparisons difficult. Further study at a larger number of sites would be useful to gain greater depth of understanding of how practices for each indicator vary within each institutional type, and how civic engagement activities differ or converge across all types of MSIs.

Conclusion

Evidence from each of the three types of MSIs that participated in the project must be considered only within the context of their own group. HBCUs, HSIs, and TCUs do not share the same mission, focus, or demographic profiles; therefore, it is not possible to produce any meaningful findings that are applicable to all institutions serving minority populations. It was for this reason that the project sought to examine practices at each institutional type rather than as a single group.

As described here, these same differences among types of institutions led to use of differing approaches in gathering and analyzing data, with the approach for HBCUs and HSIs being quite similar and the strategy for TCUs diverging. Despite these challenges, the evaluation of the evidence and applicability of the indicators of engagement has confirmed the value of the indicators in assessing the depth, impact, and sustainability of campus-based engagement efforts at minority-serving institutions.

Appendix II

Campus Compact's "Indicators of Engagement" Self-Assessment Guide

Using the Indicators to Assess and Deepen Campus Engagement

These questions seek to document civic and community engagement using the framework of the 13 indicators of engagement developed by Campus Compact. Taken together, these indicators compose the building blocks of an engaged campus. The *engaged campus* has been defined as having "an integrated approach to fostering students' citizenship skills through both educational and co-curricular programs and activities, and conscious modeling of good institutional citizenship through external partnerships and activities" (Thomas, 2000, p. 66). An engaged campus reflects full acceptance of the larger sense of institutional alignment that Ernest Boyer identified as "the scholarship of engagement"; namely, scholarship that "connect[s] the rich resources of the university to our most pressing social, civic, and ethical problems" (Boyer, 1996).

The indicators are designed to help campuses both assess their current level of engagement and create strategies to deepen their work. They recognize that institutions utilize approaches to engagement best suited to their particular culture and priorities. It is unlikely that any one campus, however engaged, will exhibit all of the indicators equally well. For this reason, the indicators are not prescriptive; their value lies primarily in the possibilities they suggest.

The questions below were adapted from the site visit protocol created for the second year of the Indicators of Engagement Project. During the site visits, Campus Compact scholars met with senior academic and administrative leaders, faculty, students, community partners, and the community service and/or service-learning director. We believe that these questions can provide valuable guidance for individuals wishing to assess civic and community engagement on their campus.

Recommended Procedure

Participants

The questions below are intended for a campus team consisting of senior academic and administrative leaders, faculty, students, community partners, and the community service and/or service-learning director.

First steps

We suggest that the campus designate a team (consisting of the stakeholders listed above) to guide the self-assessment based on the indicators of engagement. Once this team is in place, members should choose the indicators where the campus excels, and focus on those indicators and questions to begin the team's discussion.

Notes on Language

The questions have been written in a way to avoid "yes/no" answers. In almost all cases, you will want to ask participant(s) to provide illustrations, descriptions, or examples so that you will have more detailed and complete answers.

As in any interview protocol, you may modify language as necessary to better communicate with the audience, so long as the core meaning of the question does not change. Since the questions reflect the detailed content of the indicators (included with each set of interview questions), please refer to this language in order to ensure any editorial changes do not affect the original intent of the indicators.

1. Mission and Purpose

Core Question: *How do civic engagement, service-learning, and related activities reflect the mission and purpose of the institution?*

Specific language of this indicator (for reference):

- The institution's mission statement explicitly articulates its commitment to the public purposes of higher education and is deliberate about educating students for lifelong participation in their communities.

- This aspect of the mission is openly valued and is explicitly used to promote and to explain the civic engagement and community building activities on and off campus.

- The institution demonstrates a genuine willingness to review, discuss, and strengthen its commitment to civic engagement and community building.

- All members of the campus community demonstrate their familiarity with and ownership of the institution's mission.

Questions:

1. Please describe the mission and purpose of the institution in your own words.

2. How is the mission publicized on campus and around the community (billboards, signs, logos, mottos on letterhead, etc.)?

3. Does the mission reflect civic and community engagement, service-learning, and/or community service? Please give some examples.

4. Does the mission statement provide the basis for establishing effective community-university partnerships? How are you able to use your mission to support your community efforts?

5. If you have a strategic plan for the institution, is civic engagement part of the plan? If so, how is it included?

6. Have you encountered resistance either within the institution or from the community in general regarding the nature of your mission and/or strategic plan? How have you dealt with this resistance? Please give some examples.

→ **Do these questions and the resulting conversation suggest any ways to better connect the institutional mission and purpose to your engagement efforts?**

Documentation to Review

Kinds of documentation/information you may wish to review include:

- Mission statement, plus statement of the institution's vision/values/purpose
- Promotional materials
- Institution homepage/website
- Membership in Campus Compact and/or leadership roles on Campus Compact's Board of Directors or Board committees
- President's corner on website
- Annual report
- Public paper trail of community development efforts (from public relations office)
- Publications by leaders—scholarly or op/ed on civic engagement/service-learning
- Examples of speeches by leaders—e.g., to board, legislators, or faculty—that reference the mission
- Media files

APPENDIX II: SELF-ASSESSMENT GUIDE

2. Administrative and Academic Leadership

Core Question: *How do academic and administrative leaders support civic engagement, service-learning, and related forms of experiential learning at the institution?*

Specific language of this indicator (for reference):

- The president, the chief academic officer, and the trustees visibly support the campus's civic engagement and community building efforts, in both their words and their actions.

- The president and the institution's academic leaders have played a visible and committed role in helping the institution sustain and expand its community-building efforts and evolve into a genuinely engaged institution.

- The campus is publicly regarded as an important and reliable partner in local community development efforts.

- High-level administrators include community-based and service-learning in their strategic plans for enhanced academic learning.

Questions:

1. In what ways do academic and administrative leaders promote civic and community engagement and related teaching/learning strategies, both on campus and to external communities?

2. What are some examples of the ways leaders demonstrate commitment to the community (public work by leaders, speeches, community involvement, support of community initiatives, participation on boards of community organizations, etc.)? What are ways that *you* do this?

3. Are there formalized plans among institutional leaders regarding civic engagement practices? If so, please describe. Is there a strategic plan? Does it include civic or community engagement?

4. How is the commitment to engagement embedded within the institution's practice? Would this continue if key leaders left?

5. Does the institution use specific methods to assess the impact of its civic engagement activities? Please offer some examples. How do you use the results of these assessments?

Documentation to Review

Kinds of documentation/information you may wish to review include:

- Publications by leaders—scholarly or op/ed on civic engagement/service-learning

- Membership in Campus Compact and/or leadership roles on Campus Compact's Board of Directors or Board committees

- Examples of speeches by leaders—e.g., to board, legislators, or faculty—that support engagement
- President's corner on website
- Public paper trail of community development efforts (from public relations office)

3. Departments, Disciplines, and Interdisciplinary Work

Core Question: *How is the commitment to civic engagement and community-based learning reflected in and across disciplines?*

Specific language of this indicator (for reference):

- Community-based learning opportunities can be found across the entire curriculum. They are as much the concern of the arts and humanities, the natural sciences, technical disciplines, pre-professional studies, and interdisciplinary programs as it is of the social sciences.

- Students have multiple opportunities to do community-based work in their disciplinary and general education curricula.

- Formal opportunities exist for capstone experiences (including group reflection meetings, forums, and variable credit courses) focused on community-based problems or issues in most disciplines.

- Academic units (i.e., departments and programs) rather than individual faculty members have assumed ownership of partnering activities.

- Course-based community initiatives are structured and/or coordinated across disciplines.

Questions:

1. How is the commitment to civic engagement and community-based learning reflected in and across disciplines?

2. Think about a department/discipline/program where the commitment to civic engagement is particularly strong. Please describe what contributes to this strength, and how this might be further developed or enhanced.

3. Think about a department/discipline/program where the commitment to civic engagement is minimal or nonexistent. Please describe what contributes to this lack of involvement, and how a commitment to civic engagement might be encouraged and initiated.

4. Have you encountered resistance from departments regarding the implementation of service-learning, community-based experiences, or other civic engagement activities? How have you dealt with this resistance? (Please give some examples.)

5. Does the campus offer opportunities to promote best practices in civic engagement and/or to share these activities with other departments and programs? *Probe for departmentally based activities, individual faculty development, other kinds of initiatives and learning opportunities.*

6. What mechanisms exist to facilitate collaboration among departments/programs in working with specific community partners?

7. Are there specific opportunities or structures for interdisciplinary collaborations in community-based learning? If so, please give some examples. If not, are there any opportunities on campus that could facilitate the development of interdisciplinary community-based collaborations?

Documentation to Review

Kinds of documentation/information you may wish to review include:

- Departmental promotional materials
- Department/program homepage/website
- Annual report (institution and/or departments)
- Public paper trail of community development efforts (from public relations office)
- Presentations and publications of faculty
- Documentation from office of community-based learning or volunteerism
- Community partner documentation on partnerships
- Samples of student projects from community-based classes

4. Teaching and Learning

Core Question: *How are the multiple sources of knowledge and contributions of instructors valued, incorporated, and acknowledged at the institution?*

Specific language of this indicator (for reference):

- The institution recognizes that course content can be delivered in many ways and allows faculty sufficient freedom to utilize community-based strategies.

- Multiple cultural and historical perspectives on the meanings of community-based work are integrated throughout the students' curricular and co-curricular experiences.

- Community-based work provides an opportunity for students to generate knowledge, develop critical thinking skills, and grapple with the ambiguity of social problems.

- Community knowledge and community expertise are valued as essential to the education of students for meaningful participation in their communities and are incorporated in various ways throughout the curriculum.

- Experiential learning is valued both by faculty and by administrators as an academically credible method of creating meaning and understanding.

- Students are formally introduced to the concepts and skills necessary for civic engagement and community-based work early on in their academic careers.

Questions:

1. Does the institution recognize that course content can be delivered in many ways? If so, does it make these options available? Please give some examples.

2. How are multiple cultural and historical perspectives on the meaning of community-based work integrated into students' curricular and co-curricular experiences? Please give some examples.

3. What role do campus leaders and faculty play in facilitating and supporting multiple approaches to teaching and learning, especially as they support civic and community engagement? What role do others play?

4. Are community sources of knowledge valued, incorporated, and acknowledged at the institution? Please give some specific examples of community involvement in course design/delivery, participation on institution committees, and other activities.

5. Does the institution use specific methods to assess the impact of its civic engagement activities? Please offer some specific examples. How do you use the results of these assessments?

6. Are students formally introduced to the concepts and skills necessary for civic and community engagement and community-based work early in their academic careers? If so, how?

7. Does community-based work provide an opportunity for students to generate knowledge, develop critical thinking skills, and analyze the ambiguity of social problems? If so, how?

Documentation to Review

Kinds of documentation/information you may wish to review include:

- Departmental promotional materials
- Department/program homepage/website
- Faculty presentations and publications
- Documentation of teaching innovations
- Formal agreements with partners
- Inventory/report of partnership activity
- Examples of syllabi
- Community partner documentation on campus partnership
- Samples of student projects from community-based classes

5. Faculty Development

Core Question: *What resources are available to faculty members (full-time, part-time, and adjunct instructors) to enhance their efforts?*

Specific language of this indicator (for reference):

- The institution regularly provides faculty with campus-based opportunities to become familiar with teaching methods and practices related to service-learning and community-based education.

- Mechanisms have been developed to help faculty mentor and support each other in learning to design and implement service-learning and other community-based courses.

- To enhance their ability to offer quality community-based or service-learning courses, faculty have access to curriculum development grants, reductions in teaching loads, and/or travel grants to attend relevant regional and national conferences.

Questions:

1. What kinds of faculty development activities does the institution design, promote, and provide? What has been the response of faculty to these activities? What are the results of the evaluations of these activities?

2. How does the institution determine the needs of faculty for specific kinds of knowledge and skill development related to civic engagement, service-learning, and related strategies? Please describe the process. Once you get the results of these determinations, what do you do with the information? Who is responsible for translating these results into concrete development activities? *Please be sure to highlight central campus functions vs. individual departmental functions.*

3. Does the institution provide faculty with incentives such as curriculum development grants, reductions in teaching loads, and/or travel grants to attend relevant regional and national conferences to enhance their ability to offer quality community-based or service-learning courses? How many faculty are able to take advantage of these (a few, some, many, most)?

4. Without naming it, think about a department/discipline/program where the commitment to civic engagement is minimal or nonexistent. What is it about the faculty in this unit (based upon discipline, experience, etc.) that has kept them from developing such a commitment? What opportunities have you tried to provide to encourage them to develop knowledge and skills regarding civic engagement?

5. How are faculty prepared for the process of identifying suitable community partners? What support does the campus provide? What other faculty development activities exist that specifically address how to orient partners to the expectations of community-based learning opportunities; how to involve them in the design of these experiences; how to determine appropriate roles for partners in assessment of student learning; and/or how to seek partners' evaluation of the overall experience?

6. How do programs/departments identify community partners for service-learning experiences? In general, are these partners suitable for these courses? Are the partners able to provide the support students need to complete their learning experience? Do the partners appear to understand what the expectations are in order for students to complete both the community-based learning experience and the course successfully?

Documentation to Review

- Kinds of documentation/information you may wish to review include:
- Report(s) of faculty development unit (or similar center)
- Announcements of faculty development activities
- Evaluations of faculty development activities
- Lists of faculty attending various development activities
- Participation in Campus Compact training or other activities
- Other resources relevant to faculty development

6. Faculty Roles and Rewards

Core Question: *What are the specific ways the institution demonstrates the importance of civic engagement with regard to roles and rewards for faculty (full-time, part-time, and adjunct)?*

Specific language of this indicator (for reference):

- The institution's tenure, promotion, and/or retention guidelines reward a range of scholarly activities such as those proposed by Ernest Boyer (1990), including community-based teaching and scholarship.

- Faculty data forms, annual reports, and mandatory evaluations all include sections related to civic engagement, community-based teaching and research, professional service, and/or other forms of academically based public work.

- The institution explicitly encourages academic departments to include community-based interests and experience as criteria in their faculty recruiting efforts.

Questions:

1. Does the institution have policies that support and reward faculty for civic engagement and related teaching and learning strategies (such as service-learning)? Please give some examples. How are these policies publicized?

2. How did these policies regarding faculty roles and rewards develop? Were there specific events that stimulated interest in such policies (such as a speaker coming to campus or campus representatives attending a professional or disciplinary meeting)?

3. Do course evaluation forms include opportunities for students to comment on the presence, absence, and/or quality of community-based learning opportunities? Please give some illustrations.

4. Does the institution explicitly encourage academic departments to seek faculty with community-based interests and experience when they are recruiting new faculty? If so, please give some examples of how successful this strategy has been. Are community members ever involved in this recruitment? If so, how?

5. What are some of the challenges that you have encountered in implementing these policies regarding faculty roles and rewards? How have they been overcome?

6. How do your policies regarding faculty participation in civic engagement relate to the overall mission, goals, and strategic plan of the institution? Do these policies vary for full-time and adjunct faculty? If so, how?

7. In your opinion, is the institution's commitment to recognizing and rewarding faculty for civic engagement and related activities something that can be sustained? Could it be replicated elsewhere, and if so, how?

Documentation to Review

Kinds of documentation/information you may wish to review include:

- Promotion and tenure guidelines
- Recruitment materials for new faculty
- Job descriptions for recent faculty searches
- Reports on community-based scholarship, presentations, research
- Numbers of individuals tenured/promoted based on civic engagement
- Utilization of resources such as the National Review Board on the Scholarship of Engagement

7. Support Structures and Resources

Core Question: *What are the sources of tangible evidence of the institution's commitment to promoting and sustaining civic engagement and related community-based learning strategies?*

Specific language of this indicator (for reference):

- Faculty and students are kept well informed of the resources available to support community-based work. These resources are effectively included in all faculty and student orientation programs.

- The institution has developed a full range of forms and procedures that allow it to organize and document community-based work.

- The institution recognizes the unpredictable nature of work in the community and attempts to provide flexible scheduling options for faculty and students.

- The institution maintains a centralized office or center that is clearly aligned with academic affairs and is committed to community-based teaching and learning.

Questions:

1. Do you have a centralized office that supports civic engagement (such as an office of service-learning, community service, or community partnerships)? If so, what is the role of this office? How long has it been in existence? What sorts of resources (staff, budget, physical space, etc.) support it? Are these sufficient? How does it facilitate integration of various civic engagement related efforts?

2. Are faculty and students made aware of the institution's commitment to promoting and sustaining civic engagement and related community-based learning strategies in orientation programs? If so, how? What kinds of information are provided about specific policies, resources, and services?

3. How does the institution show flexibility in accommodating civic and community engagement activities? Please describe, including examples relevant both to faculty and to students (e.g., time commitments, scheduling, logistics, alternative course delivery strategies, etc.).

4. How does the institution promote and integrate civic and community engagement activities? Please describe.

5. How does the institution facilitate communication among faculty, academic units, administrators, and community partners?

6. Given the various methods the campus uses to facilitate civic engagement activities, do you think this commitment is sustainable? Why or why not? If not, what do you believe would be necessary to make it sustainable?

Documentation to Review

Kinds of documentation/information you may wish to review include:

- Center mission statement, website, annual report, activities report
- Faculty handbook
- Student handbook
- Schedules and supporting materials from faculty and student orientations
- Academic catalog
- Campus publications (reports to community, etc.)
- Media files
- Inventories of community partnerships, community-based activities
- Database summaries of community partners
- Presence/activities of community advisory boards
- Web-based resources

8. Internal Budget and Resource Allocation

Core Question: *What are the policies and practices regarding the internal allocation and stability of resources (including funding, staffing, and space) to support engagement activities?*

Specific language of this indicator (for reference):

- Adequate funding is provided to support, enhance, and deepen involvement by faculty, students, and staff in community-based work.

- The institution regularly draws upon already existing resources to strengthen community-based and civic engagement activities. Such activities are seen as priorities in the allocation of those resources.

- The institution provides sufficient long-term staffing to support all core partnerships and community-based and civic activities. It also provides adequate office space for that staff to do its work.

Questions:

1. Do you have a centralized office that supports civic engagement (such as an office of service-learning, community service, or community partnerships)? What sorts of resources (staff, budget, physical space, etc.) support it? Are these sufficient? Do you anticipate the office will continue to exist in the future?

2. What policies does the institution have in place regarding the allocation of resources to promote and sustain civic engagement and related teaching/learning strategies? Please give some concrete examples related to any of fiscal, human, physical, information, technological and/or other kinds of resources.

3. How are priorities established for the allocation of resources to support civic engagement activities? What formal positions, committees, or structures have responsibility for setting and communicating priorities? How effective are these in practice?

4. Who is responsible for allocation of these resources—in other words, how are the policies put into practice? Please give concrete examples related to fiscal, human, physical, information, technological, and/or other kinds of resources.

5. Does the institution provide scholarships, awards, fellowships, or other support for community-based work? If so, please provide examples.

6. Are any resources available to students or faculty to offset personal expenses for community-based work (such as costs related to transportation, background checks, etc.)? How do people find out about these

resources? Are the resources available sufficient? If not, what other kinds of resources are needed?

Documentation to Review

Kinds of documentation/information you may wish to review include:

- Annual report, activities report
- Budget summary statements
- Budget guidelines; other policies on resource allocation
- President's priority funding list
- Campus publications (reports to community, etc.)
- Inventories of community partnerships, community-based activities
- Web-based resources, listservs, other information about community resources

9. Community Voice

Core Question: *How do community organizations participate in shaping the institution's commitment to promoting and sustaining civic engagement and related community-based learning strategies?*

Specific language of this indicator (for reference):

- Local knowledge and expertise are honored through on-campus celebrations of and for the community. The keepers of local history and knowledge are invited to share their expertise with campus students, faculty, and staff.

- The community is deeply and regularly involved in determining its roles in, and contributions to, community-based learning.

- The community plays a significant role in helping shape institutional involvement in the community.

- The community is well represented on all relevant institutional committees.

- The community provides feedback on the development and maintenance of engagement programs and community-based work and is involved in all relevant strategic planning.

- The institution allocates resources to compensate community partners for their participation in service-learning courses and other forms of teaching and research.

Questions:

1. How does the institution facilitate communication between the campus and its community partners? What mechanisms work particularly well to involve the community with the institution?

2. How do community representatives participate in the design and delivery of community-based courses? How do they participate in assessment of their involvement in courses, committees, and other activities? Are there opportunities for them to be more involved in these activities?

3. What role do community representatives play in shaping the institution's involvement in community activities? Are community representatives involved in helping the institution seek external funding for community-based activities? If so, how?

4. Do community representatives provide feedback on the development and maintenance of engagement programs and community-based work? Are they involved in all relevant planning, development, and assessment activities?

5. To what extent are community partners represented on relevant institution committees? How are the representatives selected/appointed? What are their roles on various committees? *Probe for voting status, leadership roles, other decision-making responsibilities.*

6. Do you ever see community members on campus? In what roles?

Documentation to Review

Kinds of documentation/information you may wish to review include:

- Annual report, activities reports
- Schedules and supporting materials from faculty and student orientations
- Academic catalog
- Agreements/contracts for community organization participation
- Campus publications (reports to community, etc.)
- Media files
- Inventories of community partnerships, community-based activities
- Presence/activities of community advisory boards
- Committee descriptions, membership listings, records as appropriate
- Web-based resources

10. External Resource Allocations

Core Question: *What are the policies and practices regarding the allocation and stability of resources (including funding, staffing, and space) externally to support engagement activities?*

Specific language of this indicator (for reference):

- The institution helps the community create a richer learning environment for students working with it and assists it in accessing human, technical, and intellectual resources on campus.

- The institution makes resources available for community-building efforts in local neighborhoods.

- Campus mechanisms have been designed and developed to serve both the campus and the local community (e.g. shared-use buildings).

- The institution has developed purchasing and hiring policies that intentionally favor local residents and businesses.

Questions:

1. What policies does the institution have in place regarding the external allocation of resources to promote and sustain civic and community engagement? Please give some concrete examples related to fiscal, human, physical, information, technological, and/or other kinds of resources.

2. How does the institution assist the community in accessing human, technical, and intellectual resources on campus? Does the institution make resources available for use in local neighborhoods?

3. Are you aware of any instances where the institution has made resources available to the community that would otherwise have been unavailable or unaffordable? If so, please give examples (e.g., library privileges, donation of computers, technical assistance, grant writing, parking).

4. Does the institution allocate resources to compensate community partners for their participation in service-learning courses and other forms of community-based teaching and research? Please give some examples.

5. Have campus mechanisms been designed and developed to serve both the campus and the local community (e.g., shared-use buildings)? Does the institution give preference in purchasing and hiring to local residents and businesses?

6. How do academic and administrative leaders, faculty, and/or students participate in or contribute to community-building efforts? Please give some examples.

7. Does the institution have federal work-study students who work in the community? If so, please describe what they do (how many, in what capacity, etc.).

Documentation Reviewed

Kinds of documentation/information you may wish to review include:

- Annual report, activities reports
- Budget summary statements
- Budget guidelines, other policies on resource allocation
- President's priority funding list
- Campus publications (reports to community, etc.)
- Community partner publications (annual reports, etc.)
- Inventories of community partnerships, community-based activities
- Web-based resources, listservs, other information about community resources

11. Coordination of Community-Based Activities

Core Question: *How are the institution's efforts regarding civic engagement integrated across the campus and with the community?*

Specific language of this indicator (for reference):

- The institution effectively coordinates community-based activities across academic, co-curricular, and nonacademic programs.
- The institution helps community partners understand, access, and navigate all of its community-based activities (practica, service-learning and other community-based courses, volunteers, etc.).

Questions:

1. How well does the institution coordinate its community-based activities across academic, co-curricular, and nonacademic programs? Could coordination be improved? If so, how?

2. In what ways do you integrate civic engagement and service-learning with other community engagement activities? Are course-based civic engagement activities integrated with other community service and volunteer activities? Please give some examples.

3. Do you have a centralized office that coordinates civic engagement (such as an office of service-learning, community service, or community partnerships)? If so, how does the office promote the coordination or integration of these activities? How does it work with other campus offices such as Student Affairs, Academic Affairs, or Volunteer Services? Do you anticipate the office will continue to exist in the future?

4. What roles do other campus offices such as Student Affairs or Academic Affairs play in this coordination? Please give some examples.

5. How does the institution facilitate communication about engagement activities among faculty, academic units, campus leaders, and community partners?

6. Does the institution use specific methods to assess the impact of its civic engagement activities? Please offer some examples. How do you use the results of these assessments?

Documentation to Review

Kinds of documentation/information you may wish to review include:

- Campus calendar of events
- Academic catalog

- Campus publications (reports to community, etc.)
- Inventories of community partnerships, community-based activities
- Database summaries of community partners
- Presence/activities of community advisory boards
- Web-based resources

12. Forums for Fostering Public Dialogue

Core Question: *What does the institution do to foster public dialogue and raise awareness about its commitment to civic engagement?*

Specific language of this indicator (for reference):

- The institution plays a visible and effective role in facilitating dialogue around important public issues.
- The institution helps to bring together stakeholders from all sectors of the community.

Questions:

1. In what ways does the institution foster public dialogue in order to promote and sustain civic engagement and related teaching/learning strategies? How does the institution bring together various stakeholder groups to exchange information and participate in collective problem-solving regarding important public issues? Please provide some concrete examples.

2. What offices or positions at the institution are responsible for facilitating public dialogue? Please give some examples and describe specific roles. *Probe for centralized office, senior administrator, community outreach coordinator, faculty units or organizations, student government and other student associations, lobbyist, etc.*

3. How does the institution facilitate communication among internal and external stakeholders? What specific communication strategies and mechanisms are used regularly?

4. How does the institution become involved in community development, planning, or advocacy activities that are relevant to the institution's mission of civic engagement? What community leadership roles have campus-affiliated individuals played? Are these roles institutionalized as community expectations, or are they filled on an ad hoc basis?

5. How do students and faculty know where to go on campus to become involved in issues pertinent to the community? What mechanisms exist to inform students and faculty? How do students and faculty gain additional information about the college or university's activities in community development and outreach?

6. How do community organizations know where to go on campus to seek campus involvement in issues pertinent to the community? How do community organizations gain additional information about campus activities in community development and outreach?

Documentation to Review

Kinds of documentation/information you may wish to review include:

- Annual report, activities reports
- Academic catalog
- Campus publications (reports to community, etc.)
- Media files
- Inventories of community partnerships, community-based activities
- Presence/activities of community advisory boards
- Documentation regarding student and faculty organizations
- Committee descriptions, membership listings, records as appropriate
- Web-based resources

13. Student Voice

Core Question: *How do students participate in shaping the institution's commitment to promoting and sustaining civic engagement and related community-based learning strategies?*

Specific language of this indicator (for reference):

- Students participate on major institutional committees, including those that make personnel decisions.

- The institution provides a venue for students to discuss and act upon issues important to them and their communities.

- The institution recruits and trains student leaders to work with faculty and community partners.

- Students are formally introduced to the concepts and skills necessary for community-based work early in their academic careers.

- The institution recognizes student-initiated advocacy campaigns as legitimate forms of civic engagement.

Questions:

1. To what extent do students participate on institutional committees? How are the representatives selected/appointed? What are their roles on various committees, especially those related to civic and community engagement? *Probe for voting status, leadership roles, and other decision-making responsibilities.*

2. What support does the institution provide for student-initiated efforts with community organizations? Does the institution support student political engagement and/or issue-centered activism? If so, how?

3. Does the institution recruit and train student leaders to work with faculty and community partners? Please describe such efforts.

4. How do students participate in the design of community-based courses? How do they participate in assessing their involvement in such courses? Are there opportunities for students to play a more substantial role in design, delivery, and evaluation of the institution's civic and community engagement activities?

5. Are students formally introduced to the concepts and skills necessary for community-based work early in their academic careers? Please describe some examples.

6. Does the institution provide a venue for students to discuss and act upon issues important to them and their communities? Does the campus have

official student organizations and/or committees? What roles do these organizations and/or their leaders play in shaping the institution's commitment to civic engagement? Please give some examples.

Documentation to Review

Kinds of documentation/information you may wish to review include:

- Annual report, activities reports
- Schedules and supporting materials from faculty and student orientations
- Academic catalog
- Campus publications (reports to community, etc.)
- Media files
- Inventories of community partnerships, community-based activities
- Presence/activities of community advisory boards
- Documentation regarding student organizations
- Committee descriptions, membership listings, records as appropriate
- Web-based resources

Appendix III

Key Campus Contacts for Institutions in This Study

Gwenda Greene
Director, Service-Learning Program
Benedict College
1600 Harden Street
Columbia, SC 29204
Phone: (803) 253-5253 / (803) 806-3225
E-mail: greeneg@benedict.edu

Julie Fox
Service Learning Coordinator
CSU–Stanislaus
801 West Monte Vista Avenue
Turlock, CA 95382
Phone: (209) 667-3311
E-mail: jfox@stan.csustan.edu

Mary Alice Muellerleile
Special Assistant to the President
Heritage University
3240 Fort Road
Toppenish, WA 98948
Phone: (509) 865-8600
E-mail: muellerleile_m@heritage.edu

Angela Jeter
Service Learning Coordinator
Johnson C. Smith University
100 Beatties Ford Road
Charlotte, NC 28216
Phone: (704) 378-3558
E-mail: ajeter@jcsu.edu

Barbara S. Frankle
Dean of Faculty
LeMoyne-Owen College
807 Walker Avenue
Memphis, TN 38126
Phone: (901) 942-7363
E-mail: barbara_frankle@loc.edu

Rosa Anderson
Director, Academic Community
  Service Learning Program
North Carolina Central University
1801 Fayetteville Street
Durham, NC 27707
Phone: (919) 530-7078
E-mail: rand@wpo.nccu.edu

Ruth Bounous
Our Lady of the Lake University
411 SW 24th Street
San Antonio, TX 78207
Phone: (210) 434-6711
E-mail: bounr@lake.ollusa.edu

Richard Kinsey
Assistant to the President
St. Edward's University
3001 South Congress Avenue
Austin, TX 78704
Phone: (512) 448-8417
E-mail:
richardk@admin.stedwards.edu

Cathy Barabe
Director of Grants, Research
 and Planning
West Hills Community College District
9900 Cody Street
Coalinga, CA 93210
Phone: (559) 934-2147
E-mail:
cathybarabe@westhillscollege.com

Kimberly Reese
Assistant Dean of Students
Xavier University of Louisiana
1 Drexel Drive
New Orleans, LA 70125
Phone: (504) 520-5133
E-mail: kreese@xula.edu

References

Aguirre, Jr., A. (1996). The status of minority faculty in academe. *Equity & Excellence in Education, 28*(1), 63–68.

Ambler, M. (2003). History comes alive at Tribal colleges. *Tribal College Journal of American Indian Higher Education, 14*(3), 1.

American Indian Higher Education Consortium and the Institute for Higher Education Policy. (1999). *Tribal colleges: An introduction.* Alexandria, VA: AIHEC.

American Indian Higher Education Consortium and the Institute for Higher Education Policy. (2000). *Tribal college contributions to local economic development.* Alexandria, VA: AIHEC.

Archambault, D., & Allen, T. (2002). Politics and the presidency: Tribal college presidents share their thoughts. *Tribal College Journal of American Indian Higher Education, 13*(4), 14–19.

Barber B., & Battistoni, R. (1993). *Education for democracy.* Dubuque, IA: Kendall/Hunt.

Bowen, W.G., & Bok, D.C. (1998). *The Shape of the river: Long-term consequences of considering race in college and university admissions.* Princeton, NJ: Princeton University Press.

Boyer, E. (1990). *Scholarship reconsidered: Priorities of the professoriate.* Princeton, NJ: Carnegie Foundation for the Advancement of Teaching.

Boyer, E. (1996a). The scholarship of engagement. *Journal of Public Service and Outreach, 1*(1), 11–20.

Boyer, E.L. (1996b). Five priorities for quality schools. *Education Digest, 62*(1), 4–5.

Boyer, P. (1989). Higher education and Native American society. *Tribal College Journal of American Indian Higher Education, 1*(1), 10–14.

Boyer, P. (1995). Tomorrow's Tribal college will redefine the culture of its tribe, and help shape national policy. *Tribal College Journal of American Indian Higher Education, 7*(1), 8–17.

Boyer, P. (1997). *Native American colleges: Progress and prospects.* Princeton, NJ: Carnegie Foundation for the Advancement of Teaching.

Campus Compact (1999). *Building the service-learning pyramid.* Providence, RI: Campus Compact.

Campus Compact. (2004). *2003 service statistics: Results of Campus Compact's annual membership survey.* Providence, RI: Campus Compact.

Campus support spurs student service to record levels. (2004, Spring/Summer). *Compact Current,* 3. Available at www.compact.org/newscc/Compact_Current.

Carnevale, A.P. (2000). *Community colleges and career qualifications.* New Expeditions Issue Paper Series, #11. Washington, DC: Community College Press, American Association of Community Colleges.

Carnegie Foundation for the Advancement of Teaching. (1989). *Tribal colleges: Shaping the future of Native America.* Lawrenceville, NJ: Princeton University Press.

Chafe, W.H. (1981). *Civilities and civil rights: Greensboro, North Carolina, and the black struggle for freedom.* New York: Oxford University Press.

Clayton, D., & Born, D. (1989). R*eport to the Bush Foundation on Tribal college faculty development needs.* Duluth, MN: University of Minnesota.

Colby, A., Erlich, T., Beaumont, E., & Stephens, J. (2003). *Educating citizens: Preparing America's undergraduates for lives of moral and civic responsibility.* San Francisco: Jossey-Bass.

College campuses will grow more diverse, report says. (2000, June 2). *The Chronicle of Higher Education,* A51.

Conti, G.J., & Fellenz, R.A. (1991). Teaching adults. *Tribal College Journal of American Indian Higher Education, 2*(4), 18–23.

Cunningham, A.F., & Parker, C. (1998). Tribal colleges as community institutions and resources. *New Directions for Higher Education, 102,* 45–58.

Cunningham, A., & Redd, K. (2000). *Creating role models for change: A survey of Tribal college graduates.* Alexandria, VA: American Indian Higher Education Consortium and the Institute for Higher Education Policy.

Cunningham, A., & Redmond, C. (2001). *Building strong communities: Tribal colleges as engaged institutions.* Alexandria, VA: American Indian Higher Education Consortium and the Institute for Higher Education Policy.

Dawson, C.T., & Grayson, L.G. (2001). *Native American service-learning: Learning to serve, serving to learn.* Washington, DC: Learn and Serve America (Corporation for National Service).

Drewry, H.N., & Doermann, H. (2001). *Stand and prosper: Private Black colleges and their students.* Princeton, NJ: Princeton University Press.

DuBois, W.E.B. (1903). *The souls of black folk.* New York: Penguin.

Ehrlich, T. (Ed.). (2000). *Civic responsibility and higher education.* Phoenix, AZ: Oryx Press.

Fann, A. (2002). *Tribal colleges: An overview.* Los Angeles, CA: ERIC Digest.

Frankle, B.S., & Ajanaku, F.I. (2002). A positive impact on their lives: Service-learning and first-year students at LeMoyne-Owen College. In E. Zlotkowski (Ed.), *Service-learning and the first-year experience: Preparing students for personal success and civic responsibility.* Columbia, SC: National Resource Center for the First-Year Experience and Students in Transition.

Franklin, J.H. (2000). *From slavery to freedom: A history of African-Americans.* New York: Knopf (8th ed.).

Furco, A. (2001). *Self-assessment rubric for the institutionalization of service-learning in higher education.* Providence, RI: Campus Compact.

Gelmon, S.B. (2000, Fall). Challenges in assessing service-learning. *Michigan Journal of Community Service Learning* (Special Issue: Strategic Directions for Service Learning Research), 84–90.

Gelmon, S.B., Holland, B.A., Driscoll, A., Spring, A., & Kerrigan, S. (2001). *Assessing service-learning and civic engagement: Principles and techniques.* Providence, RI: Campus Compact.

Goetz, M. (2001). Facilities focus on Capitol Hill pays off. *Tribal College Journal of American Indian Higher Education, 12*(3), 45.

Greenleaf, R.K. (1998). *The power of servant leadership.* San Francisco: Berret-Koehler Publishers.

Harkavy, I. (2000). Service-learning, academically based community service, and the historic mission of the American urban research university. In I. Harkavy, M. Donovan, & E. Zlotkowski (Eds.), *Connecting past and present: Concepts and models for service-learning in history.* Washington, DC: American Association for Higher Education.

Hear us out: Community college students talk about their lives and dreams. (2003). Providence, RI: What Kids Can Do.

HeavyRunner, I., & Marshall, K. (2003). Miracle survivors: Promoting resilience in Indian students. *Tribal College Journal of American Indian Higher Education, 14*(4), 14–19.

Helms, A.D. (2003, November 9). Elementary students get academic boost by going to college early. *The Charlotte Observer.*

Hollander, E., & Saltmarsh, J. (2000). The engaged university. *Academe: Bulletin of the American Association of University Professors, 86*(4), 29–31.

Hollander, E., Saltmarsh, J., & Zlotkowski, E. (2001). Indicators of engagement. In L.A. Simon, M. Kenny, K. Brabeck, & R.M. Lerner (Eds.), *Learning to serve: Promoting civil society through service-learning.* Norwell, MA: Kluwer Academic Publishers.

Holmes, A. (2000). *Focus on Hispanic-serving institutions.* Washington, DC: American Psychological Association, Psychology and Ethnic Minority Serving Institutions Initiative (PEMSI). Available at www.apa.org/pi/oema/programs/pemsi_hispanic_serving_institutions.pdf

Hoyle, M.J. (2002). The college presidency: Player or spectator? *Community College Journal, 73*(1), 26–32.

Ibarra, R.A. (2001). *Beyond affirmative action: Reframing the context of higher education.* Madison, WI: University of Wisconsin Press.

Indian Nations At Risk Task Force. (1991). *Indian nations at risk: An educational strategy for action.* (Final report of the Indian Nations at Risk Task Force). Washington, DC: U.S. Department of Education.

Institute of Politics. (2000). *Attitudes toward politics and public service: A national survey of college and university undergraduates.* Cambridge, MA: Institute of Politics, Harvard University.

Jacobs, D.T. (2001). The indigenous worldview as a prerequisite for effective civic learning in higher education. *Journal of College and Character, 2.* Available at www.collegevalues.org/articles.cfm?id=461&a=1.

Johnson, V., Benham, M.K.P., & VanAlstine, M.J. (2003). Native leadership: Advocacy for transformation, culture, community, and sovereignty. In M.K.P. Benham & W.J. Stein (Eds.), *The renaissance of American Indian higher education: Capturing the dream.* Mahwah, NJ: Lawrence Erlbaum Associates.

Jones, B.W. (1998). Rediscovering our heritage: Community service and the historically Black university. In E. Zlotkowski (Ed.), *Successful service-learning programs: New models of excellence in higher education.* Bolton, MA: Anker Publishing.

Keohane, N. (1999). Majoring in diversity. *Business Mexico, 12*(1), 30–31.

The Mellman Group. (2000). *Summary of national survey of 800 college students by the Mellman Group.* Seaside, CA: The Panetta Institute. Available at www.panettainstitute.org/poll-memo.html.

Merisotis, J.P., & O'Brien, C. T. (Eds.). (1998). *New directions for higher education—Minority-serving institutions: Distinct purposes, common goals.* San Francisco: Jossey-Bass.

Miller, S. (2003). Hispanics replace African Americans as largest U.S. minority group. *The Washington File,* January 23. (U.S. Department of State, International Information Programs. Available at http://usinfo.state.gov/usa/diversity/a012303.htm.)

Mortensen, M., Nelson, C.E., & Strauss, J. (2001). Refereed research: Survey of Tribal colleges reveals research's benefits. *Tribal College Journal of American Indian Higher Education, 13*(2), 28–32.

National Association of Secretaries of State. (1999). *New Millennium Project, Part 1— American youth attitudes on politics, citizenship, government and voting: Survey on youth attitudes.* Lexington, KY: National Association of Secretaries of State.

National Commission on Civic Renewal (1998). *A nation of spectators: How civic disengagement weakens America and what we can do about it.* College Park, MD: National Commission on Civic Renewal. Available at www.pauf.umd.edu/civicrenewal.

National Committee of Inquiry into Higher Education. (1997). *Report of the National Committee, Appendix 5: Higher education in other countries.* London: NCIHE. Available at www.leeds.ac.uk/educol/ncihe.

Office of University Partnerships. (2003). *Minority serving institutions of higher education.* Washington, DC: U.S. Department of Housing and Urban Development.

Ozuna, R. (2002). Community outreach partnership center created in Toppenish. *University Week, 20*(3).

Padilla, R., & Chavez, R. (Eds.). (1995). *The leaning ivory tower: Latino professors in American universities.* Albany, NY: State University of New York Press.

Phillips, J. (2004). Financial education brightens future of tribal economies. *Tribal College Journal of American Indian Higher Education, 15*(3): 28–29.

Presidential Advisory Commission on Educational Excellence for Hispanic Americans. (2003). *From risk to opportunity: Fulfilling the educational needs of Hispanic Americans in the 21st century.* Washington, DC: PACEEHA.

Presidential Proclamation 5099. (1983). *National historically Black colleges day, 1983.* Available at www.reagan.utexas.edu/archives/speeches/1983/91983c.htm.

Reyhner, J., & Eder, J. (2004). *American Indian education: A history.* Norman, OK: University of Oklahoma Press.

Robbins, R.L. (2002). *Tribal college and university profiles.* Pablo, MT: Salish Kootenai College.

Sax, L.J., Astin, A.W., Korn, W.S., & Mahoney, K.M. (1999). *The American freshman: national norms for fall 1999.* Los Angeles, CA: Higher Education Research Institute, UCLA.

Schroeder, C.C. (1993, Sept./Oct.). New students, new learning styles. *Change,* 21–26.

Selden, R. (2004). Back from the brink. *Tribal College Journal of American Indian Higher Education, 15*(3), 22.

Sternberg, R.J. (1996). *Successful intelligence: How practical and creative intelligence determine success in life.* New York: Simon & Schuster.

Stevens, C. (2003). Unrecognized roots of service-learning in African American social thought and action, 1890–1930. *Michigan Journal of Community Service Learning 9*(2), 25–34.

Sullivan, W. (2000). Institutional identity and social responsibility in higher education. In T. Ehrlich (Ed.), *Civic responsibility and higher education.* Phoenix, AZ: Oryx Press.

Swail, W.S., Redd, K.E. & Perna, L.W. (2003). *Retaining minority students in higher education: A framework for success.* San Francisco: Jossey-Bass.

Thomas, N. (2000). The college and university as citizen. In T. Ehrlich (Ed.), *Civic responsibility and higher education.* Phoenix, AZ: Oryx Press.

Tippeconnic, J.W., & McKinney, S. (2003). Native faculty: Scholarship and development. In M.K.P. Benham & W.J. Stein (Eds.), *The renaissance of American Indian higher education: Capturing the dream.* Mahweh, NJ: Lawrence Erlbaum Associates.

United States Congress (2003). *Digital and Wireless Network Technology Program Act of 2003: 108th Congress 1st session Senate report (S.196, 108–34).* Available at www.congress.gov/cgi-bin/cpquery/?&&dbname=cp108&&db_id=cp108&&r_n=sr034.108&&sel=TOC_6710&.

U.S. Census Bureau. (2002). *Population by race and Hispanic or Latino origin for the United States: 1990 and 2000 (PHC-T-1).* Washington, DC: U.S. Census Bureau. Available at www.census.gov/population/www/cen2000/phc-t1.html.

U.S. Census Bureau. (2003). *The Hispanic population of the United States: March 2002.* Washington, DC: U.S. Census Bureau. Available at www.census.gov/prod/2003pubs/p20-545.pdf.

U.S. Department of Education. (1998). *1998 amendments to the Higher Education Act of 1965.* (P.L. 105–244). Washington, DC: U.S. Government Printing Office. Available at www.ed.gov/policy/highered/leg/hea98/sec501.html.

A vision for West Hills: Voices and values from its communities. (2003, February). *Dialogue: A West Hills College Quarterly, 2*(3), 1–8. Available at www.westhillscollege.com/district/news_&_events/dialogue/index.asp.

Voorhees, R.A. (2003). *Characteristics of Tribal college and university faculty.* Denver, CO: American Indian College Fund.

Voorhees, R.A., & Adams, N. (2004). Tribal college faculty survey: Despite lower pay, faculty tend to be content, altruistic, ambitious. *Tribal College Journal of American Indian Higher Education, 15*(3), 20–21.

Walshok, M.L. (1995). *Knowledge without boundaries: What America's research universities can do for the economy, the workplace, and the community.* San Francisco: Jossey-Bass.

Washington, B.T. (1901). *Up from slavery.* New York: Doubleday.

Webster, L. (2003). Tribal colleges and universities: Guided by tribal values, advancing academic study. *Diversity Digest, 7*(2), 3–5.

Wynia, P. (2003). SWC building will reflect Dakota renaissance. *Tribal College Journal of American Indian Higher Education, 14*(4), 33.

Young, J.R. (2000, February 18). Study counts more minority students earning degrees as of 1997. *Chronicle of Higher Education,* A60.

Young, J.R. (2002, September 27). Minority enrollment continues to rise at colleges, report says. *Chronicle of Higher Education,* A54.

Zlotkowski, E., Duffy, D.K., Franco, R., Gelmon, S.B., Norvell, K.H., Meeropol, J., & Jones, S. (2004). *The community's college: Indicators of engagement at two-year institutions.* Providence, RI: Campus Compact.